D1391152

The East German Economy, 1945–2010

FALLING BEHIND OR CATCHING UP?

By many measures, the German Democratic Republic (GDR) had the strongest economy in the Eastern bloc and was one of the most important industrial nations worldwide. Nonetheless, the economic history of the GDR has been primarily discussed as a failure when compared with the economic success of the Federal Republic and is often cited as one of the preeminent examples of central planning's deficiencies. This volume analyzes both the successes and failures of the East German economy. The contributors consider the economic history of East Germany within its broader political, cultural, and social contexts. Rather than limit their perspective to the period of the GDR's existence, the essays additionally consider the decades before 1945 and the post-1990 era. Contributors also trace the present and future of the East German economy and suggest possible outcomes.

Hartmut Berghoff is Director of the German Historical Institute, Washington, D.C., and Professor of Economic and Social History at the University Göttingen in Germany. Dr. Berghoff is a member of the editorial boards of *Business History Review* and *Enterprise and Society*.

Uta Andrea Balbier is Director of the Institute of North American Studies at King's College London and Lecturer in U.S. History. Her first book, *Kalter Krieg auf der Aschenbahn: Deutsch-deutscher Sport 1950–1972*, was a runner-up for the Carl Diem Prize for an outstanding contribution to the field of sports history.

PUBLICATIONS OF THE GERMAN HISTORICAL INSTITUTE

Edited by Hartmut Berghoff
with the assistance of David Lazar

The German Historical Institute is a center for advanced study and research whose purpose is to provide a permanent basis for scholarly cooperation among historians from the Federal Republic of Germany and the United States. The institute conducts, promotes, and supports research into both American and German political, social, economic, and cultural history; into transatlantic migration, especially in the nineteenth and twentieth centuries; and into the history of international relations, with special emphasis on the roles played by the United States and Germany.

Recent Books in the Series

Alison Efford, *German Immigrants, Race, and Citizenship in the Civil War Era*

Lars Maischak, *German Merchants in the Nineteenth-Century Atlantic*

Ingo Köhler, *The Aryanization of Private Banks in the Third Reich*

Hartmut Berghoff, Jürgen Kocka, and Dieter Ziegler, editors, *Business in the Age of Extremes*

Yair Mintzker, *The Defortification of the German City, 1689–1866*

Astrid M. Eckert, *The Struggle for the Files: The Western Allies and the Return of German Archives after the Second World War*

Winson Chu, *The German Minority in Interwar Poland*

Christof Mauch and Kiran Klaus Patel, *The United States and Germany during the Twentieth Century*

Monica Black, *Death in Berlin: From Weimar to Divided Germany*

John R. McNeill and Corinna R. Unger, editors, *Environmental Histories of the Cold War*

Roger Chickering and Stig Förster, editors, *War in an Age of Revolution, 1775–1815*

Cathryn Carson, *Heisenberg in the Atomic Age: Science and the Public Sphere*

Michaela Hoenicke Moore, *Know Your Enemy: The American Debate on Nazism, 1933–1945*

Matthias Schulz and Thomas A. Schwartz, editors, *The Strained Alliance: U.S.-European Relations from Nixon to Carter*

The East German Economy, 1945–2010

FALLING BEHIND OR CATCHING UP?

Edited by

HARTMUT BERGHOFF

German Historical Institute, Washington, D.C.

UTA ANDREA BALBIER

King's College London

GERMAN HISTORICAL INSTITUTE

Washington, D.C.

and

CAMBRIDGE
UNIVERSITY PRESS

CAMBRIDGE
UNIVERSITY PRESS

32 Avenue of the Americas, New York, NY 10013-2473, USA

Cambridge University Press is part of the University of Cambridge.

It furthers the University's mission by disseminating knowledge in the pursuit of education, learning, and research at the highest international levels of excellence.

www.cambridge.org
Information on this title: www.cambridge.org/9781107030138

GERMAN HISTORICAL INSTITUTE
1607 New Hampshire Avenue, N.W., Washington, DC 20009, USA

First published 2013

Printed in the United States of America

A catalog record for this publication is available from the British Library.

Library of Congress Cataloging in Publication Data
The East German economy, 1945–2010 : falling behind or catching up? / [edited by] Hartmut Berghoff, German Historical Institute, Washington, DC, Uta A. Balbier, King's College, London.
pages cm. – (Publications of the German Historical Institute)
Includes bibliographical references and index.
ISBN 978-1-107-03013-8 (hardback)
1. Germany (East) – Economic conditions – 1945–1990.   2. Germany (East) – Economic
conditions – 1990–3.   3. Germany (East) – Economic policy.   I. Berghoff, Hartmut.
II. Balbier, Uta A.
HC290.78.E233   2014
330.943′1087–dc23   2013020825

ISBN 978-1-107-03013-8 Hardback

Contents

Contributors

Ralf Ahrens, Zentrum für Zeithistorische Forschung, Potsdam

Dolores L. Augustine, Department of History, St. John's University

Uta Andrea Balbier, Institute of North American Studies, King's College London

Hartmut Berghoff, German Historical Institute Washington, DC, and Institute for Economic and Social History, Georg August University Göttingen

Michael C. Burda, School of Business and Economics, Humboldt Universtät zu Berlin

Burghard Ciesla, Independent Scholar

Silke Fengler, Institute for Contemporary History, University of Vienna

Rainer Karlsch, Free University of Berlin

Jeffrey Kopstein, Department of Political Science and Center for Jewish Studies, University of Toronto

Andrew I. Port, Department of History, Wayne State University

Gerhard A. Ritter, Historical Seminar, Ludwig Maximillian University, Munich

André Steiner, Zentrum für Zeithistorische Forschung, Potsdam

Ray Stokes, School of Social and Political Sciences, University of Glasgow

Holger C. Wolf, BMW Center for German and European Studies, Georgetown University

PART I

Introduction

1

From Centrally Planned Economy to Capitalist Avant-Garde?

The Creation, Collapse, and Transformation of a Socialist Economy

HARTMUT BERGHOFF AND UTA ANDREA BALBIER

During the celebrations of the twentieth anniversary of German unification in 2010, Federal Minister of the Interior and Commissioner for the New Federal States Thomas de Maizière proudly proclaimed, "Over the past few years, Eastern Germany has become one of the most competitive places for investment in Europe." He was referring to obvious successes such as the doubling of productivity since 1991 and the decision by numerous foreign firms, including more than three hundred U.S. companies, to invest in the five federal states that had previously constituted the German Democratic Republic (GDR). "Situated in the heart of Europe, this . . . location offers excellent conditions for businesses," de Maizière continued. "The main advantages of the region include the state-of-the-art research and development landscape, modern logistics and communication networks, a highly qualified and flexible workforce and access to the dynamic markets of Eastern Europe and the major Western European economies."[1] Low rates of unionization, high levels of subvention, and successful clusters of innovative industries such as renewable energies, chemicals, mechanical engineering, microelectronics, and optics could be added of the list of Eastern Germany's commercial advantages. The former GDR, according to de Maizière, has become a rejuvenated "powerhouse," an avant-garde leading the way into the future of capitalism, a model region far ahead of less prosperous sections of Western Germany that had not undergone such rigorous modernization.

The rhetoric of Eastern Germany's unique promise is not an invention of postunification politics. During the imperial era and the crisis-ridden 1920s and 1930s, politicians and writers from very different political camps saw Germany's east, which then encompassed vast regions east of the river

---

[1] Thomas de Maizière, Welcome Address, http://www.gtai.com/homepage/business-location-germany/powerhouse-eastern-germany/welcome-address/?backlink=0 (accessed August 28, 2010).

Elbe, as the key to remedying the ills of modern industrial society. Going east and settling the land was seen as an alternative to emigration and to urban poverty and lack of community. These agrarian settlers would also help alleviate Germany's dependence on food imports.[2] During the Great Depression, the idea of using the East for the emergency resettlement of unemployed city dwellers was discussed intensely, but little came of the idea. A bill introduced by the government of Chancellor Heinrich Brüning foundered on the opposition of agrarian magnates who did not want to give up parts of their lands. But as often as the East was associated with utopian visions of social renewal, it was more commonly discussed in terms of backwardness. Large stretches of Eastern Germany were thinly populated, little developed, and desperately poor. Before and after World War I, the state intervened to ease the grave political and social problems of these troubled regions.[3] These discussions included Mecklenburg and Western Pommerania, which are among the poorest regions of today's East Germany.

Germany's East shifted westward after 1945. As a result of the redrawing of borders, the region known during the interwar period as Central Germany (Mitteldeutschland) became East Germany.[4] This area included some of Germany's most important industrial centers, especially in Saxony but also in parts of Thuringia, Brandenburg, and East Berlin. This new East was characterized by a sharp north-south divide. The north (Brandenburg and Mecklenburg-West Pommerania) was primarily agrarian, whereas the south (Thuringia, Saxony, and Saxony-Anhalt) was home to numerous industrial centers. This heterogeneity provided a basis for the GDR to take up the traditional rhetoric of eastern promise and to combine it with the belief in the superiority of socialism. The GDR would become the "better Germany," if not a shining example for the rest of the world. Spurred by the Sputnik euphoria, the GDR's Socialist Unity Party (Sozialistische

---

[2] Rita Gudermann, "'Bereitschaft zur totalen Verantwortung' – Zur Ideengeschichte der Selbstversorgung," in *Der Lange Weg in den Überfluss. Anfänge und Entwicklung der Konsumgesellschaft seit der Vormoderne*, ed. Michael Prinz (Paderborn, 2003), 375–411.

[3] Uwe Müller, "Die sozialökonomische Situation in den ostdeutschen Grenzregionen und die Beziehungen zu Polen im 20. Jahrhundert," in *Politische Ökonomie Deutch-Polnischer Beziehungen im 20. Jahrhundert*, ed. Dieter Bingen, Peter Oliver Loew, and Nikolaus Wolf (Wiesbaden, 2008), 58–77; Uwe Müller, "Die Industrialisierung des agrarischen Ostens. Motive, Erfolge und Grenzen staatlicher Industrieförderung in Westpreußen um 1900," *Jahrbuch für Regionalgeschichte* 28 (2010): 99–115.

[4] The GDR comprised East Berlin as its capital city and Mecklenburg, Brandenburg, Saxony-Anhalt, Thuringia, Saxony, and the western parts of two provinces, Pomerania and Lower Silesia. Still, there was some overlap with the "old East."

Einheitspartei Deutschlands, or SED) announced in 1958 at its tenth congress that the "superiority of the socialist model" vis-à-vis "the imperialist forces in the Bonn state" could be "unambiguously proven." Consumption in the GDR, the party predicted, would reach and then surpass the level of West Germany by 1961.[5] The frustration caused by the utter failure of this promise was among the main reasons behind the mass exodus of East Germans to the Federal Republic that led to the erection of the Berlin Wall in 1961. Apparently undeterred by the failure of the SED's earlier promise, party General Secretary and GDR head of state Walter Ulbricht made an even bolder prediction in 1970 when he famously announced that the GDR would overtake the West economically without bothering to catch up. This declaration became the rallying cry in the GDR's attempt to find its own path to industrial progress without copying Western products or strategies.[6]

Even if this eagerness could not prevent the economic decline of the GDR, we still have to consider the relative success and longevity of the East German economic system. By many measures, the East German economy was the strongest economy in the Eastern bloc, and the GDR ranked as one of the twenty most important industrial nations worldwide. But the economic history of the GDR is nonetheless usually presented as a history of failure, a failure all the more conspicuous when contrasted to the Federal Republic's record of economic success. From this perspective, the GDR stands as the preeminent example of the deficiencies of central planning. It was not a foregone conclusion in 1945, however, that East Germany would fall behind Western Germany economically or that the gap between them would steadily widen. Loss of productive capacity to Allied bombing was far less extensive in what became the Soviet occupation zone than in the western part of the country. That difference was more than offset, however, by Soviet dismantling and removal of factories during the occupation. The establishment of central planning, the nationalization of large industrial companies, and the emigration of business and technical elites further weakened Eastern Germany. As econometric research by Albrecht Ritschl has shown, the transition to central planning triggered a shock that immediately pushed down productivity levels. A considerable gap had emerged vis-á-vis

---

[5] Quoted in Annette Kaminsky, *Wohlstand, Schönheit, Glück. Kleine Konsumgeschichte der DDR* (Munich, 2001), 49.

[6] See André Steiner, *Von Plan zu Plan: Eine Wirtschaftsgeschichte der DDR* (Munich, 2004); published in English as *The Plans That Failed: An Economic History of the GDR* (New York, 2010).

West Germany by 1950.[7] Central planning means in essence to do without
market signals, feedback from strong competitors and critical consumers,
and constant incentives to improve quality and raise productivity. It is undis-
putable that central planning has a built-in tendency to self-destruction, but
to summarize the economic history of the GDR as an "exercise in futility,"
as Ritschl put it, is deterministic and ahistorical. Nor does underscoring the
limitations of central planning explain the comparative economic success
the GDR achieved or how its economy managed to continue functioning
for as long as it did.

The time is ripe to set aside the simplistic narrative that regards the
GDR economy primarily as a failure and as nothing but an example of
the inherent deficiencies of central planning, especially when contrasted
with the outstanding economic success of the Federal Republic. The story
is much more complicated. Accordingly, this volume does not propose
an alternative narrative but rather stresses the coexistence of continuity
and upheaval, the concurrence of contradictory trends, the fragmentary
nature of East Germany's economic development, and the persistence of
regional disparities. The contributors explore the factors behind both the
strengths and weaknesses of the East German economy. The time period
considered here is not limited to the years of the GDR's existence. This
volume takes the decades before 1945 as well as the post-1990 era into
account to consider longer historical trends, the effects of several changes of
political regime, and the fate of distinct regional economic structures over
the *longue durée*. Just as the GDR did not begin with a blank slate in 1949,
the dissolution of the GDR in 1990 did not simply wipe away the legacy
of four decades of central planning. This volume shows, in short, that the
GDR was by no means isolated from the course of German history.

This book is interdisciplinary. The contributors come from the fields of
history, economics, political science, and business history. Their methodological approaches range from biographical and business case histories to
macroeconomic analyses. This book sets out to do three things: to take stock
of the research on the economic history of the GDR published since the
early 1990s, assess trends in research, and integrate the history of the Eastern
German economy within one narrative that encompasses the socialist past,
the process of unification and transformation, and the capitalist future.

With the opening of the East German archives in the early 1990s, scholars
were at last able to study the GDR's economic history in depth and thereby

---

[7] Albrecht Ritschl, "An Exercise in Futility: Growth and Decline of the East German Economy, 1945–
1989," in *Economic Growth in Postwar Europe*, ed. Nick Crafts and Gianni Toniolo (Cambridge, 1996),
498–540.

gained new insights. André Steiner and Jeffrey Kopstein were the first historians to present narratives that spanned the decades from the Soviet occupation and the beginnings of central planning through the economic experiments of the 1960s to the period of rapid decline after 1970 and the end of the East German state in 1990.[8] Both authors explored the functioning of the socialist planned economy with its internal processes, ideological limitations, historical legacies, and external challenges.

In the opening essay of this collection, Steiner builds on and extends his basic narrative. He integrates recent research on price policy[9] and consumerism[10] in the GDR, and he continues his narrative beyond 1989 to consider the economic situation of the "new eastern states" in united Germany. Steiner outlines the major economic decisions by the Soviet occupation authorities in the immediate postwar period and, later, by the SED. He traces the history of the major crises in the 1950s, the reform programs of the 1960s, the challenges of the 1970s, and the attempts at industrial innovation in the 1980s. The key factor behind the GDR's ultimately disastrous economic performance, Steiner argues, was the inflexibility of the SED's economic plans, which rested on incomplete or inadequate information, eschewed competition, and stifled innovation. Taking stock of the period of transformation in the 1990s, Steiner concludes that the results were largely positive despite the high social costs and the burdens of adaptation borne by East German citizens.

BEGINNINGS, CRISES, AND REFORMS: THE PLANNED ECONOMY, 1945–1971

Of all the different phases of the separated East German territory's history, the years of Soviet occupation are the period we know the least about. In the mid-1990s, Norman Naimark opened the way to a deeper understanding of

---

[8] Jeffrey Kopstein, *The Politics of Economic Decline in East Germany, 1945–1989* (Chapel Hill, NC, 1997). Steiner, *Von Plan zu Plan.* Even broader in regional and chronological scope is Jaap Sleifer, *Planning Ahead and Falling Behind: The East German Economy in Comparison with West Germany 1936–2002* (Berlin, 2006).

[9] Jennifer Scevardo, *Vom Wert des Notwendigen: Preispolitik und Lebensstandard in der DDR der fünfziger Jahre* (Stuttgart, 2006); Jonathan R. Zatlin, *The Currency of Socialism: Money and Political Culture in East Germany* (Cambridge, 2007).

[10] No aspect of the economic and the cultural history of the GDR has received as much scholarly attention as the consumption. See, e.g., Philipp Heldmann, *Herrschaft, Wirtschaft, Anoraks: Konsumpolitik in der DDR der Sechzigerjahre* (Göttingen, 2004); Mark Landsman, *Dictatorship and Demand: The Politics of Consumerism in East Germany* (Cambridge, MA, 2005); Judd Stitziel, *Fashioning Socialism: Clothing, Politics, and Consumer Culture in East Germany* (Oxford, 2005); Eli Rubin, *Synthetic Socialism: Plastics and Dictatorship in the German Democratic Republic* (Chapel Hill, NC, 2008).

the hopes and fears that shaped Soviet policy in the wake of the war.[11]
Several recent German publications have broadened our understanding of
the reasoning behind agrarian reform during the Soviet occupation and
reparation policies.[12] In his contribution to this volume, Burghard Ciesla
analyzes the Soviet's strategic economic decisions in their occupation zone
and the mind-set – a mixture of fear and revenge – that led them to impose
an often-contradictory reparations policy that made economic success in
East Germany impossible in the long run. Ciesla describes in detail the
dismantling of factories in the Soviet zone and its economic consequence.
The memory of earlier hunger crises, he notes, was a guiding force in the
Soviet's economic decision making in Germany.

The essays on the period 1945–1971 that follow Ciesla's analyze the interconnections between central factors in the GDR's economy – labor, enterprises, technology, and trade – that have usually been discussed separately.[13]
Rainer Karlsch's article on autarky projects in Eastern Germany shows how
Nazi-era autarky projects in the "Chemical Triangle" near Halle influenced
the economic structure of the GDR and created unhealthy path dependencies. Karlsch also analyzes projects that originated in the GDR but had
the same aim as Nazi autarky projects, namely import substitution and the
alleviation of the badly strained foreign exchange balance. These projects
included copper and iron mining; the production of crude oil and natural
gas; and, later on, microelectronics. All of these projects turned out to be a
burden on the GDR economy, and none proved viable under free market
conditions after unification.

The long-term studies by Karlsch and Silke Fengler in this collection
point to the constraints on enterprises in the GDR. They tell a story of
strong Soviet influence, inflexible plans, lagging innovation, and eventual
decline.[14] But more than that, they provide insights into the more complex
power play between ruling, planning, controlling, and resisting on the level
of everyday work life. Andrew Port shifts attention to the field of workers'
history, which has gained the most attention of all topics in the spectrum of

---

[11] Norman M. Naimark, *The Russians in Germany: A History of the Soviet Zone of Occupation, 1945–1949* (Cambridge, MA, 1995).

[12] Rainer Karlsch and Jochen Laufer, eds., *Sowjetische Demontagen in Deutschland 1944–1949: Hintergründe, Ziele und Wirkungen* (Berlin, 2002); Elke Scherstjanoi, *SED-Agrarpolitik unter sowjetischer Kontrolle 1949–1953* (Munich, 2007).

[13] A comparable attempt was published in German: André Steiner, ed., *Überholen ohne einzuholen: Die DDR-Wirtschaft als Fussnote der deutschen Geschichte?* (Berlin, 2006).

[14] On the very special case of uranium mining, see Juliane Schütterle, *Kumpel, Kader und Genossen: Arbeiten und Leben im Uranbergbau der DDR. Die Wismut AG* (Paderborn, 2010).

the GDR's economic history.[15] That is understandable, as Kopstein argued in his 1995 book, as the "social compact" between state and working class had given the latter a kind of veto power. In addition, the lives and actions of the working class are a key to understanding the unique picture of social conflict and consent in the GDR that can in the end even explain the curiously long stability of the economically and ideologically declining dictatorship.[16]

In his contribution on workers' life in Saalfeld, Port makes use of Alf Lüdtke's concept of *Eigensinn*. Port shows how the state's attempt to create artificial competition among workers to stimulate productivity failed. The promise of special gratifications had a contrary outcome: socialist workers began to sabotage the work of their colleagues in the struggle for benefits and honors – a process Port terms the "dark side of *Eigensinn*." His essay shows how fragile and self-destructive the economic system was on the basis of everyday work life and shop-floor practices. Morale was notoriously low, and the workers' party did not reach the proletarians it claimed to represent. There was no constructive element in their frustration. It was not only the plans that failed but also the people who were supposed to use them as guidelines.

Dolores Augustine's work on microelectronics tells a similar story at the management level and its relation to the political leadership. By choosing a biographical approach, she also highlights the combined social, economic, and political changes that marked the transition from Ulbricht to Erich Honecker in 1971. Analyzing the biography of Werner Hartmann, the "father of GDR's microelectronics," Augustine outlines the shifts in the GDR's culture of technological innovation that undermined the regime's economic viability as early as the 1960s. Lack of access to Western technological developments, she argues, was not the only obstacle impeding the GDR's microelectronics industry. The increasingly restrictive security measures in the realm of technology imposed by the SED and the Stasi also had a deadening impact on scientific and technological productivity. The further tightening of control over scientific research during the Honecker years is one reason why the GDR's competitive potential in the technological sector hit a new low point in the 1980s. Hartmann started off as a

---

[15] Renate Hürtgen and Thomas Reichel, eds., *Der Schein der Stabilität: DDR-Betriebsalltag in der Ära Honecker* (Berlin, 2001); Jeannette Z. Madarász, *Working in East Germany: Normality in a Socialist Dictatorship, 1961–1979* (New York, 2006); Christoph Kleßmann, *Arbeiter im "Arbeiterstaat" DDR: Deutsche Traditionen, sowjetisches Modell, westdeutsches Magnetfeld (1945–1971)* (Bonn, 2007).

[16] Andrew Port, *Conflict and Stability in the German Democratic Republic* (Cambridge, 2007).

dedicated and highly motivated scientist, but, as Augustine explains, he was ultimately worn down by his frustration with the SED regime.

LIVING BEYOND ONE'S MEANS: THE LONG DECLINE, 1971–1989

The third section of this volume concentrates on the last two decades of the GDR's existence. These essays increase our understanding of the economic changes that followed after Honecker supplanted Ulbricht as the GDR's head of state and leader of the SED. They highlight the different factors at play during a period that, for very good reason, has typically been characterized as a time of stagnation and decline. Compared to the 1960s, when the state tried to implement several economic reforms and create artificial competition within the planned economy, the 1970s and 1980s saw a number of initiatives to assuage public discontent, including increased production of consumer goods and the extension of social welfare benefits, but few serious attempts to address the fundamental structural problems hobbling the GDR's economy.

Reflecting a trend in recent scholarship on the GDR, the essays in this section take the international dimensions of the GDR's economic history into consideration. Technological competition with the West, the challenges posed by global economic crises, and the GDR's all-important but difficult trade relations with the Federal Republic are central topics in this section. These essays also highlight the inner-bloc dependencies and the Soviet Union's role as de facto occupier, sometime generous but often-unreliable business partner, and competitor. The GDR's planned economy did not operate solely within the protected cocoon of the Council for Mutual Economic Assistance (COMECON). The deficiencies of economic cooperation within the Eastern bloc spurred increased cooperation with the West, which brought with it new international dependencies. Indeed, "inner-German economic relations," which rested on massive loans from Bonn to East Berlin, helped postpone the GDR's economic collapse.

In his contribution to this volume, Ray Stokes analyzes the impact of the 1970s oil crises on the GDR. The surge in oil prizes in 1973 and 1978 upset the world economy at large and also deeply affected the countries of the Eastern bloc and their trade relations with each other. The GDR's demand for oil increased sharply with the SED's new emphasis on satisfying consumer demand after Honecker came to power. Stokes shows how heavily the GDR relied on the Soviet Union as it principal supplier and how the Soviet Union initially supported the GDR by selling it oil on extremely favorable terms. After the Soviet Union began to cut back on oil deliveries in the late 1970s, however, the GDR had to change course. The regime rose to the new challenge by investing money into short-term solutions like increasing brown coal production, which threatened further harm to the environment, and expanding the GDR's debt to foreign lenders. The regime simply did not consider long-term solutions to economic problems and energy needs but tried to cling to an unsustainable pattern of consumption and trade. Its collapse was only a matter of time.

Cooperation within the framework of COMECON was envisioned as a motor of economic development, but the results often fell short of expectations, as Fengler shows in her study here of the VEB Filmfabrik Wolfen. The Wolfen film works' difficulties were compounded by the SED's decision in 1958 to make the country's photochemical industry independent of Western suppliers. The result was a decline in the quality of Wolfen's products, which hurt sales not only in the West but also in the other COMECON member states. The Wolfen works fell steadily behind its capitalist competitors technologically during the 1960s and 1970s. Plans to trade its film products for Soviet goods and raw materials, above all oil, did not halt the firm's decline. The opening of the Eastern German economy to international competition with unification spelt the end for the Wolfen film works.

Ralf Ahrens's essay analyzes the vicious circle that developed in the GDR's foreign trade during the Honecker years. The more heavily the GDR depended on the other COMECON states as an export market for its outmoded, low-quality products, the less capable it was to pursue technological innovation, which in turned fueled an "import hunger" for Western goods to meet domestic consumer demand. The Soviet Union supported the GDR by buying East German products that could not be sold in the West, for example, and by providing raw materials at below world-market prices. The Soviet Union could not, however, prevent the GDR from spiraling into debt caused by its trade with Western countries. Rising prices for raw material on the world market contributed to the problem and lead to a predictable breakdown of the GDR's economic system in the late 1980s. Taken together, the contributions by Ahrens and Stokes shed light on the complex relations between the GDR and the Soviet Union by calling attention to the Soviet Union's dual role as protector but also competitor for market share.

With Kopstein's essay, attention shifts from the micro- to the macrolevel. Offering a new reading of the GDR's political economy, Kopstein examines the nature of the economic order that evolved from occupation-era Soviet influence and the legacy of National Socialism. Drawing on the work of the political economist Andrew Janos, he considers the question of continuity between the Third Reich and the GDR by looking at their economic systems as "militarized economies." Although weapons production did not figure prominently in its economy, the GDR was a major supplier of militarily relevant products – ranging from machine tools and optical technology to chemicals and uranium – to the Soviet Union. More important, Kopstein suggests, was the militarization of East German society and its impact on labor relations. The SED's attempts to spur workers to greater productivity with militaristic sloganeering met with considerable resistance. Both the Nazi and SED dictatorships responded to worker discontent with social bribery because both feared the prospect of challenge by mass protests: 1919 and 1953, in short, cast long shadows.

TRANSFORMATION, SUBVENTION, AND RENEWAL, 1989–2010

This volume extends the history of the Eastern German economy into the postunification period and offers for the first time an integrated narrative of the socialist economic past and the difficult transformation process during the first decades of the Berlin Republic. Going a step further, several contributors also offer their thoughts on the long-term effects of the socialist experiment and the transformation process on Eastern Germany's economic future.

Although Helmut Kohl's famous 1990 promise of "flourishing landscapes" and de Maizière's "powerhouse" metaphor might not have been much more realistic than Ulbricht's 1971 vision of a socialist land of plenty, some scholars have nonetheless identified distinct advantages that the East German economy possesses. Rather than extolling such advantages uncritically or making unrealistic claims for East Germany's prospects, these scholars balance signs of promise against the glaring indications of decline, notably persistently high unemployment; continuing emigration of the young and skilled; heavy dependence on subsidies; and comparatively high levels of support for radical political forces on both the left and the right. They either constitute legacies of older regional advantages or emerged only in the transformation process. Instead of extolling these factors in a one-sided fashion and founding unrealistic claims of an avant-garde model region on them, these scholars balance these factors against the still-glaring signs of decline such as high unemployment figures, high numbers of emigration especially of young and well-qualified people, the continued dependence on subventions, and a marked overrepresentation of political radicalism.

Karl-Heinz Paqué, an economist who served as economics minister in the state of Saxony-Anhalt from 2002 to 2006, has stressed the magnitude of the challenge in integrating East Germany into the global market economy.[17] This venture, in Paqué's view, was hampered by the lasting damages of forty years of socialist economic planning. Decades of isolation from Western markets and from cutting-edge research and development, of running down the country's capital stock, and of horrific environmental contamination could not be overcome in a couple of years. Productivity was deplorably low and competitive products almost nonexistent. Political oppression and propaganda left their scars on Eastern society and habits of thought. A dictatorship that encouraged conformism and discouraged initiative had created a culture of compliance and passivity. Consequently, free markets and individual responsibility were viewed more as threats than as opportunities. Many former GDR citizens expected much from the welfare state and deeply mistrusted the market. When millions of industrial jobs were axed in the first postunification years, bitterness and resentment loomed large. Overcoming this mental legacy will take many years, Paqué contends, and the coming of age of younger generations that escaped the influence of the SED dictatorship. Considering the severity of these challenges, East Germany has, with the help of massive transfers from West Germany, done rather well in Paqué's view, although many problems persist. Average per capita productivity in Germany's Eastern states, for example, is still well below the level of the Western states but higher by large margins than the Polish, Hungarian, Slovakian, Slovenian, and Czech averages.[18]

Political scientist Wolfgang Streeck has also concluded that unification has had mixed results. In his view, unification not only radically changed the former GDR but also paved the way for a new type of capitalism that spells the end of the Federal Republic's model of cooperative capitalism.[19] Under extreme time pressure during the heady days of 1989–90, when the window of opportunity for uniting Germany opened unexpectedly and the rapid pace of stunning developments required immediate decisions, there was no chance to pursue a "third way" or to design a radically new political or economic system. Instead, in a rare historical experiment, the complete institutional system of one state was transferred to another. For interests vested in the preservation of West Germany's social system of production, unification was "a unique opportunity to protect the West German welfare state from mounting pressures for reform by extending it"[20] to the former

---

[17] Karl-Heinz Paqué, *Die Bilanz. Eine wirtschaftliche Analyse der Deutschen Einheit* (Munich, 2009).

[18] Ibid., 198–207.

[19] See Wolfgang Streeck, *Re-Forming Capitalism: Institutional Change in the German Political Economy* (Oxford, 2009), esp. 207–16. See also Peter A. Hall and David Soskice, eds., *Varieties of Capitalism: The Institutional Foundations of Comparative Advantage* (Oxford, 2001).

[20] Streeck, *Re-Forming*, 212.

GDR. The result was an unhealthy cocktail composed of unsustainable demands on the social welfare system, the overextension of parafiscal budgets, the need to subsidize them out of the state budget, and an escalating debt burden for the enlarged Federal Republic. Unification thus at first aggravated the massive problems that the West German system already had and brought the cautious attempts at institutional reform of the 1980s virtually to a standstill. Ironically, this temporary triumph of vested rights set in motion a "gradual process of transformative institutional change" that undermined some pillars of West German cooperative capitalism and created, according to Streeck, the opportunity for creating a new system that might be more sustainable under conditions of globalization. Organized labor and capital were substantially weakened in East Germany during the 1990s, and centralized collective wage agreements were frequently replaced by more flexible local agreements, which led to substantially lower wages. In Streeck's view, unification was a shock that – after a phase of high expectations and futile attempts to preserve the status quo – revealed the undeniable need for institutional reform and set into motion first steps toward a fundamental transformation of the German variety of capitalism. Even though this process is still far from completion, the unique historical event of unification opened the way to institutional renewal.[21]

Both optimistic and pessimistic assessments of the unification process are represented in this volume. Social historian Gerhard A. Ritter emphasizes the negative consequences of transferring the social system of the Federal Republic to the new states. Drawing on his study *Der Preis der Einheit*,[22] he demonstrates how the transfer of the West German system to the economically weaker East produced higher wages and inflated the cost of unification. Western options for early retirement and short-term employment became important parts of the labor market policy toward the East. The result, Ritter notes, was a vicious circle in which high social welfare costs led to increasing unemployment.

Ritter's negative take on German economic unification stands in contrast to the more positive assessment offered here by economist Michael Burda. Surveying economic developments in the different regions of the former GDR since unification, Burda underscores the dramatic improvements of

---

[21] This argument is also put forward in Michael Burda, "What Kind of Shock Was It? Regional Integration and Structural Change in Germany after Unification," *Journal of Comparative Economics* 36 (2008): 557–67; Michael Burda, "Factor Reallocation in Eastern Germany after Reunification," *American Economic Review* 96 (2006): 368–74.

[22] Gerhard A. Ritter, *Der Preis der deutschen Einheit: Die Wiedervereinigung und die Krise des Sozialstaats* (Munich, 2006); published in English as *The Price of German Unity: Reunification and the Crisis of the Welfare State* (Oxford, 2011).

living standards in the East over the last two decades and the convergence of consumption patterns in the East and West. He also points to the relocation of firms to the Eastern states resulting from the wage differential between Eastern and Western Germany. The economic future of new states, Burda predicts, will be characterized by growth, not decline.

The final essay in this volume takes up a question that countless Germans, ordinary citizens as well as economists and policy makers, have asked: Why did the currency union of 1990 and economic reforms introduced with unification fail to trigger a second *Wirtschaftswunder*? To answer that question, Holger Wolf compares the West German currency reform of 1948 and the reform of 1990. In both instances, economies stifled by wage and price controls, heavy governmental debt, and extensive state influence were to be invigorated by monetary reform and price liberalization. The reform of 1990 had a very different outcome than that of 1948. In 1990, Wolf notes, currency reform did not introduce a hard but undervalued currency as in 1948 but rather a hard and high-valued currency; most industrial firms were simply priced out of the market as a result. Moreover, the favorable real labor cost dynamics of the postwar period could not be recreated for political reasons. Wolf points also to differences in the international settings in which the reforms took place. The liberalization of world trade, the push for European integration, and strong global demand for capital goods helped turn the D-Mark boom of 1948 into the sustained West German economic miracle of the 1950s and 1960s. Although global trade was expanding rapidly during the 1990s, East German firms found it difficult to gain a foothold in intensely competitive international markets. Acknowledging the difficulties that the East German economy experienced in the years immediately following the 1990 reforms, Wolf, like Burda, sees the more recent growth in manufacturing output and exports as encouraging signs for the future.

It is clear that former chancellor Helmut Schmidt's warning in 2005 that East Germany might become a "Mezzogiorno without the mafia" was unrealistic and too gloomy.[23] There have been many positive developments: spectacular productivity gains, flexible labor market arrangements, low real labor costs, and the successful rejuvenation of old regional specializations. Nevertheless, East Germany's successful regions can still be seen as mere pockets within a larger area of relative depression and backwardness. Twenty years after unification, East Germany continues to suffer from high unemployment and net emigration, especially of the young and the skilled.

---

[23] Quoted in Paqué, *Bilanz*, 181.

A government brochure celebrating the twentieth anniversary of unification bemoans that "inner unity" has still not been fully achieved. The "equalization of living conditions in the East and the West," which is mandated by the Germany constitution, remains an unfinished task "of national priority."[24] But what is the real significance of the findings presented in this book? The coexistence of prosperous regions with strong industrial and services sectors alongside less affluent regions dominated by agriculture and tourism might not be such a disaster. That is probably a rather normal situation and a pattern very much in line with the regional economic structures of pre-1945 Germany as well as of other nations such as Britain, France, and the United States.

---

[24] *Magazin-deutschland.de. Forum on Politics, Culture and Business* No. 3, 2010, 3.

2

From the Soviet Occupation Zone to the "New Eastern States"

A Survey

ANDRÉ STEINER

The independent Eastern German economy resulted from the division of Germany following World War II, and it disappeared in the wake of Germany's political unification in 1990.[1] A consequence of the onset of the Cold War, the division of Germany was the decisive development in the shaping of the Eastern German economy. A Soviet-style planned economic system was established in the East that regarded itself as the alternative to the Western free market system. It derived its legitimacy from the claim that, after the experience of the international depression of the early 1930s, it would prevent economic crises, unemployment, and homelessness. When that system failed, the Eastern German state lost its claim to legitimacy, and this economic area was incorporated within a united Germany. Beginning with the starting conditions of the Eastern German economy, this essay traces the development of this region from the time of the Soviet occupation, through the existence of the German Democratic Republic (GDR), and into the first two decades of the unified Federal Republic.[2]

STARTING CONDITIONS

The region that became the Soviet occupation zone was already highly industrialized before World War II. For strategic reasons, the National Socialists began to expand the industrial sector in Central Germany in

---

[1] The term *Eastern Germany* is used here to refer to the area that constituted the Soviet occupation zone and that, in turn, became the GDR and the new states of the Federal Republic of Germany after unification.

[2] On the period of the Soviet occupation and the GDR era, see the detailed account and source references in André Steiner, *The Plans That Failed: An Economic History of the GDR* (New York, 2010). In this essay, I limit citations to the sources of the figures, statistics, and quotations given in the text and to some important scholarly studies.

1936 to increase arms production and to prepare for war.[3] At the end of the war, it was estimated that only 15 percent of the industrial capacity that had existed in the Soviet zone in 1944 had been destroyed. On the whole, damage to industry was less extensive there than in the zones occupied by the Western allies. The regions that fell within the Soviet zone did, however, experience heavy losses of livestock, transportation infrastructure, and housing stock.[4]

Another starting condition of the Soviet zone was that it was almost entirely dependent on deliveries of important industrial raw and input materials from elsewhere, either from other parts of Germany or from abroad. Inadequate local supplies of coal, iron ore, and raw steel were the decisive structural weakness in the Soviet zone's economy. Only brown coal and potash were available in abundance. The dependence on iron and steel produced elsewhere was a hindrance to the highly developed machine tool and metal-working industries in the Soviet zone. The chemical industry was dominated by the manufacture of primary products, and there was little further processing. The paper, food, and textile industries were also well represented in the Soviet zone. Before the war, the sections of Central Germany that became the Soviet zone had been much more dependent on trade with other parts of Germany than were the areas occupied by the Western Allies. After the war, the region's trade increasingly shifted eastward as relations between the wartime Allies deteriorated and the division between the Western and Soviet zones hardened. The more pronounced these developments became, the stronger the negative effects of these imbalances on the economic structure of the Soviet zone. A further aggravating factor was that the planned economy established in the East tended to inhibit foreign trade, making it impossible to use this means to fill gaps in the economic structure brought about by the division of Germany.

Despite these imbalances, the Soviet zone had substantial economic potential at the end of the war. It had, however, to bear the considerable burden of reparations to the Soviet Union. By 1948, the Soviets had dismantled and appropriated approximately 3,400 factories. Taking investments, war damages, and depreciation into account as well, the value of Soviet zone gross capital assets was 25 percent lower in 1948 than in 1936. In addition to the capital assets dismantled and removed to the Soviet Union,

---

[3] Bruno Gleitze, *Ostdeutsche Wirtschaft. Industrielle Standorte und volkswirtschaftliche Kapazitäten des ungeteilten Deutschlands* (Berlin [West], 1956), 173.

[4] Rainer Karlsch, *Allein bezahlt? Die Reparationsleistungen der SBZ/DDR 1945–1953* (Berlin, 1993), 44–6; Werner Matschke, *Die industrielle Entwicklung in der Sowjetischen Besatzungszone Deutschlands (SBZ) von 1945 bis 1948* (Berlin [West], 1988), 301.

the direct and indirect reparations that the Soviet zone and East Berlin paid between 1945 and 1953 are estimated to have been worth at least U.S. $14 billion in 1938 prices. The burden of reparations diminished only gradually. In 1946, reparations amounted to nearly half of the gross national product; in 1953, they still comprised 13 percent. In all, the per capita burden on the Soviet zone/GDR was many times higher than that on the Western zones.[5] Eastern Germany paid more in reparations than any other defeated combatant of World War II. That burden seriously impaired the economic development of the Soviet zone/GDR, but high reparations alone do not explain the GDR's later lag in growth vis-à-vis the Federal Republic. That was, rather, primarily a consequence of the economic system.

ESTABLISHING THE PLANNED ECONOMY

The first steps toward nationalizing the economy took place in the context of the processes of denazifying and democratizing Germany that the Allies had agreed upon. In connection with these processes, the structure of property ownership in Eastern Germany was transformed. The Soviets initiated these processes, and German agencies, often led by communists, implemented and frequently intensified them. They started with land reform in agriculture, seizing large estates and redistributing the land. In part a punitive measure against old elites, this change was expected to better secure the food supply as private ownership by many individuals was supposed to provide incentive to increase production. The new farmers were expected to be able to earn a livelihood from the allotments of expropriated land and equipment they received. But in the end, they did not receive sufficient supplies of land, livestock, or equipment, and only a few of them were able to sustain themselves successfully. This shortcoming was to have a long-lasting impact on agricultural production in the GDR.[6]

In the industrial sector, National Socialist activists and war profiteers were to be dispossessed. Their assets and German state assets were the Soviet occupiers' first confiscations. Firms were supposed to be evaluated on a case-by-case basis, but, as it turned out, any firm that had achieved a certain size was regarded as "deserving of expropriation" (*enteignungswürdig*). Consequently, all large firms as well as numerous medium-sized businesses had been expropriated by 1948. De jure, they became *Volkseigentum*, "the

---

[5] On reparations to the Soviet Union, see Karlsch, *Allein bezahlt?*
[6] See Arnd Bauerkämper, ed., *"Junkerland in Bauernhand"? Durchführung, Auswirkungen und Stellenwert der Bodenreform in der Sowjetischen Besatzungszone* (Stuttgart, 1996).

people's property"; de facto, they were in the hands of the state. Subsequently, an ever larger share of supplies and investment was allocated to the burgeoning state sector. At the same time, private firms were disadvantaged, particularly as authorities directed the full force of tax regulations and laws on economic crimes against them. By 1948–9, growing numbers of private business owners were declaring bankruptcy, giving up, and/or fleeing to the West. In 1950, the state sector accounted for three-quarters of industrial production, and by 1955, the proportion had risen to more than four-fifths.[7]

The Soviets regarded the expropriations and the first steps toward a planned command economy as necessary above all to secure reparations. These steps were also in line with the ambitions of the Communist Party (Kommunistische Partei Deutschlands, or KPD) and, in turn, its successor, the Socialist Unity Party (Sozialistische Einheitspartei Deutschlands, or SED). These parties sought ultimately to restructure Eastern German society along communist lines; initially, however, they pursued another tactic in light of Soviet policy toward Germany. Many people throughout Europe saw state economic intervention as necessary to address extreme poverty. Moreover, as state-owned firms accounted for an ever larger share of economic activity, greater state control over the economy became necessary. The initial attempts at economic planning – production orders at first, then quarterly plans – were impeded by the Soviets' uncoordinated dismantling of factories and their reparations demands as well as by their random seizures of goods, supplies, and equipment. Consequently, planning efforts were often at cross-purposes. Although production increased quickly at first after the war, it collapsed during the exceptionally hard winter of 1946–7. Employees were undernourished, and wartime industrial reserves of raw materials and supplies had been used up. The distribution system was unable to provide relief – a situation exacerbated by a transportation crisis – and worker performance and productivity declined. The Eastern German communists and the Soviet occupiers responded to this crisis by tightening economic controls and by developing more effective incentives to improve worker performance. A central body for steering economic policy, the German Economic Commission, was established, along with a hierarchical state apparatus. Economic planning was expanded to cover longer spans of time. A six-month plan for 1948 was followed by a two-year plan for 1949–50. The German Economic Commission formed the core of

---

[7] Based on Werner Krause, *Die Entstehung des Volkseigentums in der Industrie der DDR* (Berlin [East], 1958), 108; Staatliche Zentralverwaltung für Statistik, ed., *Statistisches Jahrbuch der DDR 1955* (Berlin [East], 1955), 126.

the new government when the GDR was founded in 1949.[8] In November 1950, the State Planning Commission was formed. It assumed leadership over all other institutions dealing with economic matters. Ministries were created to manage individual branches of industry and other sectors of the economy, and large enterprises were directly subordinated to them. Nevertheless, the SED leadership and the economic departments of the party headquarters still had the final say in economic decision making.

It quickly became apparent that motivating workers to increase their productivity would be difficult in an economy dominated by state-owned enterprises. The ideal of the socialist "New Man" that the authorities' espoused quickly proved to be illusory as formal worker ownership of the means of production failed to provide motivation to work harder. Consequently, the SED faced a fundamental contradiction between the pressures of economic necessity and the legitimating principles upon which socialist rule rested. The promise of full employment was a cornerstone of SED ideology, but it prevented the use of the *ultima ratio* when workers or enterprises failed to perform as desired, namely dismissal in the case of workers and closure in the case of enterprises. Moreover, the SED leadership legitimized its rule as by designating the GDR the "Workers' and Peasants' State," but it also had to act as an employer vis-à-vis the workforce − an employer who kept demanding greater effort and output. Each additional coercive measure potentially endangered the SED's legitimacy, but so did refraining from coercion, which resulted in reduced economic efficiency.

The SED attempted to solve this problem by decree as part of its program to accelerate the development of socialism in 1952–3. That program, however, ended up triggering a popular uprising on June 17, 1953.[9] Traumatized, the SED leadership was extremely cautious in its efforts to promote productivity thereafter. It tried to develop economic incentives beyond mere coercion and ideologically camouflaged pressure.

Another fundamental issue for a Soviet-style planned economy was the information problem.[10] In the perfect market economy, prices, determined by the free interplay of supply and demand, are a form of uncertain information that firms utilize in making decisions. In a planned economy, by contrast, authorities seek to consciously direct economic activity in advance;

---

[8] André Steiner, "Die Deutsche Wirtschaftskommission − ein ordnungspolitisches Machtinstrument?" in *Das letzte Jahr der SBZ. Politische Weichenstellungen und Kontinuitäten im Prozeß der Gründung der DDR*, ed. Dierk Hoffmann and Hermann Wentker (Munich, 2000), 85–105.

[9] On the uprising, see Christoph Buchheim, "Wirtschaftliche Hintergründe des Arbeiteraufstandes vom 17. Juni 1953 in der DDR," *Vierteljahrshefte für Zeitgeschichte* 38 (1990): 415–33.

[10] On the fundamental problems of this economic system, see János Kornai, *The Socialist System: The Political Economy of Communism* (Oxford, 1992).

prices, therefore, are not a source of uncertainty. Consequently, actors in the planned economy could not use prices as an independent source of information derived from the economy itself. The central authorities gathered the information necessary for economic decision making only in the process of preparing the plans. Much of the information came from enterprises and other bodies directly affected by the plans, and they often gave false information to protect their own interests. For that reason and because of the complexity of the economic process, the central planning authorities were not in a position to make optimal decisions. Unsurprisingly, they thus took their orientation from political priorities in accordance with their claim to leadership. In other words, the structure of the economic system called for political decisions in economic affairs.

Because enterprises that fulfilled the centrally set goals could pay bonuses or make investments from either their profits or special government funding, they usually had an interest in meeting at least the minimum requirements of the plans. Consequently, enterprises and their management teams sought to be assigned the lowest possible planning goals and the largest possible resource allocations. Taking advantage of the asymmetrical distribution of information, they often concealed their available capacities and inventories, and they tended to hoard equipment, materials, and even workers in anticipation of spikes in demand and future increases in production quotas. These practices could already be observed in the late 1940s as inventories of materials and unsold products rapidly expanded. As a result of this tendency toward "soft" plans inherent in the system, officials in the higher reaches of the planning apparatus never had a complete picture of the economic situation or of available resources. The "people's enterprises" could try to secure as many resources as possible without worrying about costs because they knew the state would support them even if they operated at a loss. The state felt obliged to prevent any enterprise from going bankrupt and to cover enterprises' financial needs in its efforts to secure full employment and to demonstrate socialism's superiority to Western capitalism. Consequently, the GDR's economic system was characterized by soft budget constraints; in other words, money, or at least the national currency, was never in short supply. It was, rather, the uneven distribution of goods in short supply that set the limits of economic activity.

The planning mechanism in the 1950s was set up so that enterprises were rewarded primarily for fulfilling a specific, quantified gross production target. This approach encouraged maximum utilization of capacity and resources because all production costs and inputs were included in the value of enterprises' output, and rewards (or penalties) were determined by that value. But this measure of performance also encouraged wastefulness and, often, the subordination of quality to quantity. From the perspective engendered by the planning system, any change in products or manufacturing processes appeared to be a disruption, which is why, with few exceptions, enterprises were little interested in innovation. Nor was that a problem, as the general scarcity of goods allowed them to sell their products regardless of quality. That scarcity was a structural problem that resulted from the abundance of money and the concomitant prevalence of hoarding as well as from the absence of incentives for firms to use resources efficiently. The state's monopoly on foreign trade, intended to protect the economy from external "disruptions" also played a role by shielding enterprises from competition. In short, the structure of the system was the major impediment to innovation in the East German economy.[11]

Governmental and party officials were aware of these problems, but they did not regard them as inherent to the system; rather, they saw them as "teething pains." They aimed to solve these issues over the course of the 1950s by expanding planning to all areas of economic activity. Although focused on production and investments, the plans also arranged for the distribution of labor and materials as well as technical development and sales.

In 1950, Western experts estimated the economic output of the GDR (the per capita gross national product) to be about two-thirds of its prewar level and also of West Germany's gross national product per capita.[12] Several factors contributed to this early lag. First, production capacity had been lost to wartime destruction and, to a greater extent, to postwar dismantling and removal. Second, reparations had to be paid out of current production, which had a negative impact in the mid- and long terms. The third major factor was the cost of establishing the planned economy. The attrition of elites robbed the Soviet zone/GDR of entrepreneurial potential and professional expertise. By 1953, more than four thousand East German industrial firms – roughly one out of every seven – had relocated to the West, along with their managers and skilled workers.[13] This situation was exacerbated by the unrealistic assumptions, limitless optimism, widespread

---

[11] Hans-Jürgen Wagener, "Zur Innovationsschwäche der DDR-Wirtschaft," in *Innovationsverhalten und Entscheidungsstrukturen. Vergleichende Studien zur wirtschaftlichen Entwicklung im geteilten Deutschland*, ed. Johannes Bähr and Dietmar Petzina (Berlin, 1996), 21–48.

[12] Wolfgang F. Stolper, *The Structure of the Eastern German Economy* (Cambridge, 1960), 436, 440.

[13] Johannes Bähr, "Die Firmenabwanderung aus der SBZ/DDR und aus Berlin-Ost (1945–1953)," in *Wirtschaft im Umbruch. Strukturveränderungen und Wirtschaftspolitik im 19. und 20. Jahrhundert*, ed. Wolfram Fischer, Uwe Müller, and Frank Zschaler (St. Katharinen, Germany, 1997), 229–49.

incompetence, and occasional chaos of the planning attempts, which were dismissed as start-up difficulties.

FORMING ITS OWN NATIONAL ECONOMY?

The division of Germany tore through a historically developed economic area. As the East and the West increasingly shut themselves off from one another as the Cold War unfolded, the SED leadership decided – in part on Soviet advice – to fill the gaps in existing production lines with new capacities. Soviet reparations demands had already prepared the way for such a structural policy. Since 1947, the Soviets had demanded deliveries of a broad range of industrial goods, particularly from the automotive and heavy engineering sectors. Entire industries, such as ocean-going ship building, were built from the ground up. Others were considerably expanded. Consequently, branches not affected by reparations demands, by contrast, grew more slowly. Carried forth from the Two-Year Plan of 1949–50 to the Five-Year Plans of 1951–5 and 1956–60, this forced structural shift was supposed to forge a national economy for the Soviet zone/GDR. Metallurgy, heavy engineering, and energy were to be the main areas of industrial development.[14] The central authorities concentrated enterprises' profits and invested them in prioritized branches. Heavy industry profited from this policy at the expense of light industry and food production. Even when the forced expansion of heavy industry led to the popular uprising in June 1953, this course was only temporarily abandoned.[15]

Although structural policies continued to prioritize heavy industry, their main emphasis shifted somewhat in the 1950s. Beginning in the middle of the decade, SED economic policy focused more on technological development because the poor quality and outmoded technology made East German products difficult to sell on the domestic and international markets. Technologically, the GDR fell behind the West primarily because the planned economy impeded innovation. Instances of successful innovation were usually the achievement of individual scientists or engineers who managed to overcome systemic hurdles. The orientation of the GDR's

---

[14] Rainer Karlsch, "Die Auswirkungen der Reparationsentnahmen auf die Wettbewerbsfähigkeit der Wirtschaft in der SBZ/DDR," in *Wirtschaftsordnung und Wirtschaftspolitik in Deutschland (1933–1993)*, ed. Jürgen Schneider and Wolfgang Harbrecht (Stuttgart, 1996), 139–72; here, 148–50.

[15] Jörg Roesler, *Die Herausbildung der sozialistischen Planwirtschaft in der DDR. Aufgaben, Methoden und Ergebnisse der Wirtschaftsplanung in der zentralgeleiteten volkseigenen Industrie während der Übergangsperiode vom Kapitalismus zum Sozialismus* (Berlin [East], 1978), 18; André Steiner, "Wirtschaftliche Lenkungsverfahren in der Industrie der DDR Mitte der fünfziger Jahre. Resultate und Alternativen," in *Die Wirtschaftlichen Folgelasten des Krieges in der SBZ/DDR*, ed. Christoph Bucheim (Baden-Baden, 1995), 271–93; here, p. 283.

foreign trade toward the Eastern bloc, the Soviet Union in particular, also inhibited innovation because demand in that market centered on simple, sturdy products. Last but not least, the Cold War also impeded technological development: the flow of information was blocked by both the West's embargo policies and the East's self-imposed isolation.

Starting in the mid-1950s, some of the more modern sectors – the machine tool, engineering, and automation technology industries, for example, and, later, the electronics industry – received more resources. The chief beneficiary was the chemical industry. A program, based on a Soviet model, was adopted in 1958 under the slogan "Chemistry provides bread, prosperity, beauty." It followed a two-pronged strategy to develop the traditional coal-based chemical industry as well as the petrochemical industry, which relied on Soviet petroleum deliveries. Although the former was already falling behind internationally, the local availability of raw materials made support of this industry desirable. However, the development of a power-supply industry and the chemistry program overburdened the capacities of the machine tool, engineering, and construction industries. Moreover, they also consumed more than half of all industrial investment funds.[16]

The heavy concentration of investment changed the structure of industry less than expected because many sectors still had unutilized capacity. The primary and capital goods industries profited most from these investments.[17] As noted previously, structural change was not driven primarily by innovation. Consequently, declining productivity and anemic growth went hand in hand, and the lag behind the Federal Republic did not diminish. In 1958, per capita private consumption still remained below the prewar level and was about half that of West Germany.[18] That the lag behind West Germany in consumption was greater than the lag in output is indicative of the GDR's priorities in the 1950s.

The relatively low standard of living was only one of the reasons why many people turned their backs on the GDR and fled to the West. In light of the inefficient organization of labor and the production standstills caused by economic shortages, many simply wished to "work in an orderly manner"

[16] Wolfgang Mühlfriedel and Klaus Wießner, *Die Geschichte der Industrie der DDR bis 1965* (Berlin [East], 1989), 238–45.

[17] See Manfred Melzer, *Anlagevermögen, Produktion und Beschäftigung der Industrie im Gebiet der DDR von 1936 bis 1978 sowie Schätzung des künftigen Angebotspotentials* (Berlin [West], 1980), 183.

[18] Stolper, *Structure*, 417f., 440; André Steiner, "Preispolitik und ihre Folgen unter den Bedingungen von Diktatur und Demokratie in Deutschland im Vergleich," in *Preispolitik und Lebensstandard. Nationalsozialismus, DDR und Bundesrepublik im Vergleich*, ed. André Steiner (Cologne, 2006), 171–203; here, pp. 196–7.

again.[19] Other factors driving *Republikflucht* (flight from the republic) were despotism and political repression. By the early 1960s, the GDR had lost about 15 percent of its 1950 population,[20] and most of those who had left were young and highly qualified people. This ongoing flight was not only a consequence of the GDR's lag behind the Federal Republic but also a contributing cause: the East's loss in human capital was the West's gain.

To close this gap once and for all and to stem the flight to the West, SED leader Walter Ulbricht announced the "main economic task" at the Fifth SED Party Congress in 1958. The "working population" of Eastern Germany was to "reach and surpass the per capita consumption of the entire West German population" in respect to "all important foodstuffs and consumer goods" by 1961.[21] Behind this optimism lay the belief in socialism's potential – a potential symbolized by the Soviet Union's launch of the Sputnik satellite in October 1957. SED leaders saw this achievement as proof of the superiority of their own system. They also called attention to recent improvements in the GDR's economy, and they interpreted the temporary economic downturn in the Federal Republic in 1958 as the beginning of a serious economic crisis that would make surpassing the Western rival all the easier. Consequently, the SED leaders probably did assume that the country would achieve this challenging goal. They also expected the Soviet Union to help them significantly. Toward meeting the goal of increased food consumption, the SED planned to extend the collectivization of agriculture. Socialist structures of property ownership, they believed, were per se more productive than private ownership. Extending agricultural collectivization also aimed to contribute to the triumph of "socialist relations in production."[22]

In the end, the GDR failed to fulfill this "main economic task" for a number of reasons. The forced total collectivization of agriculture did not produce the intended results. To the contrary, it spurred an increase in the number of farmers fleeing to the West in 1960–1 and led to a crop failure in 1961, which was exacerbated by unfavorable weather. It took the new cooperatives several years to become economically viable. Another cause was the Soviet Union's failure to provide the goods and raw materials

[19] Bericht der Kommission zu Fragen der Republik-Flucht, 25.5.56; Auszug aus dem Protokoll Nr. 29/56 des Politbüro vom 19.6.56; Stellvertreter des Vorsitzenden an Leuschner: Republik-Flucht, 25.9.56, Bundesarchiv Berlin (hereafter referred to as BA) DE1/6109.

[20] The figures presented here are based on Hans-Hermann Hertle, Konrad H. Jarausch, and Christoph Kleßmann, eds., *Mauerbau und Mauerfall. Ursachen – Verlauf – Auswirkungen* (Berlin, 2002), 312.

[21] See *Protokoll der Verhandlungen des V. Parteitages der Sozialistischen Einheitspartei Deutschlands. 10. bis 16. Juli 1958* (Berlin [East], 1959), 68, 70.

[22] See Jens Schöne, *Frühling auf dem Lande? Die Kollektivierung der DDR-Landwirtschaft* (Berlin, 2005).

necessary to achieve planning goals. Some of the partners in the Eastern bloc did not hold to the terms of trade agreements, and trade with the Federal Republic was hobbled by the GDR's difficulties in fulfilling its obligations. Under these circumstances, production in the GDR fell even further behind planning targets, which in turn increased the difficulty of supplying enterprises and the populace with needed goods. An economic vicious circle ensued that political factors only intensified: the supply problems confronting enterprises and the limited range of goods on offer to consumers increased Eastern Germans' dissatisfaction and fueled the wave of flight to the West, which in turn exacerbated the problems of supply and production by reducing the number of workers. The Federal Republic's threat in September 1960 to abrogate the intra-German trade agreement at the end of the year aggravated the situation. Lacking any feasible economic response to this situation, SED leaders sought a political solution: the construction of the Berlin Wall in August 1961 suppressed by force the departure of people "voting with their feet."[23] With that step, the SED leadership in effect acknowledged that the planned economy could not continue to function within open borders because it could not provide the prosperity the government had promised and the populace wanted.

THE DAWN OF A NEW FOUNDATION?

Building the Wall solved neither the basic problem confronting the GDR nor the economic crisis of 1960–1. It did, however, provide protection to those in power, who opted for short-term solutions to the crisis. One initiative was the policy of *Störfreimachung*, that is, the "elimination of disruptions" in the economy by reducing imports from the Federal Republic and other NATO member states. They had demanded something like this from the enterprises before, but now they formulated it programmatically. The West German government's threat to terminate the intra-German trade agreement had demonstrated to those responsible in East Berlin and in Moscow the extent to which the West could use trade for political ends.[24] Yet the entire program reinforced the country's tendency to isolate itself from world markets. Moreover, the products it made often replaced Western imports of

---

[23] André Steiner, "Vom Überholen eingeholt. Zur Wirtschaftskrise 1960/61 in der DDR," in *Sterben für Berlin? Die Berliner Krisen 1948–1958*, ed. Burghard Ciesla, Michael Lemke, and Thomas Lindenberger (Berlin, 1999), 245–62.

[24] Apel an Ulbricht, 4.7.63: Analytische Einschätzung des Standes der Abhängigkeit der DDR . . . , 27.6.63, Stiftung Archiv der Parteien und Massenorganisationen der ehemaligen DDR im Bundesarchiv (hereafter referred to as SAPMO-BA) NY4182/969.

better quality, which had a further detrimental effect on the technological level of production.

SED leaders also utilized the protection provided by the Wall to increase the performance demands on the workers, a step they would scarcely have been able to take with an open border. A campaign to raise work norms was supposed to eliminate the discrepancy between the development of productivity and of wages as well as to redress the imbalance between purchasing power and the availability of goods. The response to this step was growing worker dissatisfaction and a jump in the number of strikes in 1962. Workers often defended themselves by working less productively. Although the program succeeded in raising productivity more than average wages in the short term, wage increases again outpaced productivity growth in the intermediate term.[25] This campaign too showed those in charge that fundamental changes were needed in the economic control mechanisms to make the Eastern German system attractive. Moreover, SED leaders decided they had no choice but to reform the economic system after the Soviet Union rejected their appeal for financial assistance for economic modernization.

After long discussions and preliminary experiments, SED leaders announced the launch of the "New Economic System of Planning and Management of the Economy" in 1963.[26] Ostensibly intended to modernize the economy and increase productivity, this reform program sought above all to present the East German system as a competitive alternative to Western capitalism. Toward that end, the authorities responsible for individual industrial sectors as well as the enterprises were to be given more responsibility in focusing plans on key indicators and in setting goals for the medium term. Economic incentives were to be structured to bring the interests of branches and enterprises in line with those of the central authorities. This made profit the core of a "system of economic levers," which meant that new standards for cost accounting would have to be created. Consequently, industrial prices were to be fixed according to uniform principles, and capital assets were to be revalued. Under the rubric *Eigenerwirtschaftung der Mittel* (self-generation of funding), branches and enterprises were to earn more of their own financing, especially for investment, in order to limit waste and to defuse the problem of soft budget constraint.

---

[25] See Peter Hübner, *Konsens, Konflikt und Kompromiß. Soziale Arbeiterinteressen und Sozialpolitik in der SBZ/DDR 1945–1970* (Berlin, 1995), 79–82; André Steiner, *Die DDR-Wirtschaftsreform der sechziger Jahre. Konflikt zwischen Effizienz- und Machtkalkül* (Berlin, 1999), 280–1, 313.

[26] *Richtlinie für das neue ökonomische System der Planung und Leitung der Volkswirtschaft* (Berlin [East], 1963). On the implementation and results of the "New Economic System of Planning and Management of the Economy," see Steiner, *Die DDR-Wirtschaftsreform.*

Furthermore, a production fund charge was introduced; it was a sort of interest charge on the buildings and facilities that the state made available to enterprises. Charging this form of "interest on capital" was supposed to push enterprises to generate at least minimal profits and to reduce reserve capacity. The state also wanted to spur innovation and structural change, but it offered only weak incentives. With these and other regulations, the reformers sought to simulate market mechanisms without introducing the foundations of a market economy. Inevitably, this led to new inconsistencies and contradictions. In the end, the plan remained the decisive instrument of control, and neither the dominance of state ownership of the means of production nor the SED's monopoly of power was called into question.

The problems caused by the internal contradictions of the reform were compounded by the policy of gradual implementation. Old and new regulations were in effect simultaneously, which created friction and made it difficult for managers to comply with the new rules. The branches and enterprises used the new "freedoms" to pursue their own interests, which were often inefficient on the macroeconomic level. For example, branch leaders were now in charge of deciding where to deliver their products, but they lacked the information necessary to prioritize the orders they received. At the same time, in the absence of hard budget constraints, enterprises demanded as many resources of all kinds as possible. Together, these factors led to inefficient resource allocation; consequently, nearly all enterprises struggled to meet their needs for raw materials and supplies. A variety of producers in monopoly positions exploited shortages by applying price surcharges merely for delivering goods within a certain period of time. The higher levels of the hierarchy reacted to these and other problems by once again intervening in planning and economic processes from above in 1965.[27]

The difficulties in enacting the reform were exacerbated in 1964–5 when the Soviet Union, responding to its own economic problems, gave greater priority to its own interests. It cut deliveries of agricultural products and made increases in raw materials deliveries dependent on return favors. Goods the Soviet Union no longer supplied had to be imported from the West. At the same time, Moscow reduced the number of chemical plants it wanted delivered, even though the GDR had expanded production capacity at the Soviets' request. Along with the insufficient competitiveness of GDR products in international markets, this Soviet shift worsened the terms of

---

[27] See, e.g., SPK: Information über Aussprachen mit leitenden Genossen aus VVB und Betrieben über Fragen der Durchführung des NÖS . . . , 13.11.65, BA DE1/45454.

foreign trade for the reform and impeded work on a medium-term plan that was supposed to put the more modern sectors of the economy into center.

As of the mid-1960s, the tangible results of the reform had fallen far short of initial expectations. Industrial growth rates and productivity rose steadily, but those gains were the result of increased investment and the entry of several major projects into the production phase in 1964 – not of the changes in the system of control. Moreover, enterprises continued to hoard resources; until 1967, their stores grew more rapidly than production.[28] This outcome must have given the reformers pause because the improved utilization of inputs was supposed to be one of the advantages of their plan. As for innovation, the results were ambiguous. Enterprises worked harder to update their production methods and products, but these efforts alone were not sufficient to modernize the East German economy.

The designers of the reform found themselves under pressure to justify their ideas in light of the modest results it had achieved. The ensuing discussion led to a revision of the reform plan in 1967–8. The new "Economic System of Socialism" aimed to achieve a limited number of fundamental innovations and structural changes under central control. It would focus on industries and fields seen as strategic in bringing about a scientific-technological revolution: the modern sectors of chemicals (in particular petrochemicals and artificial fibers), engineering (machine tools and plant construction), electronics, data processing equipment, and automation technology. A central "structure-determining plan" would direct and prioritize the selected technological developments; in practice, that meant the state would preferentially allocate resources and funding to these sectors. A framework of overall planning for the economy would take care of other sectors not included in the "structure-determining planning," allowing enterprises to organize their own economic activity through marketlike relations but in accordance with central guidelines.[29] This framework would give most enterprises autonomy, whereby central and subordinate responsibilities needed to be balanced out. This was in line with the system and rational within this framework.

But this configuration resulted in a strong interest of the subordinate economic entities to get their products and investments included in the sphere of structure-determining projects so that they would be favorably treated. The higher authorities could not escape this pressure, particularly

---

[28] See Steiner, *DDR-Wirtschaftsreform*, 562–77.

[29] *Protokoll der Verhandlungen des VII. Parteitages der SED, 17. bis 22. April 1967*, vol. 1 (Berlin [East], 1967), esp. 112–19, 137–42.

because they profited from it. At the same time, Ulbricht used the slogan "overtake without catching up" during the last third of the 1960s to inspire scientists and engineers as well as economic officials and workers to achieve "maximum performance" in the competition between the systems. He also hoped to persuade the East German population of the system's potential for the future. Under pressure to succeed, the SED turned to ever more radical ideas to spur economic development. The party wanted to demonstrate the GDR's economic capabilities and the effectiveness of its reform to the Soviet leadership in the wake of the Prague Spring. It was also eager to present a picture of prosperity to the West at time when movement in intra-German relations seemed possible.[30]

As result of the interests of the branches and enterprises, on the one hand, and, on the other, the central authorities' fixation on growth, the number of projects deemed strategically important grew continuously. Investment was increased at the expense of consumption, but it was still not sufficient to achieve the SED's goals. Given the political competition with the Federal Republic next door, however, consumption could not be further restricted. The GDR's economic capacities were thus overstretched by the tension between resource hunger on the part of the prioritized industries and enterprises, the SED's growth fetishism, and the citizenry's consumption. All three factors limited the resources available for sectors and enterprises not included in the structure-determining planning. Moreover, incomplete and inadequate information impeded decision making and resulted in less than optimal resource allocation. The central authorities thus found themselves intervening in the nonstructure-determining sector more frequently, which undermined efforts to partially decentralize decision making and to give enterprises more autonomy. The reform, in short, seized up. This problem was reflected in industrial growth and productivity: 1970 saw a drop in growth and productivity from the high rates realized in the two preceding years. Moreover, given the accelerated structural policy, the plan did not adequately take the manufacturers of semifinished goods and energy into account as it did not provide them with enough investment. The especially hard winter of 1969–70 then did its part to set production back, disrupting transport and power supply. This renewed crisis at the end of the 1960s and the beginning of the 1970s was reflected above all in a shortage of semifinished goods and the perceptibly deteriorating supply of goods for the population; the growth rate, however, remained high.

[30] On the following, see also Steiner, *DDR-Wirtschaftsreform*, 442–520.

Despite policy inconsistencies and difficulties in enacting the reform, the East German economy performed better in the 1960s than it had previously, primarily as a result of increased investment starting in 1963 and improved returns on investment. Living standards for the population fundamentally improved, even if the supply of consumer products continued to lag behind demand. Incomes rose, households rapidly equipped themselves with consumer durables, and the five-day workweek became a reality. This improvement in living conditions and the SED leadership's willingness to change, as evidenced by the economic reform, are probably key reasons why the 1960s are often remembered rather positively by Eastern Germans.

The structural development of the GDR's economy during this period followed much the same trends that prevailed during the 1950s. Industry accounted for a growing share of the gross national product because of the SED's industry-oriented economic policy; in the Federal Republic, by contrast, industry's share of gross national product had already begun to decline. Capital goods industries were the most dynamic sectors of the economy, a consequence not least of an ideology that assigned greater priority to growth in the means of production than to growth of consumption. Consequently, smokestack industries continued to be structure determining in the GDR at a time when Western countries were beginning to turn away from them. The structural change prompted by the technology and structure offensive in the last third of the 1960s increased industrial productivity compared to the previous and following years, but its contribution to productivity growth remained very low. It was not the economic process so much as pressure from the central authorities that drove innovation and structural change. At the same time, however, the authorities shrank from closing down enterprises or sectors. That step would have promoted structural change, but it would also have been associated with localized and temporary unemployment, which was as strong a political-ideological taboo in a socialist economy as was an enterprise going bankrupt. Ultimately, the state always bore operating losses, which made it nearly impossible to induce structural change economically and which also minimized the effects of structural change on growth and productivity when it occurred.[31] Despite improved economic performance, the reform did not succeed in laying the foundation for a thorough modernization of the economy.

---

[31] André Steiner, "Beständigkeit oder Wandel? Zur Entwicklung der Industriestruktur der DDR in den sechziger Jahren," *Jahrbuch für Wirtschaftsgeschichte* (1995, pt. 2): 101–18.

POLITICS AT THE EXPENSE OF ECONOMIC SUBSTANCE

Ulbricht's growth and technology offensive of the late 1960s resulted in a growth crisis that was also a supply crisis. In accelerating the development of high-tech sectors, the SED's economic policy had neglected consumption-oriented branches. The very limited success of the reforms and the outbreak of worker revolts in Poland in December 1970 led the leaders of the SED, like their counterparts in the other Eastern bloc countries, to shift course in social and economic policy. Under Erich Honecker, Ulbricht's replacement at the head of the SED, the party sought to secure its power through a policy of appeasing the public rather than through economic modernization. Better supplies of consumer goods at stable prices, along with more generous social welfare benefits, were supposed to pacify the workers and motivate them to be more productive in the absence of direct financial incentives.[32]

Abandoning the reform experiments, the SED leadership once again reoriented the economic control mechanism toward more centralized and direct planning of production and distribution.[33] The renewed centralization of the control mechanism in the early 1970s resulted in greater inflexibility, a development that was exacerbated by the nationalization of the last of the mainly small and medium-sized firms in private or partially private ownership in 1972.[34] Toward the end of the decade, the state completely concentrated industrial enterprises in combines. Although that step made sense in some instances, it was often a purely technocratic move that allowed the state to deliberately create monopolies and eliminate competition among the combines. As a result, the combines were able to dictate delivery terms while ignoring innovation and product quality. The combines thus tended to develop into autarkic economic entities, which significantly reduced the division of labor and efficiency for the economy as a whole. In a similar manner, agriculture was further concentrated in two pillars, crops and livestock. That tore apart natural interconnections in agrarian production. The policy of concentration had a negative effect on agricultural production, and the state thus cautiously changed course in the 1980s.

---

[32] See Peter Hübner and Jürgen Danyel, "Soziale Argumente im politischen Machtkampf: Prag, Warschau, Berlin 1968–1971," *Zeitschrift für Geschichtswissenschaft* 50 (2002): 804–32.

[33] Ian Jeffries and Manfred Melzer, "The New Economic System of Planning and Management 1963–70 and Recentralisation in the 1970s," in *The Eastern German Economy*, ed. Ian Jeffries and Manfred Melzer (London, 1987), 35–7.

[34] Frank Ebbinghaus, *Ausnutzung und Verdrängung. Steuerungsprobleme der SED-Mittelstandspolitik 1955–1972* (Berlin, 2003), 183–327.

The economic situation stabilized in the early 1970s with the help of additional imports. Even more imports would be needed, however, to maintain the SED's consumption and social welfare policies. Given the continuing uncompetitiveness of East German products on international markets, export revenues were not adequate to finance imports, and efforts to increase export sales fell short. Economic advisors repeatedly warned SED leaders about the discrepancy between political objectives and economic possibilities that lay behind this state of affairs, but under Honecker, they disregarded this information.[35] Expanded expenditure on consumption also limited the funds the state could make available for scientific and technological research. As a result, a number of promising innovations had to be abandoned and the technological gap between the GDR and the Western industrial nations widened.[36] The growing sales problems in foreign markets were one major reason the central authorities tried once again to reduce this gap.

In the second half of the 1970s, the SED leadership initiated a program to spur the development of a microelectronics industry. The West's embargo on exports of advanced technology, although of limited effectiveness, made this initiative necessary. This program took up a considerable portion of the funds available for investment, however, and the memory chips that the GDR finally brought to market were not only obsolete but also much more expensive than those produced elsewhere.[37] Programs like this – notably an initiative for the automotive industry in the 1980s – failed to eliminate the obstacles to innovation inherent in the system. To the contrary: they actually reinforced them in the branches they did not promote, which, in turn, limited the possible productivity gains. The goal of expanding consumption and social welfare expenditures while modernizing select branches of the economy strained the GDR's economic capacities and led to an increase in the country's burden of debt.

Furthermore the GDR was not immune to changes in the world economy during the 1970s. An explosion in the prices of raw materials on world markets affected the GDR – though belatedly because of the principles of the Council for Mutual Economic Assistance (COMECON) price

---

[35] Hans-Hermann Hertle, "Die Diskussion der ökonomischen Krisen in der Führungsspitze der SED," in *Der Plan als Befehl und Fiktion. Wirtschaftsführung in der DDR. Gespräche und Analysen,* ed. Theo Pirker, M. Rainer Lepsius, Rainer Weinert, Hans-Hermann Hertle (Opladen, 1995), 309–45.

[36] Ralf Ahrens, *Gegenseitige Wirtschaftshilfe? Die DDR im RGW – Strukturen und handelspolitische Strategien 1963–1976* (Cologne, 2000), 323–5.

[37] See Günter Kusch, Rolf Montag, Günter Specht, and Konrad Wetzker, *Schlußbilanz – DDR. Fazit einer verfehlten Wirtschafts- und Sozialpolitik* (Berlin, 1991), 37–8; Charles S. Maier, *Dissolution: The Crisis of Communism and the End of Eastern Germany* (Princeton, NJ, 1997), 73–5.

setting – and narrowed the scope of its economic opportunities.[38] The state could not pass the rising costs of raw materials on to the citizens because the SED wanted to continue the policy of social pacification. But it also wanted to press forward with technological development for economic sustainability, and because it could not increase exports, debt grew. A rise in interest rates worldwide in the late 1970s and another dramatic increase in the prices of raw materials exacerbated this problem. Moreover, the Soviet Union became a steadily less reliable source of economic support as it found itself under growing economic and political pressure. Reality caught up with the GDR when Poland declared itself bankrupt, East–West relations took a turn for the worse, and the West imposed a de facto credit boycott on the Eastern bloc. The country found itself in a debt trap. No one had expected such a dramatic development a decade earlier, although there had been no dearth of warnings about the possible economic consequences of the new policy.

In the end, the Federal Republic helped the GDR out of its early 1980s debt crisis. The GDR managed to reduce its obligations to the West but did so at the expense of its capital as it maintained existing levels of consumption and social spending despite the changing international economic situation. The government changed the pattern of foreign trade, reducing imports from the West and shifting purchases to countries with which it ran a trade surplus. It also pushed exports at all cost under the motto "Liquidity before profitability." In this way, it achieved trade surpluses but deprived the domestic market of capital and consumer goods as well as foodstuffs. In addition, the Honecker government also sold Soviet crude oil abroad to earn foreign currency. That policy led to an increase in the use of domestically produced brown coal, which aggravated environmental pollution. Crude oil sales became a less successful source of income in the second half of the 1980s as a result of changes in the world economy.[39]

It was not possible to replace the declining revenues from the sale of crude oil products by offering other products. The GDR's engineering industry had not kept up with technological advances, and it suffered from inadequate investment. This resulted in ever more wear and tear on plants and eventually – particularly in the GDR's main export branches – to a drop in the competitiveness of its products on the world market. For the most

---

[38] Harm G. Schröter, "Ölkrisen und Reaktionen in der chemischen Industrie beider deutscher Staaten. Ein Beitrag zur Erklärung wirtschaftlicher Leistungsdifferenzen," in *Innovationsverhalten und Entscheidungsstrukturen. Vergleichende Studien zur wirtschaftlichen Entwicklung im geteilten Deutschland*, ed. Johannes Bähr and Dietmar Petzina (Berlin, 1996), 109–38.

[39] Maier, *Dissolution*, 66–7.

part, East German products could be sold only in the Eastern bloc. This made the GDR especially dependent on demand from the Soviet Union, which more or less dictated what the GDR was to deliver. Soviet demand had considerable impact on many combines' product lines, especially in engineering. Low productivity growth and rising relative manufacturing costs contributed to a decline in foreign currency revenues. In 1980, the GDR managed to earn only 0.45 Valutamarks with the products it exported to the West for every mark spent domestically producing them, and in 1988, earnings had dropped to a mere 0.25 Valutamarks.[40] Thus the state had based all plans to reduce the debt substantially on unrealistic foundations.

Against this background of limited technological innovation and ineffective use of resources, growth rates declined. In this situation, there was growing competition between three areas of expenditure: investment, consumption, and debt service to the West. To preserve the (apparent) political stability of the GDR, the SED wanted to avoid a decline in the standard of living. The debt to Western lenders had to be serviced to guarantee the country's creditworthiness. Investment thus fell by the wayside, with the result of further undermining the prospects for growth in the future. The total volume of investment between 1982 and 1986 fell below the level of 1981. Moreover, the available funds went primarily to certain branches. The hoped for results did not appear in those branches, and other sectors were, consequently, often unable to replace old, worn-out equipment. The wear rate on plants and equipment in industry rose from 43.4 percent in 1980 to 46.4 percent in 1988, and even these figures do not give a complete picture of the deterioration because the depreciation rates in the GDR were relatively low. In other economic sectors, such as construction and transportation, the situation was even more dramatic. At the same time, at the end of the 1980s, about 30 percent of the stock of machines and equipment had been put into operation within the preceding five years. This contrast reflected the selective investment policies that led to islands of modern manufacturing existing alongside completely outdated plants and factories. The proportion of fully depreciated machines and facilities that were still in use in industry was 18.8 percent.[41]

---

[40] H. Jörg Thieme, "Notenbank und Währung in der DDR," in *Fünfzig Jahre Deutsche Mark. Notenbank und Währung in Deutschland seit 1948*, ed. Deutsche Bundesbank (Munich, 1998), 609–53; here, p. 648; Albrecht O. Ritschl, "An Exercise in Futility: Eastern German Economic Growth and Decline, 1945–89," in *Economic Growth in Europe since 1945*, ed. Nicholas Crafts and Gianni Toniolo (Cambridge, 1996), 498–540. The Valutamark was an internal calculation unit that, for political reasons, was equated with the West German D-Mark. Subsequently this economically uncovered exchange rate was internally corrected by additional charges.

[41] All figures are taken from Statistisches Amt der DDR, ed., *Statistisches Jahrbuch der DDR 1990* (Berlin [East], 1990), 110, 113, 120–1.

One particularly neglected sector of the economy was the consumer goods industry. The range of goods available to consumers was limited but, because of the GDR's already high debt to the West and uncompetitiveness as an exporter, could not be expanded by increasing imports. Although most of the demand for foodstuffs could be satisfied, highly noticeable temporary and localized gaps in the food supply could not always be avoided. There was also was a dearth of high-quality products, especially technological durable goods. New and increasing demands from the younger generations could not be satisfied, nor was there any attempt to do so. As incomes grew rapidly and the state sharply increased subsidies for basic necessities, Eastern Germans found themselves with every greater "excess purchasing power." Ever more dissatisfied with the inadequate range of consumer products, people turned to bartering to obtain scarce goods and services, or they increasingly used the D-Mark as a means of exchange.[42] This demonstrated the loss of trust in the GDR currency as well as the erosion of the SED leadership's control over the economic behavior of the people. In sum, the system had failed economically, ideologically, and even morally.

Another indicator of the system's failure was the state's domestic and foreign debt. In 1988, the state owed 123 billion marks – more than half of its budget for that year – to the country's credit system.[43] It silently financed this debt primarily by drawing upon the people's savings deposits and by taking most of the profits generated by state enterprises as well as funds intended for maintaining their fixed assets. Enterprises had to take out loans from the state for investments, allowing the latter to issue additional money. At the time of the fall of the Wall, the GDR had a balance-of-payments deficit of approximately $10.8 billion vis-à-vis the West. That figure included $8.2 billion in convertible currencies government debt, which was the politically relevant debt. This represented 175 percent of the value of the country's exports to the Western industrial nations (excluding the Federal Republic) and about one-fifth of its gross domestic product.[44] Going simply by the

---

[42] See Jonathan R. Zatlin, *The Currency of Socialism: Money and Political Culture in Eastern Germany* (Cambridge, 2007).

[43] Gerhard Schürer, Gerhard Beil, Alexander Schalck, Ernst Höfner, and Arno Donda, "Vorlage für das Politbüro des Zentralkomitees der SED: Analyse der ökonomischen Lage der DDR mit Schlußfolgerungen vom 30.10.1989," *Deutschland Archiv* 25 (1992): 1112–20; here, p. 1115. Calculations based on André Steiner, *Statistische Übersichten zur Sozialpolitik in Deutschland seit 1945. Band SBZ/DDR* (Bonn, 2006), Table 0.2.0.1.

[44] Deutsche Bundesbank, *Die Zahlungsbilanz der ehemaligen DDR 1975 bis 1989* (Frankfurt, 1999), 60; Arnim Volze, "Zur Devisenverschuldung der DDR-Entstehung, Bewältigung und Folgen," in *Die Endzeit der DDR-Wirtschaft – Analysen zur Wirtschafts-, Sozial- und Umweltpolitik*, ed. Eberhard Kuhrt (Opladen, 1999), 151–83; here, pp. 180f. Calculations based on Statistisches Bundesamt, ed., *Entstehung und Verwendung des Bruttoinlandsprodukts 1970 bis 1989*, Sonderreihe mit Beiträgen für das Gebiet der ehemaligen DDR 33 (Wiesbaden, 2000), 89.

numbers, that level of debt should have been manageable; the GDR, in other words, was not bankrupt in the strict sense of the term. It had, however, already encountered serious difficulties in maintaining export sales to the West as its products grew ever more uncompetitive on international markets. With no real prospect of improvement in sight, most East German products would be saleable in market economies only under very specific conditions, namely at dumping prices. Clearly, the GDR would find it increasingly difficult to earn the foreign currency it needed to service its debts.

COLLAPSE AND TRANSFORMATION

The SED found its room for maneuver in economic policy ever more limited as a result of the structural inflexibility of the economic system and as a consequence of earlier policy decisions. By 1989, productivity in the GDR had fallen to only about one-third of the West German level.[45] This obvious discrepancy in the economic performance and consumption levels of the two countries played a considerable role in eroding the party's power. The deterioration of the GDR's economic capital and the tangible economic hardships that the population endured also contributed to mass flight and mass protests in the summer and fall of 1989 that led ultimately to the collapse of SED rule. With the fall of the Berlin Wall in November 1989, the largely closed economy opened up.

The fall of the Wall accelerated the decline of the GDR economy. As the number of people fleeing to the West rose once again, the number of workers declined, and those who remained went on strike with growing frequency. At the same time, combines and enterprises found it increasingly difficult to obtain supplies, and planning authorities lost all control over distribution. All these factors contributed to a decline in production. Growing production shortfalls compounded the supply problems faced by enterprises and individuals, which in turn fueled migration to the West. Meanwhile, D-Marks were flowing into the country from commuter incomes, social transfers, and other transactions. As the D-Mark grew more valuable on the black market, the exchange of D-Mark transfers for GDR marks increased the amount of money circulating in the GDR considerably. Consumer

---

[45] Udo Ludwig, Reiner Stäglin, and Carsten Stahmer, *Verflechtungsanalysen für die Volkswirtschaft der DDR am Vorabend der deutschen Vereinigung*, Deutsches Institut für Wirtschaftsforschung. Beiträge zur Strukturforschung 163 (Berlin, 1996), 44. If the Statistisches Bundesamt's figures for 1991 are correct and 1991 marks the nadir, then this figure is too low. Heske arrives at 48 percent: Gerhard Heske, "Bruttoinlandsprodukt, Verbrauch und Erwerbstätigkeit in Ostdeutschland 1970–2000. Neue Ergebnisse einer volkswirtschaftlichen Gesamtrechnung," *Historical Social Research*, Supplement 17 (2005): 69–70.

demand grew accordingly. Both of these developments further exacerbated the discrepancy between supply and demand and further undermined people's trust in the GDR's currency.

To stop the ongoing flight to the West and to stabilize the situation, the West German government proposed an economic and monetary union to the GDR in February 1990. Following the first free elections for the GDR's parliament, the Volkskammer, on March 18, 1990, the new noncommunist government swiftly negotiated a treaty on monetary, economic, and social union with the Federal Republic. This union, which went into effect on July 1, 1990, made the D-Mark the currency of the GDR and established the West German social market economy the country's economic order, thus sealing the fate of the GDR's economy. Monetary, economic, and social union was a decisive step toward political unification, which followed on October 3, 1990.[46]

The monetary union converted salaries, wages, and other income at a rate of 1:1. Other claims and liabilities were generally to be converted at a rate of 2:1. Private individuals could exchange a certain amount from their savings at the rate of 1:1; the amount varied according to age, and savings beyond that age-graded amount were converted at 2:1. On average, this resulted in an overall exchange rate of 1.8:1 and a rate of 1.5:1 for private household assets.[47] After obtaining the longed-for Western currency, GDR citizens did not endanger monetary stability by their behavior. The inflation experts had feared thus did not come to pass. Nevertheless, for Eastern Germans the currency union meant not only an abundance of new consumption opportunities or even an increase in real income – in which, however, the unemployed and single parents did not participate – but also a loss of monetary assets, especially for the surviving remnant of the *Mittelstand*. The wealth situation of Eastern German households, already sharply curtailed by GDR governmental policies, deteriorated further, which in turn impeded the economic development of the new federal states later on. The monetary union also dealt a blow to the Eastern economy by raising export prices to levels what wiped out foreign demand. Domestic demand fell dramatically as well, as East Germans took advantage of the opportunity to buy Western-made goods. The problems created by the fall in demand

---

[46] See Dieter Grosser, *Das Wagnis der Währungs-, Wirtschafts- und Sozialunion.* Vol. 2, *Politische Zwänge im Konflikt mit ökonomischen Regeln* (Stuttgart, 1998); André Steiner, "Der Weg zur Wirtschafts- und Währungsunion vom 1. Juli 1990," in *Revolution und Vereinigung 1989/90. Als in Deutschland die Realität die Phantasie überholte,* ed. K.-D. Henke (Munich, 2009), 441–55.

[47] Erik Gawel, *Die deutsche Währungsunion. Verlauf und geldpolitische Konsequenzen* (Baden-Baden, 1994), 227ff.

for East German goods were compounded by the wage increases negotiated by West German–dominated unions and the management of Eastern enterprises. Aimed at raising Eastern incomes to Western levels as quickly as possible, the wage increases cut into profits, limited investment, and created a gap between productivity and pay. The Eastern economy collapsed as industrial production plummeted and unemployment soared.

It was against this background that the agency established by the last SED government to oversee the restructuring of property ownership, the Treuhandanstalt (commonly called the Treuhand), began work. This agency was originally supposed to preserve the "people's property" and manage it according to market-oriented principles. In June 1990, however, the new noncommunist government passed a law that changed the Treuhand's mandate, giving priority to the privatization of "the people's property." The Treuhand was now to privatize enterprises as quickly as possible, resolutely restructure them, or, if necessary, shut them gently down. It quickly became apparent, however, that there was not as much interest in taking over former GDR firms as had been expected. Most firms in Western Germany had sufficient capacity to supply both the "old" and the "new" federal states and thus had little incentive to purchase Eastern enterprises. Few of the Eastern Germans interested in participating in the privatization of enterprises had access to the necessary capital. In the end, the Treuhand had to subsidize privatization massively. Formally, the process of privatization was completed by the end of 1994. Thirteen percent of the firms under the Treuhand's stewardship were returned to their former owners; most were small and medium-sized businesses that had been nationalized in 1972. A small number of firms were transferred to local authorities. Somewhat more than half of the firms (54 percent) were sold to private investors: 22 percent to West Germans investors, 7 percent to foreigners, and the remaining 24 percent to the firms' management – that is, to East Germans. Most of the firms acquired by Eastern managers were small or medium sized. The firms under West German or foreign control generally had more employees and larger turnovers. Finally, nearly one-third of the firms were liquidated.[48] All of the jobs they had provided disappeared. Taken together, liquidations and layoffs at privatized firms resulted in the loss of roughly 60 percent of the jobs that had existed at the time the Treuhand began its work.[49] This massive loss of jobs and the enormous deficit the Treuhand left behind are

---

[48] Institut für Wirtschaftsforschung Halle, "Eigentums- und Vermögensstrukturen in den neuen Bundesländern," in *Materialien der Enquete-Kommission "Überwindung der Folgen der SED-Diktatur im Prozeß der deutschen Einheit."* Vol. 3, pt. 2, *Wirtschafts-, Sozial- und Umweltpolitik*, ed. Deutscher Bundestag (Baden-Baden, 1999), 1792–1923; here, p. 1841.

[49] Karl-Heinz Paqué, *Die Bilanz. Eine wirtschaftliche Analyse der Deutschen Einheit* (Munich, 2009), 48–9, 67.

the negative side of the story of economic reconstruction in Eastern Germany. The Treuhand's deficit amounted to approximately DM 264 billion; initial estimates, by contrast, had anticipated revenues of DM 600 billion.[50]

This tremendous discrepancy had several causes. First, the products manufactured by the GDR firms that were up for sale generally proved less marketable than initially assumed. Second, the oversupply of Eastern German enterprises depressed their price. Third, the GDR-era "debts" of firms, which had not, in Western style, originated in credits, were not written off in the currency union. The interest and principal payments connected with those "debts" were a burden on firms and on the Treuhand's balance sheet. Fourth, the subsidies the Treuhand had to offer buyers and its expenditures in overhauling firms had a negative impact on its revenues. And fifth, the privatization process offered numerous opportunities for corruption and crime. Although it is difficult to judge how widespread illegal activity might have been, it did bite into revenues.[51]

The Treuhand was severely criticized for its strategy of first privatizing and then restructuring firms. Reversing that procedure would probably not have been feasible, however; it would likely have led to substantial long-term subsidies that would have been difficult if not impossible to maintain and that, moreover, would have acted as a misdirected financial incentive. In any event, some of the problems that arose in the privatization process might have been avoided or at least alleviated if the Treuhand had been given more time to fulfill its mandate. Another point of criticism was the small proportion of businesses owned by Eastern Germans – in terms of turnover and employment – as well as the modus operandi of the Treuhand. Together with the loss of jobs, the agency's handling of "the people's property" had a lasting negative psychological impact. Nevertheless, the Treuhand did succeed in laying the foundations for a market economy in Eastern Germany by transferring state-owned firms to private ownership. It functioned as a lightning rod for criticism of the socioeconomic transformation of the new federal states and thus served to protect the federal government.[52]

---

[50] Karl Brenke and Klaus F. Zimmermann, "Ostdeutschland 20 Jahre nach dem Mauerfall: Was war und was ist heute mit der Wirtschaft?" *Vierteljahreshefte zur Wirtschaftsforschung* 78, no. 2 (2009): 32–62; here, pp. 33–5.

[51] Hans-Werner Sinn and Gerlinde Sinn, *Kaltstart. Volkswirtschaftliche Aspekte der Deutschen Vereinigung* (Munich, 1993), 144–6; Paqué, *Bilanz*, 49–50, 60; Ingo Techmeier, "'Verkaufen um jeden Preis'. Korruption in der Treuhandniederlassung Halle," *Deutschland Archiv* 43, no. 5 (2010): 816–24; Klaus Boers, Ursula Nelles, and Hans Theile, eds., *Wirtschaftskriminalität und die Privatisierung der DDR-Betriebe* (Baden-Baden, 2010).

[52] See Klaus Schroeder, "Deutschland nach 1990: Probleme der Einheit," in *Die Bundesrepublik Deutschland: Eine Bilanz nach 60 Jahren*, ed. Hans-Peter Schwarz (Cologne, 2008), 205–26; here, p. 213.

The East German economy, in short, abruptly underwent a series of structural changes that had taken place in the West over a period of between ten and twenty years. The outmoded economy experienced the shock of suddenly being opened up to competition for which it was largely unprepared. In this respect, the economic and social upheavals and problems in the 1990s resulted primarily from GDR economic policy. But they were also consequences of the organization of privatization and of the currency union – of the way they were forced through politically – as well as of the acceleration of globalization after the collapse of the Eastern bloc. Methodologically, these factors are difficult to separate from one another.[53]

ECONOMIC DEVELOPMENT ON A NEW SYSTEMATIC BASIS

The euphoria of 1989 began to give way to fear and resignation in 1991 as the postunification economic boom ebbed, the structural backwardness of the former GDR economy became fully apparent, and unemployment skyrocketed.[54] The Eastern German economy hit its nadir in 1991. No one could fail to notice that the federal government's naïve and optimistic expectations that introducing the D-Mark would start a long-lasting boom – as happened after the West German currency reform of 1948 – had not been fulfilled. Those expectations had also led Bonn to reject the assistance for structural adjustment that the East German representatives had pressed for in the negotiations on currency union.[55] The liberal market-oriented privatization policies of the Treuhand were likewise unsuccessful in spurring an economic upturn. Realizing that the economic transformation of Eastern Germany would not be so easy after all and, confronted with the constitutional imperative to ensure equality of living conditions throughout the country, the government decided in 1991 to launch the stimulus initiative "Gemeinschaftswerk Aufschwung Ost" (Common Project Eastern Upturn). This comprehensive program called for tax increases to fund state investment (particularly in infrastructure), job-creation measures, and support for private investment. As much as half of a firm's investment in Eastern Germany might be covered by state assistance.[56] As the illusion that

---

[53] Gerhard A. Ritter, *Der Preis der deutschen Einheit. Die Wiedervereinigung und die Krise des Sozialstaats* (Munich, 2006), 101–3; Christoph Kleßmann, "'Deutschland einig Vaterland'? Politische und gesellschaftliche Verwerfungen im Prozess der deutschen Vereinigung," *Zeithistorische Forschungen/Studies in Contemporary History* 6, no. 1 (2009): 2 (online edition, http://www.zeithistorische-forschungen.de/16126041-Klessmann-1-2009 [accessed April 18, 2013]).

[54] Ibid., 8.

[55] See Steiner, "Weg zur Wirtschafts- und Währungsunion," 451–5.

[56] *Frankfurter Allgemeine Zeitung*, March 9, 1991; June 27, 1991; August 27, 1991; June 19, 1992.

German unification could finance itself through a quick *Wirtschaftswunder* evaporated, the state increased taxes. But it also relied more heavily on borrowing because the politicians, with an eye toward elections, thought increasing debt more opportune.[57] Although the package of stimulus measures was modified in the following years, its essential features remained the same. Four main instruments were supposed to revive the Eastern German economy: special tax incentives to encourage investment; generous special tax write-offs for capital investments; investment subsidies from national and European Union programs; and low-cost loans and start-up funding from the European Recovery Program (ERP).[58] Agreements between the federal government and the states established a financial framework for the special funding: Solidarity Pact I (1995–2004) and Solidarity Pact II (2005–19). Nowhere in the various instruments was there any trace of a coherent general plan. The politicians probably did not have one, fearing that they might arouse suspicions of trying to reintroduce central planning through the backdoor. Eventually, the state reduced aid to certain sectors little by little and then cut it off entirely on the grounds that that they had developed sufficiently. The manufacturing sector, however, continues to remain highly dependent on state assistance.

State assistance was one cause that helped the Eastern states quickly catch up to the western states in several indicators of economic performance until the middle of the 1990s. The point of reference for those measurements, however, was always the low point of economic performance recorded in 1991, which, because of the pressure of market competition, was considerably below the level of 1989. Because of complicated methodological problems, views on the extent of the economic collapse in the East differ, which also has consequences for judging the backwardness of the GDR economy in 1989. One estimate calculated the drop in total economic output from 1989 to 1991 at 23.5 percent.[59] The assumption that the crash cut production by between 20 and 25 percent is plausible. Taking the resulting low figures for 1991 as a point of reference explains in part Eastern Germany's high growth rates during the first half of the 1990s and its rapid progress in catching up to Western Germany.

Furthermore, the construction industry was the first motor of economic growth in the new Eastern states. From 1991 to 1994, the average annual gross value added in the Eastern German construction industry rose

---

[57] See Reimut Zohlnhöfer, "Der lange Schatten der schönen Illusion: Finanzpolitik nach der deutschen Einheit, 1990–1998," *Leviathan* 28 (2000): 14–38.

[58] Paqué, *Bilanz*, 92–3.

[59] Heske, "Bruttoinlandsprodukt," 78.

22 percent. It was above all the state and governmental bodies that initially invested in East German infrastructure to overcome serious deficiencies. But there were also numerous private investors. Driven by expectations that Eastern Germany would rapidly catch up with the western half of the country and fueled with governmental subventions, they poured money into commercial and residential construction. As it became clear in the mid-1990s that such expectations had been exaggerated and as the state cut back on infrastructure investment, the construction industry went into a slump. By that point, not only had the most urgent needs been satisfied but also there were also signs that a bubble, fed by the special assistance funds, had developed, particularly in housing construction. The construction boom nonetheless did help improve living standards in Eastern Germany and provided considerable numbers of people with jobs, which kept them from unemployment and pushed the already high unemployment rate down. Although state aid was not appreciably reduced until 1999, the construction industry began reducing surplus capacity as soon as the building boom came to an end, and real estate investors concentrated on reducing the stock of vacant properties.[60]

Despite the expansion of the services sector, the revival of industry was decisive in lifting the performance of the Eastern economy. The number of jobs in the industrial sectors began to stabilize in the mid-1990s, albeit at levels much lower than before unification, and then held steady; in Western Germany, by contrast, industrial employment continued to decline during this period. Manufacturing output in the East grew sharply from an extremely low base: added value in 2010 stood at 3.2 times the level of 1992, the sector's low point.[61] Industry, in short, increasingly became a driving force of the Eastern economy. Productivity in the Eastern German manufacturing sector was nonetheless still 26 percent lower, measured on an hourly basis, than in Western Germany in 2010. At the same time, gross wages per worker stagnated some time ago at roughly two-thirds of the West German level. This was possible because a tremendous number of firms no longer participated in industrywide wage agreements after the aggressively generous terms negotiated in 1991 and because the high rate of unemployment curbed wage growth. Unit labor costs in the East dropped dramatically vis-à-vis the West, raising the competitiveness of Eastern German producers. Unit labor costs have been lower in the East

---

[60] Paqué, *Bilanz*, 99–109; Brenke and Zimmermann, "Ostdeutschland," 39–40.
[61] Based on Arbeitskreis "Volkswirtschaftliche Gesamtrechnungen der Länder," ed., *Bruttoinlandsprodukt, Bruttowertschöpfung in den Ländern und Ost-West-Großraumregionen Deutschlands 1991 bis 2010*, series 1, vol. 1, Table 7.3.1.2.

than in the West since 2000; in 2010, they were approximately 17 percent less.[62]

The productivity gap that continues to exist between Germany's Eastern and Western states can be attributed primarily to the fact that the products made in the East create less value added per unit of labor input. That, once again, is a consequence of the Treuhand's privatization policies. The agency generally broke up the GDR's large combines and enterprises and divided them into smaller units. That move, it was hoped, would accelerate the privatization process. As a result, small and medium-sized firms have dominated in the manufacturing sector in the East. Production facilities in the East are often only workshops for Western firms, however. Companies' research and development remains concentrated in the West. That has led to the westward migration of scientists and engineers, which further hobbles innovation in the East. Moreover, Eastern manufacturers are still not oriented toward exports or capable of exporting, which is in part a consequence of the breakup of large enterprises. Furthermore, industries with extremely high levels of productivity, such as the software industry, typically have fewer employees in the East than in the West. In general, the Eastern German economy has shown little capacity for innovation and thus creates a small proportion of added value.[63] Structurally, however, it has largely adapted to the West.

The Eastern German economy collapsed in 1990–1 largely because the currency union had abruptly opened it to the pressures of international competition without providing protection. Having developed outside of the market system and dependent on structures that were obsolete even by its own standards, the Eastern economy could not stand up to that pressure. But after the crash, Eastern Germany experienced a boom that lasted until the mid-1990s. It was driven by state infrastructure investment and promises of private investment in connection with the Treuhand's privatization of state-owned assets as well as by state-subsidized private investment, by the resulting demand for capital goods, by the building boom, and, not least, by private household consumption resulting from growing purchasing power. Gross capital investment per resident in the East stood at 1.5 times the level

---

[62] Paqué, *Bilanz*, 147–8. Data from Arbeitskreis, *Bruttoinlandsprodukt*, Table 9.3.1.2, 10.3.1.1; Arbeits-kreis "Volkswirtschaftliche Gesamtrechnungen der Länder," ed., *Arbeitnehmerentgelt, Bruttolöhne und -gehälter in den Ländern und Ost-West-Großraumregionen Deutschlands 1991 bis 2010*, series 1, vol. 2, Table 3.3.1.2, 5.3.1.2.

[63] Brenke and Zimmermann, "Ostdeutschland," 44–7; Paqué, *Bilanz*, 158–60; Wendy Carlin, "Good Institutions Are Not Enough: Ongoing Challenges of Eastern German Development (October 13, 2010)," CESifo Working Paper Series No. 3204, http://ssrn.com/abstract=1691496 (accessed April 18, 2013).

in the West and per capita capital stock at more than 3.5 times in the mid-1990s.[64] The flow of both state investment and promised private investment dwindled after the mid-1990s. Investment declined in comparison with the West, and since the turn of the century per resident investment in the East has again been lower than in the West. Private consumption has also been growing more slowly than in the mid-1990s. Consequently, the economic performance of the Eastern states – measured by per capita gross domestic product – stagnated vis-à-vis the Western states in the second half of the 1990s; after 2000, the East began slowly to gain ground of the West again. Normalization in growth can be seen; because of the structural disadvantages described here, it is not to be expected that economic performance of the East will quickly match that of the West.

Unemployment increased dramatically, primarily as a consequence of deindustrialization. The official unemployment rate hit 15 percent by the mid-1990s and had passed the 20 percent mark by the end of the decade. The jobless figures would have been even worse if "underemployment" were taken into account. The state massively expanded active job market policies to check the rise in unemployment. Measures included subsidies to retain workers on reduced hours, early retirement packages, retraining and continuing education programs, and a host of job-creation initiatives. A rough calculation of underemployment in 1994 puts it at twice the level of the official unemployment figures; in 1997–8, it was still one-third higher.[65] The total rate of unemployment in Eastern Germany in the 1990s reached dimensions comparable to the nearly 40 percent of the Great Depression of the 1930s. The Eastern states, hobbled by poor economic performance, did not have the resources to address mass unemployment or other social problems. Substantial financial transfers from the western states were thus necessary. That assistance, in turn, had a profound impact on domestic demand, which, after the construction industry, became the second force driving the domestic market during the 1990s. Pension and unemployment benefits at that time added about 30 percent more purchasing power to the total economic performance in Eastern Germany. Moreover, the new states

[64] Based on Arbeitskreis "Volkswirtschaftliche Gesamtrechnungen der Länder," ed., *Bruttoanlageinvestitionen in den Ländern und Ost-West-Großraumregionen Deutschlands 1991 bis 2008*, series 1, vol. 3, Table 1; Arbeitskreis "Volkswirtschaftliche Gesamtrechnungen der Länder," ed., *Anlagevermögen in den Ländern und Ost-West-Großraumregionen Deutschlands 1991 bis 2009*, series 1, vol. 4, Table 2.1.1; Arbeitskreis "Volkswirtschaftliche Gesamtrechnungen der Länder," ed., *Entstehung, Verteilung und Verwendung des Bruttoinlandsprodukts in den Ländern und Ost-West-Großraumregionen Deutschlands 1991 bis 2010*, series 1, vol. 5, Table 1.4, 2.4, 6.7.
[65] See Paqué, *Bilanz*, 117; Brenke and Zimmermann, "Ostdeutschland," 42–3; Klaus Schroeder, *Die veränderte Republik. Deutschland nach der Wiedervereinigung* (Stamsried, 2006), 210.

were highly dependent on transfers from the West for investment,[66] a situation that has been characterized as a "consumption-oriented path toward transformation."[67] During the second half of the 1990s, Eastern German households' disposable income reached approximately 80 percent of the Western German level, whereas primary income came to 65 percent.[68] The disparity between primary and disposable income was a result primarily of social transfers. The situation had not substantially changed by 2010.

In the course of the 1990s, in sum, Eastern Germany became a transfer economy dependent on the influx of funds from outside the region.[69] As in the later years of the GDR, Eastern Germany consumed more than it produced. The most problematic aspect of this was the financing: only part of the "Aufbau Ost" program to rebuild Eastern Germany was funded by increased taxation, namely, by the imposition of the so-called solidarity tax. Most of the money for Aufbau Ost came from increasing the federal deficit and, in particular, from the social welfare insurance programs; consequently, the heaviest share of the cost of unification was borne by employees required to make payroll social welfare contributions. The cost of unification varies according to what is included. Strictly speaking, the figure should include the special allocations made to the new federal states to cover the exceptional financial burdens arising from Germany's division and unification. These allocations began to be incrementally reduced in 2009 and are scheduled to come to an end in 2019. Transfers to the Eastern states, including special funding provided immediately following unification, the debt incurred by the Treuhand, and a variety of subsidies, had come to approximately €500 billion by 2008. That was the amount provided to bring the living conditions in the Eastern states to Western levels. In addition, at a rough guess another €700 billion flowed to the East in the form of unemployment and pension benefits.[70] One question that cannot be addressed here is how much should be deducted from the total transfers to the East for the profits Western firms earned filling the Eastern production gap – the gap between Eastern production and consumption – and the taxes paid on those profits.

---

[66] Paqué, *Bilanz*, 110, 117.
[67] Schroeder, "Deutschland nach 1990," 209.
[68] Based on Arbeitskreis "Volkswirtschaftliche Gesamtrechnungen der Länder," ed., *Entstehung, Verteilung und Verwendung des Bruttoinlandsprodukts in den Ländern und Ost-West-Großraumregionen Deutschlands 1991 bis 2009*, series 1, vol. 5, Table 7.16, 7.18 (May 2010). Statistics vary widely depending on the basis of calculation and the data source, but the trends remain the same.
[69] Paqué, *Bilanz*, 121.
[70] Ibid., 190–1. These figures vary in the literature, which can be attributed to the difficulties of definition. Consequently, they can only give an indication of the total cost of the support.

What did the money provided to the East achieve? The economic parameters of the new federal states have certainly improved significantly. The gross value added per worker in 2010 was more than double that of 1991, adjusting for inflation. But this brought it up to only 77 percent of the West German level, and in 1991, it was only 42 percent.[71] In this respect, the widely held expectation at the time of unification that the economic gap between Eastern and Western Germany would be quickly closed – an expectation not limited to Easterners and encouraged by many politicians – has not been fulfilled. That expectation must be understood against the backdrop of the long habit of GDR citizens of taking the preunification Federal Republic as their point of reference. Still, we must nonetheless ask whether expectations were not too high from the outset. It thus makes sense to consider what other former Eastern bloc states have achieved without the support of West Germany. In the Czech Republic, for example, productivity and per capita income are still significantly lower today than in Eastern Germany. Using the difference between the levels in the two former East bloc countries, we can calculate the annual return on the Aufbau Ost program to be about one-tenth of the total cost, which can hardly be characterized as a bad investment.[72]

The results of the economic efforts made after reunification are thus ambiguous. Since the end of the GDR, economic performance and Eastern Germans' living standards have improved. A modern infrastructure has been created. Nonetheless, the unemployment rate is still almost twice as high in the East as in the West.[73] Economic growth has normalized: a rapid catch-up process is probably not to be expected. Finally, a range of problems rooted in the GDR period persists, notably underdeveloped entrepreneurship, Eastern firms' limited capacity for innovation, and the firms' weak equity bases. The economic policies of the past twenty years have not reduced these problems; rather, they have made them worse. For these reasons above all, it seems questionable whether the East will fully catch up to the West in the foreseeable future. Lying behind such comparisons is the notion that reunification will not have succeeded until the East matches the West – a notion that essentially extends the idea of competing systems from the era of the divided Germany into the present. All in all, the transformation of Eastern Germany from a planned to a market economy can be regarded

---

[71] Based on Arbeitskreis, *Bruttoinlandsprodukt*, Table 4.1, 9.1. Due to the longer working hours in the East, the value in relation to work hours is somewhat lower.

[72] On the details of this calculation, see Paqué, *Bilanz*, 204.

[73] Statistik der Bundesagentur für Arbeit, *Arbeitsmarkt in Deutschland – Zeitreihen bis 2010* (Nuremberg, 2011).

as a success, even though the high social costs and adaptation efforts that Eastern Germans had to put into it cannot be overestimated. At the same time, the West had to raise substantial financial transfers to compensate for the consequence of Germany's division and the SED's economic policies, although it also managed to profit considerably from this. Without being able to take exact quantitative stock, we can nonetheless conclude that, from a long, historical perspective, this process of transformation has reallocated the burdens of the postwar period. Whereas Eastern Germany had borne the brunt of these encumbrances (including its planned economy) that should have been apportioned to all of Germany, the West–East transfers have now redistributed them to all of Germany. Viewed in this way, the GDR's planned economy and the economic development associated with it represent a detour on the country's way to becoming a market economy that originated in the specific historical properties of the European postwar situation. Now all of Germany is paying for it.

PART II

Beginnings, Crises, and Reforms

The Planned Economy, 1945–1971

3

Winner Takes All

The Soviet Union and the Beginning of Central Planning in Eastern Germany, 1945–1949

BURGHARD CIESLA

At the close of the two-week Potsdam conference on August 2, 1945, the delegations of the victorious Allied powers presented a "Protocol of Proceedings" to the public.[1] Whether that document had legal force was to become a point of dispute between them. In the Soviets' understanding, the Potsdam protocol was a contract under international law; the Americans, British, and French, by contrast, viewed it as a communiqué that merely summarized the resolutions and recommendations agreed upon at the conference. This disagreement notwithstanding, the protocol became "the Magna Carta of postwar policy on Germany."[2]

Under the Potsdam agreement, the four Allied powers would each establish an occupation authority that, paradoxically, would excise power both individually in their respective occupation zones and collectively through an Allied Control Council. The occupation powers thus received the de facto freedom to pursue their own policies independent of one another. This set the stage for the division of Germany because the cohesion of the four occupation zones depended on the occupation powers' willingness to cooperate.[3]

---

[1] At the Yalta Conference (February 4–11, 1945), the "big three" powers – the Soviet Union, the United States, and Great Britain – announced that France would be a fourth occupation power after the war. On May 1, 1945, France entered into the London Agreements of 1944 concerning the Allied control system in Germany. The three-zone arrangement of July 26, 1945, assigned France its own occupation zones in Germany and Austria as well in Berlin and Vienna. France was not represented at the Potsdam Conference. Afterward, France endorsed the Potsdam Protocol in several memoranda (August 7, 1945). Ernst Deuerlein, ed., *Potsdam 1945. Quellen zur Konferenz der "Großen Drei"* (Munich, 1963), 349–50; Presse- und Informationsamt der Bundesregierung, ed., *Die Berlin-Regelung. Das Viermächte-Abkommen über Berlin und die ergänzenden Vereinbarungen* (Bonn, 1971), 211–14; Matthias Uhl, *Die Teilung Deutschlands. Niederlage, Ost-West-Spaltung und Wiederaufbau 1945–1949* (Berlin, 2009), 12.

[2] Wolfgang Benz, *Potsdam 1945. Besatzungsherrschaft und Neuaufbau im Vier-Zonen-Deutschland*, 4th rev. ed. (Munich, 2005), 118.

[3] Ingo von Münch, ed., *Dokumente des geteilten Deutschland. Quellentexte zur Rechtslage des Deutschen Reiches, der Bundesrepublik Deutschland und der Deutschen Demokratischen Republik*, 2nd ed. (Stuttgart,

With an eye to the future, the victors wanted to maintain strict control over the economic development of their occupation zones. The cornerstones of their economic directives were the destruction of Germany's arms production capability, securing maximum reparations, maintaining control of the German economy, reducing Germany's economic power by decentralization, and fostering a peacetime economy capable of surviving on its own once reparations had been made. In agreeing that they should each settle their reparations demands within their own zones, the Allies set the course for the division of Germany. Their initial intention to control the German economy jointly thus turned out to be illusory. This compromise on reparations necessarily affected the future economic order in the occupation zones and contributed significantly to the fragmentation of Germany. The Allies' incompatible economic systems, their diametrically opposed interests, and their differing understandings of basic concepts rendered the idea of common control unrealistic. The Allies had come together in Potsdam to divide the spoils of war; when they parted, they had in effect laid the foundations for the division not only of Germany but of Europe and the world as well.[4]

The Allies' division of Germany for purposes of reparations policy in 1945 was followed by the monetary division of 1948 and political division of 1949. Four years after the war, two German states with different political and economic systems had emerged: the Federal Republic of Germany (FRG), with a market-oriented economy, and the German Democratic Republic (GDR), with a centrally planned economy. These two German states remained under Allied supervision, and they had to adapt to their respective victors. Control by the Allied powers would shape the political, social, and economic development of the two German states for nearly half a century.[5]

In this essay, I will explore the Soviet Union's actions in its occupation zone and its influence of the development of a planned economy there between 1945 and 1949. First, I will address the question of why Soviet

1976), 32–43; Manfred Görtemaker, "Die Potsdamer Konferenz 1945," in *Schloß Cecilienhof und die Potsdamer Konferenz 1945*, ed. Chronos-Film and Stiftung Preußische Schlösser und Gärten (Berlin, 1995), 84.

[4] George F. Kennan, *Memoirs 1925–1950* (Boston, 1967), 262; Jörg Fisch, *Reparationen nach dem Zweiten Weltkrieg* (Munich, 1992), 69–80; Rolf Steininger, *Deutsche Geschichte seit 1945. Darstellung und Dokumente in vier Bänden*. Vol. 1, *1945–1947* (Frankfurt, 1996), 90–7; Peter Bender, *Deutschlands Wiederkehr. Eine ungeteilte Nachkriegsgeschichte 1945–1990* (Stuttgart, 2007), 23–31; Hans-Ulrich Wehler, *Deutsche Gesellschaftsgeschichte*. Vol. 4, *Vom Beginn des Ersten Weltkriegs bis zur Gründung der beiden deutschen Staaten 1914–1949* (Munich, 2003), 941–77; Benz, *Potsdam 1945*, 119.

[5] Bender, *Deutschlands Wiederkehr*, 23–31; Wehler, *Deutsche Gesellschaftsgeschichte*, 941–2; Benz, *Potsdam 1945*, 135.

occupation policy was initially so tough and uncompromising, and I will look at the forces that shaped and transformed Soviet policies between 1945 and 1949. I will also examine the psychological state of the losers and early postwar conditions. Above all, the Soviets' extremely harsh reparations policy explains why and how in effect "path-dependent" structures were established that promoted the shift to a centrally planned economy in Eastern Germany. The financial and supply crisis that had begun in Germany during the war and continued into the postwar period, in turn, clearly illustrates that money and diet functioned as the nerve of things. Poor conditions determined what people wanted, did, and suffered in occupied Germany, forcing the occupying powers to soften their stance in the East-West conflict. The per capita daily caloric intake was a political issue of the highest order, and the "moral standard of 1,000 calories" prevailed: How many calories did it take to make one communist? How many to make one believe in democracy?[6] I will finish by focusing on the regulatory policies that set the course for the development of structures for a planned economy in the Soviet zone. What ideas about economic policy did the actors have? What role did security, Germany, and economic policy issues play in the expansion of Soviet economic control? How did the looming Cold War influence the socioeconomic transformation of Eastern Germany? Did the incipient Cold War unleash forces that drove the socioeconomic transformation of Eastern Germany?

THE PSYCHOLOGICAL STARTING POSITION

National Socialist Germany had waged a racially motivated war of extermination against the Soviet Union marked by unfettered violence and harshness toward combatants and civilians alike. This war claimed unimaginable numbers of victims and caused massive destruction. Some twenty-seven million Soviet citizens were killed – thirteen million soldiers and fourteen million civilians – in the course of World War II. The section of the Soviet Union occupied by German troops was among the most heavily devastated during the war. On September 13, 1945, the government newspaper *Izvestia* published the first concrete numbers of the Soviet Union's material war losses. According to official sources, more than 1,700 cities and urban areas, seventy thousand villages, about thirty-two thousand industrial enterprises, sixty-five thousand kilometers of railway, one thousand railway bridges,

---

[6] Rainer Gries, *Die Rationen-Gesellschaft. Versorgungskampf und Vergleichsmentalität: Leipzig, München und Köln nach dem Kriege* (Münster, 1991), 197.

more than four thousand train stations, and thousands of schools and hospitals were destroyed. About twenty-five million people in the Soviet Union had no homes. The standard of living had fallen to the lowest imaginable level. All in all, the Soviets estimated at that time that about 30 percent of the national wealth had been lost. Against the backdrop of Allied disagreements on reparations and the developing East-West conflict, the Western powers dismissed these figures as inflated for propaganda purposes. Present-day estimates of the Soviets' material losses largely confirm Moscow's initial reckoning, however.[7]

In the fall of 1944, Soviet troops crossed the eastern border of the Reich. On November 6, 1944, in a speech marking the twenty-seventh anniversary of the October Revolution, Stalin outlined the future Soviet occupation policy in a single sentence: "After its defeat, Germany will, of course, be economically, as well as militarily and politically, disarmed."[8] Soviet economic policy, in short, would mean a Carthaginian peace for Germany.[9] The goal was to ensure that Germany would never again be able to launch a war.[10]

"Enjoy the war; the peace will be terrible," Germans told one another as it became increasingly clear that the end of the war was drawing near.[11] In the fall of 1944, Germans could learn from the reports of the "enemy broadcasters" what the Allies intended to do with Germany after they

---

[7] Figures from Dimitri Wolkogonow, *Stalin. Triumpf und Tragödie. Ein politisches Porträt* (Düsseldorf, 1993), 681–2; Rainer Karlsch and Jochen Laufer, eds., *Sowjetische Demontagen in Deutschland 1944–1949* (Berlin, 2002), 31–2; Uhl, *Teilung*, 7–9. On the validity of the figures, see the more recent publications Jochen Laufer, *Pax Sovietica. Stalin, die Westmächte und die deutsche Frage 1941–1945* (Cologne, 2009), 263; Bogdan Musial, *Stalins Beutezug. Die Plünderung Deutschlands und der Aufstieg der Sowjetunion zur Weltmacht* (Berlin, 2010), 249, 452.

[8] Quoted in Karlsch and Laufer, *Sowjetische Demontagen*, 44.

[9] The demands the Romans made on the Carthaginians after the First and Second Punic Wars (264–241 and 218–201 BCE) are considered synonymous with a hard peace. Since then, one speaks of a "Carthaginian Peace" when the victor establishes harsh conditions for peace. The Third Punic War (149–146 BCE), by contrast, demonstrates "that an extremely hard peace excludes such reparations. Carthage was destroyed and could not afford any payments. Victors often find themselves torn between attempting to get the vanquished opponent to work for them as much as possible and the intention, dictated by revenge or security needs, to destroy him. This was also the dilemma of the victors of 1945, at least concerning Germany and Japan." Fisch, *Reparationen*, 19. See also Rudolf Walther, "Die Torheit der Sieger. John Maynard Keynes' brillante Streitschrift über den Versailler Vertrag," *Die Zeit*, August 24, 2006.

[10] On the goals of Soviet policy, see Fisch, *Reparationen*, 104–5; Rainer Karlsch, *Allein bezahlt? Die Reparationsleistungen der SBZ/DDR 1945–53* (Berlin, 1993), 16–21; Rainer Karlsch and Burghard Ciesla, "Vom 'Karthago-Frieden' zum Besatzungspragmatismus. Wandlungen der sowjetischen Reparationspolitik und ihre Umsetzung 1945/46," in *Erobert oder befreit? Deutschland im internationalen Kräftefeld und die sowjetische Besatzungszone (1945/46)*, ed. Hartmut Mehringer, Michael Schwartz, and Hermann Wentker (Munich, 1999), 71–92.

[11] Sven F. Kellerhoff and Wieland Giebel, eds., *Als die Tage zu Nächten wurden. Berliner Schicksale im Luftkrieg* (Berlin, 2003), 66.

won.[12] In the London Protocol of September 12, 1944, and in the additional protocol and agreement of November 14, the "big three" – Churchill, Roosevelt, and Stalin – settled on an occupation and control system for Germany. Unlike after World War I, Germany was to be occupied in its entirety and divided into zones of occupation. Meanwhile, German propaganda described the behavior of Soviet troops as they crossed border into the Reich, engendering little hope among the populace about what was to come. During the final months of the war, those able to make their way westward did so.

After the conclusion of the Yalta Conference in February 1945, Allied radio broadcasts indicated how terrible the peace would be in concrete terms. The Allies intended nothing less than the eradication of Nazism and militarism – the elimination of all Nazi and military influences in German political, economic, and cultural life. Toward that end, they planned to strip Germany of its arms production capabilities and to punish all war criminals. They also intended to seek compensation for the destruction Germany had caused in the form of nonmonetary reparations.[13]

Three months after Yalta, peace arrived. With the Wehrmacht's unconditional surrender,[14] the victorious Allies took over governance of Germany. The areas of Germany that lay east of the Oder and Neiße Rivers were ceded to the Soviet Union and Poland. The remainder of German territory, in accordance with the London and Yalta agreements, was divided into American, British, French, and Soviet occupation zones, each with its own military government. The "special Berlin area" was similarly divided into four occupation sectors.[15] The Soviet zone, excluding Berlin, comprised 23 percent of the Reich's 1937 territory and incorporated the states of Mecklenburg-West Pommerania, Thuringia, and Saxony along with the Prussian provinces

---

[12] Alliiertenmuseum, ed., *The Link with Home – und die Deutschen hörten zu. Die Rundfunksender der Westmächte 1945 bis 1994* (Berlin, 2001).

[13] Münch, *Dokumente des geteilten Deutschland,* 8, 25–32; Merieth Niehuss and Ulrike Lindner, eds., *Deutsche Geschichte in Quellen und Darstellung. Vol. 10, Besatzungszeit, Bundesrepublik und DDR 1945–1969* (Stuttgart, 1998), 27–31.

[14] On May 9, 1945, at 12:16 A.M., General Field Marshall Keitel signed the unconditional German surrender in Berlin-Karlshorst. On May 7, at 2:41 A.M., a document certifying the unconditional surrender of all German military forces was signed at the U.S. headquarters in Reims in the name of the German high command, but the Soviet leadership insisted on a second ratification on May 8 in Berlin. It took until after midnight to secure the final signature. Manfred Overesch, *Deutschland 1945–1949* (Königstein, 1979), 177–81; Benz, *Potsdam 1945,* 63–4; Uhl, *Teilung,* 7.

[15] On July 9, 1945, Austria and Vienna were also divided by agreement into occupation zones. On the Allies' postwar plans and regulations concerning Austria, see Rolf Steininger, *Der Staatsvertrag. Österreich im Schatten von deutscher Frage und Kaltem Krieg 1938–1955* (Innsbruck, Austria, 2005), 35–62.

of Brandenburg and Saxony. After Prussia was dissolved,[16] the two provinces became the states of Brandenburg and Saxony-Anhalt. An Allied Control Council was formed to jointly administer the four occupation zones. This body held the central power in occupied Germany through March 1948. A common military command administered the four sectors of Berlin.[17]

THE ECONOMIC STRUCTURES OF THE SOVIET ZONE

Economically, there was a noticeable divide between the north and the south of the Soviet zone. The north was predominantly agricultural. The south, traditionally known as Central Germany (Mitteldeutschland), had been the Third Reich's industrial core. Saxony had played a pioneering role in the industrial revolution in Germany. Parts of Thuringia and Saxony-Anhalt were highly industrialized, as were a number of centers in and around Berlin. Between 1936 and 1945, the Nazis had considerably expanded industrial capacity in arms production and the war economy. The focus of the Central German economy was manufacturing: the metal working, electrical, chemical, machine tool, and optical industries were highly developed there. The paper, food, and textile industries likewise played a significant role. As for raw materials, the Soviet zone was in a much less favorable position than the other zones. Some important raw materials – such as copper, iron ore, and hard coal (anthracite) – were not available or available in insufficient quantities. Brown coal (lignite), potash, and gravel, by contrast, were plentiful. After the war, the deposits of uranium ore in Central Germany became very important for the Soviet nuclear industry. To the detriment of the region's inhabitants and the environment, the Soviets began exploiting the uranium deposits there with all available means in 1946. The GDR was to become the third-largest uranium producer in the world.[18]

At the end of the war, the Soviets and the other occupying powers could temporarily fall back on the extensive reserves that the National Socialists had built up during the war by exploiting the conquered territories and ruthlessly mobilizing all possible German resources. The occupiers exhausted these reserves within a few months, using them for their own

---

[16] The dissolution of Prussia was carried out in accordance with Control Council Act No. 46 of February 25, 1947.

[17] Münch, *Dokumente des geteilten Deutschland*, 25–62; André Steiner, *Von Plan zu Plan. Eine Wirtschafts-geschichte der DDR* (Munich, 2004), 19; Uhl, *Teilung*, 17–24; Werner Abelshauser, *Deutsche Wirtschaftsgeschichte seit 1945* (Munich, 2004), 60–74.

[18] Rainer Karlsch, *Uran für Moskau. Die Wismut – Eine populäre Geschichte* (Berlin, 2007), 231–7; Matthias Judt, ed., *DDR-Geschichte in Dokumenten* (Berlin, 1997), 89–91; Karlsch, *Allein bezahlt*, 35; Steiner, *Plan zu Plan*, 19–24.

needs (plunder and provisioning troops) and for provisioning the Germans. Partly as a consequence of this "policy of the empty store," the hard winter of 1945–6 had a catastrophic impact.[19]

Allied air strikes and combat had caused substantial damage in Central Germany. In June 1945, Otto Grotewohl, a Social Democrat who later became prime minister of the GDR, described the situation:

Our economy is shattered, our transport routes are wrecked, our raw material basis is destroyed. We have no roof over our heads, no clothing on our bodies. Every last person able and willing is required to cover our basic needs and to still the hunger.[20]

In all the zones, Germans were confronted by the demoralizing scene of cities lying in ruins. Niehuss and Lindner provide figures for the extent of the damage and underscore the apparent hopelessness of reconstruction, in both the Soviet and Western zones:

Fifty million cubic meters of rubble lay in the greater Berlin area, six million in Munich, twelve million in Frankfurt, eight million in Stuttgart, etc. In order to remove eight million tons of rubble, for example – that is how one calculated it at the time – 200,000 freight trains would be required; in other words, twenty trains a day every workday for forty years. Moreover, any clean-up work seemed illusory in light of the destroyed railway systems, unusable streets in the cities, and the completely inadequate transport capacities. The proportion of totally destroyed housing in the cities ranged in the occupation zones from 25 to well over 40 percent.[21]

The destruction aggravated urban housing shortages. Thirty percent of all families in the Soviet zone did not have living quarters of their own.[22] It is estimated that 14 percent of the housing stock in the Soviet zone – some 650,000 units – had been heavily damaged or completely destroyed during the war. In the Western zones, where British and American air raids had begun earlier and had had a greater impact, the figure stood at 24 percent. Although the Soviet zone had lost less of its housing stock, the per capita supply was lower than in the West because of the influx of refugees and displaced persons. At the beginning of the war in 1939, fewer than seventeen million people lived in the area that the Soviets occupied. The population was nearly eighteen million a year after the war's end, and

---

[19] Wolfgang Benz, ed., *Deutschland unter alliierter Besatzung 1945–1949/55* (Berlin, 1999), 120–2; Paul Erker, *Ernährungskrise und Nachkriegsgesellschaft. Bauern und Arbeiterschaft in Bayern 1943–1953* (Stuttgart, 1990), 23–55; Gries, *Rationen-Gesellschaft*, 41–54.

[20] Steininger, *Deutsche Geschichte*, 1:189.

[21] Niehuss and Lindner, *Geschichte in Quellen*, 6.

[22] Uhl, *Teilung*, 43.

by 1948 it had risen to more than nineteen million. At the start of 1949, refugees and displaced persons constituted nearly 25 percent of the total population. Population growth and loss of housing drastically reduced the per capita living space available in the Soviet zone. On average, residents of Central Germany had almost fourteen square meters of living space in 1939; by 1948, the figure had dropped to only 7.6 square meters. The figures were much the same in the Western zones. In all, Germany had to absorb more than twelve million refugees and displaced persons after 1945. Five years later, 4.4 million of them were living in the GDR and 7.9 million in the FRG.[23]

Central Germany lost about 15 percent of its 1944 industrial capacity to war damage. More damage was done to housing than to industry in the Soviet zone, although some industrial sectors, notably automobile manufacturing and electrical engineering, were hard hit. In general, the damage to German industry as a whole was not as severe as widely assumed. The country's industrial capital stock may have been at least half of the level of 1939 in 1945. Industrial production came to a standstill throughout Germany at the end of the war. The transportation system faced collapse. In the Soviet zone alone, 970 railway bridges and 530 road bridges had been destroyed. In addition, the financial system was in shambles. In sum, the Soviet zone confronted imbalances in economic structure and access to raw materials in 1945. Had the Allies administered the zones jointly, they could have redressed the financial imbalances relatively quickly by means of domestic and foreign trade.[24]

TROPHIES, DISMANTLING, AND REPARATIONS

In the Allied negotiations during the war, the Soviets calculated that they were due U.S. $20 billion in reparations, in cash and kind, at 1938 prices. That figure was challenged by the Western Allies, however. Having failed to reach an agreement on the question of reparations by the end of the war, the Allies hoped to find a solution at the Potsdam Conference. On

---

[23] Rolf Dieter Müller, ed., *Das Deutsche Reich und der Zweite Weltkrieg. Der Zusammenbruch des Deutschen Reiches 1945: Die Folgen des Zweiten Weltkrieges*. Vol. 10, pt. 2 (Munich, 2008), 651; Uhl, *Teilung*, 41–3; Wehler, *Deutsche Gesellschaftsgeschichte*, 944–5; Michael von Prollius, *Deutsche Wirtschaftsgeschichte nach 1945* (Göttingen, 2006), 20.

[24] Wolfgang Zank, *Wirtschaft und Arbeit in Ostdeutschland 1945–1949* (Munich, 1987), 30–8; Andreas Hilger, Mike Schmeitzer, and Clemens Vollnhals, eds., *Sowjetisierung oder Neutralität? Optionen sowjetischer Besatzungspolitik in Deutschland und Österreich 1945–1955* (Göttingen, 2006), 418–20; Karlsch, *Allein bezahlt*, 35–40; Steiner, *Plan zu Plan*, 20–4; Judt, ed., *DDR-Geschichte in Dokumenten*, 89–91; Abelshauser, *Wirtschaftsgeschichte seit 1945*, 60–74; Prollius, *Wirtschaftsgeschichte*, 18–22; Uhl, *Teilung*, 45.

July 23, 1945, the Soviet delegation presented a "Plan for the Reparations from Germany" whereby Germany was to pay a total of $20 billion in reparations, approximately half in the form of one-time withdrawals from its national wealth during the period 1945–7 and the other half in the form of goods delivered over the course of a decade. A week later, the Soviets proposed that each of the Allied powers should extract reparations from its own zone. The Americans and British agreed to that proposal after the Soviets agreed to cut their reparations demands by half. To supplement the reparations from its own zone, the Soviet Union was to receive equipment and goods, with and without reciprocation, from the Western occupation zones.[25] The protocol issued at the close of the conference summed up the agreement concisely: "Reparation claims of the U.S.S.R. shall be met by removals from the zone of Germany occupied by the U.S.S.R. and from appropriate German external assets. . . . The reparation claims of the United States, The United Kingdom and other countries entitled to reparations shall be met from the Western Zones and from appropriate German external assets."[26] The principle of separate reparation payments formulated in the summer of 1945 was in effect a decision on the future of the occupation zones' economic systems.[27]

The Soviets initially concentrated on dismantling and removing industrial assets and other trophies. They relied in large part on German labor in carrying out these one-time extractions from Germany's national wealth. At the same time, they took goods from current production, which made the rebuilding of the zone's economy all the more difficult. The contradictory practices of industrial dismantlement and utilization of the local economy quickly became the most serious problem in Soviet occupation policy.[28]

Moscow's main policy instrument in its occupation zone was a special committee within the Soviet State Defense Committee. Stalin had ordered the formation of the committee on February 25, 1945, after the serious disagreement with the British and the Americans on reparations policy at the Yalta Conference earlier that month. The special committee was tasked with the dismantling and removal of industrial assets and military as German territory fell to the Red Army. After the German surrender, the

---

[25] Fisch, *Reparationen*, 69–80; Chronos-Film and Stiftung Preußische Schlösser und Gärten, *Schloß Cecilienhof*, 251–2, 257; Steininger, *Deutsche Geschichte*, 1:32–3, 91–7.

[26] Münch, *Dokumente*, 39.

[27] Fisch, *Reparationen*, 69–80; Karlsch, *Allein bezahlt*, 16–34, 239–40; Steininger, *Deutsche Geschichte*, 1:32–3, 91–7; Münch, *Dokumente*, 39–40.

[28] Hans-Erich Volkmann, ed., *Ende des Dritten Reiches – Ende des Zweiten Weltkrieges. Eine perspektivische Rückschau* (Munich, 1995), 530–3; Karlsch and Ciesla, "Karthago-Frieden," 72–5; Karlsch and Laufer, *Demontagen*, 33–44.

special committee served a policy oriented toward the demilitarization and deindustrialization of Germany.[29]

Soviet troops dismantled a large number of industrial facilities in the "trophy campaigns" during the Red Army's advance into Germany. As the Allies remained at odds on the issue of reparations, the special committee operated under high pressure to complete as many removal operations as possible before the approaching Potsdam Conference. According to Soviet statistics, Red Army troops had removed about four million tons of goods, armaments, raw materials, and supplies by July 8, 1945. The official Soviet reparations calculations did not take this seized material into account, counting it instead as war booty. The special committee was disbanded in early 1947, by which time its crews had transported 6.2 million tons of booty to the Soviet Union. More than 65 percent of the booty taken under the committee's supervision was removed from the Soviet zone before the Potsdam Conference began.[30]

The special committee soon came into conflict with the Soviet Military Administration in Germany (Sowjetische Militäradministration in Deutschland, SMAD), which had been established in June 1945. The speed and scope of the special committee's operations deprived the SMAD of resources that it needed. As the special committee removed tons of industrial equipment, the SMAD had to secure reparations deliveries from current production and to ensure supplies for both Soviet occupation troops and the residents of the Soviet zone. Interested perforce in preserving the zone's industrial infrastructure, the SMAD feared the removals would create an economic vacuum. The special committee's position was initially stronger than the SMAD's position. That the committee handled technology transfer from the Soviet zone was decisive. It established a number of scientific and technological centers to reconstruct German wartime weapons research and to build upon that research. The Soviet government was especially interested in avoiding having to create the industrial infrastructure for the production of missiles and nuclear weapons from the ground up at home.[31]

For the reconstruction of German missile technology, for example, the Soviets established a development center employing nearly seven thousand people in their occupation zone. The Soviet aviation industry maintained four special technology centers that had eight thousand employees by October 1946. Powerful members of the circle of leaders around Stalin who held

---

[29] Karlsch and Ciesla, "Karthago-Frieden," 74.
[30] Karlsch and Laufer, *Demontagen*, 45–77.
[31] Horst Möller and Alexandr O. Tschubarjan, eds., *SMAD-Handbuch. Die Sowjetische Militäradministration in Deutschland 1945–1949* (Munich, 2009), 91–9.

decisive positions on the special committee were responsible for the appropriation of sophisticated military technologies. At the end of October 1946, its work in the zone done, the special committee transferred approximately two thousand German specialists from its centers in Germany to the Soviet Union. Its facilities in Germany were then decommissioned and dismantled, and the special committee was disbanded a few weeks later.[32]

The transportation system suffered the most under the contradictory reparation policies in the Soviet zone. The SMAD wanted to reestablish rail traffic quickly, on the one hand, but, on the other, the removal of equipment and supplies – not least 6,200 kilometers of track – had depleted the rail system's infrastructure. The French – whose reparations policy some historians have likened to the Soviets' policy – removed only about 250 kilometers of track. The resumption of rail service was also impeded by the Soviets' use of German rail crews for transporting seized goods and industrial equipment as well as troops. At the end of 1945, thirty of these *Lok-Kolonnen* (train convoys) – staffed by more than ten thousand railway workers and using nearly nine hundred locomotives – were being used exclusively to serve the transport needs of the Soviet occupiers and were thus not available for passenger or freight traffic in the Soviet zone.[33]

Soviet reparations policy shifted focus in the early summer of 1946. SMAD Order No. 167 of June 5, 1946, increased the importance of making use of the Soviet zone's industrial capacity. Consequently, more than two hundred German industrial facilities slated for dismantling and removal were instead maintained as Soviet corporations. With the creation of these corporations, the economy of Central Germany came under direct Soviet control. The Soviet corporations accounted for more than 30 percent of the Soviet zone's industrial production by the end of the 1940s. There were, though, marked regional differences in the concentration of these corporations. In Saxony-Anhalt, for example, they accounted for more than 60 percent of industrial production and employed roughly half of all workers there in early 1947. Soviet corporations took care of most of the reparations deliveries from the Soviet zone/GDR. In the early 1950s, they supplied approximately 70 percent of in-kind reparations. Production at the Soviet corporations placed a disproportionate burden on the economy

[32] Karlsch and Laufer, *Demontagen*, 187–225; Möller and Tschubarjan, *SMAD-Handbuch*, 328–31.

[33] Christoph Buchheim, ed., *Wirtschaftliche Folgelasten des Krieges in der SBZ/DDR* (Baden-Baden, 1995), 46–9; Rüdiger Kühr, *Die Reparationspolitik der UdSSR und die Sowjetisierung des Verkehrswesens der SBZ. Eine Untersuchung der Entwicklung der Deutschen Reichsbahn 1945–1949* (Bochum, Germany, 1996), 35–50, 191–217; Burghard Ciesla, *Als der Westen durch den Osten fuhr. Die Geschichte der Deutschen Reichsbahn in Westberlin* (Cologne, 2006), 83–91; Möller and Tschubarjan, *SMAD-Handbuch*, 298–300.

and siphoned off considerable resources. They received larger allocations of materials and energy as well as significant subsidies from state budgets in the Soviet zone. In addition, they were able to entice scarce specialist talent by offering higher wages and better working conditions than other enterprises in the zone. According to one estimate, about 20 percent of annual industrial investment flowed into the Soviet corporation sector until 1954. At first glance, the Soviet corporations might appear to have been "model plants of the planned economy" – the term used at the time for factories organized on the Soviet pattern – but nothing could be further from the truth. Viewed as businesses, these firms differed little from capitalist companies and preserved traditional business structures.[34]

The automobile industry exemplifies the consequences of the shift in Soviet reparations policy from removal of industrial assets to reparations from current production. Before World War II, manufacturers in Central Germany turned out approximately 27 percent of the cars, 30 percent of the motorcycles, and nearly 40 percent of the trucks manufactured in the Third Reich. Allied air strikes in 1944–5 did heavy damage to some firms in the sector. The Bavarian Motor Works (BMW) factory in Eisenach, Thuringia, for example, lost about two-thirds of its buildings and one-third of its machinery and equipment. At the Wanderer factory of the Auto Union Corporation in Chemnitz, 75 percent of the buildings and 20 percent of the machinery were destroyed. The automobile companies Audi and Horch in Zwickau, Saxony, by contrast, were largely intact at the war's end. They lost only about 15 percent of their buildings and 5 percent of their machinery. Although suppliers to the automobile industry had also lost plant and equipment during the war, it appeared in May 1945 that most auto makers in Central Germany would be able to resume production in a short period of time.

Soviet dismantling led to lasting asset erosion, however. The Soviet occupiers completely stripped auto industry factories in the region except for the BMW plant in Eisenach and the Saxon railcar factory in Werdau that also produced auto bodies. In all, the Soviets dismantled and removed about 80 percent of the capacity in the automobile sector by 1948. At the largely intact Horch works in Chemnitz, for example, they seized 3,800 machines – 98 percent of its total machine stock – by March 1946. The removal crews

---

[34] Karlsch and Ciesla, "Karthago-Frieden," 71–92; Möller and Tschubarjan, *SMAD-Handbuch*, 387–412; Rainer Karlsch and Johannes Bähr, "Die Sowjetischen Aktiengesellschaften (SAG) in der SBZ/DDR," in *Mikropolitik im Unternehmen. Arbeitsbeziehungen und Machtstrukturen in industriellen Großbetrieben des 20. Jahrhunderts*, ed. Karl Lauschke and Thomas Welskopp (Essen, Germany, 1994), 214–55.

at the automobile factories in Zwickau proceeded in a similar manner. This approach to reparations undermined the chances of most automobile manufacturers in the Soviet zone to resume production quickly. The subsequent shift in Soviet reparations policy resulted in the formation of a Soviet corporation for the automotive sector. Named AWTOWELO, the new firm included the BMW factory in Eisennach, the railcar plant in Werdau, and the Simson and Co. motorcycle plant in Suhl. As other automakers in the Soviet zone struggled to resume production, AWTOWELO was soon turning out vehicles, primarily for the Soviet Union. In 1946, it produced nearly nine thousand passenger cars, of which 60 percent were sent to the Soviet Union, 20 percent were sold abroad under Soviet orders, and 20 percent remained in the Soviet zone. For six years, vehicle production for the Soviet Union ran in high gear at AWTOWELO.

When the Soviet Union handed the AWTOWELO factories back to the GDR in July 1952, there were significant adaptation problems. For example, Soviet orders, material deliveries, and financing ceased. East German auto makers did not have the structures, capacities, or resources to simply take over Soviet-oriented manufacturing programs. They had to revamp their product lines – a costly undertaking – and reorganize sales. Similar problems of adaptation arose in other industries when the GDR took over Soviet corporations.[35]

The waves of Soviet expropriation in the years 1945–8 were marked by several paradoxes. For example, dismantling and construction often took place at the same time. Some companies and factories that were rebuilt after having been dismantled were dismantled a second or even third time. Although a shift in Soviet reparations policy was becoming apparent in 1946, dismantling continued on a grand scale. This seriously undermined reconstruction efforts in the Soviet zone. The people grew increasingly bitter as the removal of industrial infrastructure made economic reconstruction all the more difficult. In January 1947, the Soviet occupation government appeared to relent, announcing publicly with great fanfare that it would halt dismantling and drastically reduce the reparations from current production. But nothing changed in the weeks and months that followed. Dismantling continued as before, and there was no noticeable reduction in the reparations extracted from current production. The people grew ever more annoyed,

---

[35] Wolfgang Schröder, *AWO, MZ, Trabant und Wartburg. Die Motorrad- und PKW-Produktion der DDR* (Bremen, 1995), 34–8; Reinhold Bauer, *Pkw-Bau in der DDR. Zur Innovationsschwäche von Zentralverwaltungswirtschaften* (Frankfurt, 1999), 49–58; Peter Kirchberg, *Plaste, Blech und Planwirtschaft. Die Geschichte des Automobilbaus in der DDR*, 2nd ed. (Berlin, 2001), 21–9, 31–96; Manfred Grieger, Ulrike Gutzmann, and Dirk Schlinkert, eds., *Towards Mobility: Varieties of Automobilism in East and West* (Wolfsburg, Germany, 2009), 87–100.

and the Soviets rationalized their behavior as remaining work from before. At this point, even the leaders of the Socialist Unity Party (Sozialistische Einheitspartei Deutschlands, or SED) voiced criticism. The situation was so serious that Saxon Minister of the Economy and Economic Planning Fritz Selbmann decided in May 1947 to draft a memorandum about the critical economic situation in the Soviet zone and the consequences of Soviet reparations policy. Skirting the SMAD, he sent the memo directly to Stalin in Moscow. Hunger gripped the land, he warned, the economy was feeding off itself, and the people's mood had reached a dangerous low. Selbmann's memo might have influenced Soviet policy. In any event, the Soviets had dismantled approximately 3,400 factories in their occupation zone by the spring of 1948. That figure in itself reveals little about the consequences of Soviet policy. Changes in Central Germany's gross capital industrial assets are indicative, though, of the direction of the region's economic development. In 1948, they stood at about 75 percent of the level of 1936; in the British-American bizone formed in 1947, by contrast, industrial capital assets were 111 percent the 1936 level. One reason for this difference was that far fewer factories had been dismantled in the bizone. In the Soviet zone, between 75 and 100 percent of core industries had been dismantled.[36]

Dismantling and the extraction of reparations in kind from current production resulted in enormous losses of assets and productive capacity in the Soviet zone, and those losses were much greater than those suffered by the Western occupations zones. The Soviet zone/GDR could not fully compensate for the reduced capital assets in the years that followed on account of perpetual deliveries to the Soviet Union, which systematically deprived it of means for reconstruction, as well as of urgently necessary investment goods. The Soviet zone/GDR was not able to fully compensate for the capital assets it lost in the war and through postwar dismantling because delivery of in-kind reparations to the Soviet Union systematically deprived it of resources for reconstruction and urgently needed investment goods. Meeting Soviet reparations demands led to the neglect of infrastructure and production capacity for years and brought about an adverse shift in the

---

[36] *Neues Deutschland*, January 16, 1947; Rainer Karlsch, "Das 'Selbmann-Memorandum' vom Mai 1947. Fritz Selbmann und die Reparationslasten der sächsischen Industrie," *Beiträge zur Geschichte der Arbeiterbewegung* 2 (1993): 88–125; Rolf Badstübner and Wilfried Loth, eds., *Wilhelm Pieck – Aufzeichnungen zur Deutschlandpolitik 1945–1953* (Berlin, 1994), 100–8; Karl Eckart and Jörg Roesler, eds., *Die Wirtschaft im geteilten und vereinten Deutschland* (Berlin, 1999), 11; Hilger, Schmeitzer, and Vollnhals, *Sowjetisierung oder Neutralität*, 420–5; Karlsch and Laufer, *Demontagen*, 31–77, 147–86; Steiner, *Plan zu Plan*, 28–9.

Soviet zone/GDR's industrial framework. Only in the mid-1950s was the GDR able to complete the reconstruction process. Some economic sectors were never able to fully recover from the consequences of dismantling, such as the once leading automotive manufacturing and transportation industries. The reparations and dismantling alone do not explain why the GDR's economy grew so much more slowly than the pre-1990 Federal Republic's economy did. The consequences of economic planning must also be taken into consideration.[37]

MONEY AND SUPPLY CRISIS

Memories of famine, the black market, and the turmoil of inflation during and after World War I were the reference points for monetary and supply policies for the Nazi leadership during the war and for the victorious Allies after 1945.[38] Severe shortages of food and housing were the central fact of economic life in all four occupation zones. Survival entailed a daily struggle for food, shelter, and fuel. Hunger became the focal point of society. As noted earlier, the word *calories* became a magical term of great political significance in the emerging East–West conflict. The Americans and Russians, struggling for advantage, engaged in a "calorie war."[39] In March 1946, General Lucius Clay, the head of the American military government in Germany, wrote Washington,

It is our belief that the Russian Zone is feeding approximately 1,500 calories and will continue to do so until the next harvest season. We have insisted on democratic processes in the U.S. zone and have maintained a strict neutrality between political parties. As a result the Communist Party has made little inroad [*sic*]. However, there is no choice between becoming a Communist on 1,500 calories and a believer in democracy on 1,000 calories. It is my sincere belief that our proposed ration allowance in Germany will not only defeat our objectives in middle Europe but will pave the road to a Communist Germany.[40]

---

[37] Jürgen Schneider and Wolfgang Harbrecht, eds., *Wirtschaftsordnung und Wirtschaftspolitik in Deutschland, 1933–1993* (Stuttgart, 1996), 139–72; Dierk Hoffmann, Michael Schwartz, and Hermann Wentker, *Vor dem Mauerbau. Politik und Gesellschaft in der DDR der fünfziger Jahre* (Munich, 2003), 157–8; Karlsch, *Allein bezahlt*, 223–40; Karlsch and Laufer, *Demontagen*, 147–86; Steiner, *Plan zu Plan*, 24–35; Hilger, Schmeitzer, and Vollnhals, *Sowjetisierung oder Neutralität*, 425.

[38] Erker, *Ernährungskrise*, 23; Gries, *Rationen-Gesellschaft*, 21–8; André Steiner, ed., *Preispolitik und Lebensstandard. Nationalsozialismus, DDR und Bundesrepublik im Vergleich* (Cologne, 2006), 24, 85; Malte Zierenberg, *Stadt der Schieber. Der Berliner Schwarzmarkt 1939–1950* (Göttingen, 2008).

[39] Gries, *Rationen-Gesellschaft*, 197, 323; Hermann Glaser, *1945. Ein Lesebuch* (Frankfurt, 1995), 127–31; Thomas Ahbe and Michael Hofmann, *Hungern, Hamstern, Heiligabend. Leipziger erinnern sich an die Nachkriegszeit* (Leipzig, 1996), 93–127.

[40] Quoted in Gries, *Rationen-Gesellschaft*, 383n19.

Germans had also been suffering from a national trauma about money since the hyperinflation of 1923.[41] During World War II, many once again feared a recurrence of devastating inflation because the Nazi regime was financing the war in large part by printing money. German banks, savings associations, and insurance companies – the regime's most important creditors – maintained a system of "silent war financing" by using money from private individuals' savings and investments. Financing the war became an acute problem in 1942 because the Reichsmark (RM) fell rapidly in value and increasingly lost its function as a means of exchange and of storing and calculating value. There was a vast quantity of worthless money and a scarcity of available products.[42] The Nazis had to resort to a comprehensive price and wage freeze to stop this development. They also maintained the rationing system by means of a mix of taxation policy, forced savings, and restrictive controls. By the end of the war, a tremendous and unstable monetary structure comprised of cash, bank credits, savings deposits, and debts had accumulated. The volume of money had increased from about RM 40 billion in 1933 to about RM 320 billion in 1945. Cash in circulation rose from RM 6 billion (1935) to more RM 73 billion (1945). In the same period, bank credits increased from RM 30 billion to more than RM 190 billion, and the Reich's debts soared from RM 14 billion to RM 380 billion more than 80 percent of which wound up being charged to private account holders at German financial institutions.

The disordered monetary situation led not only to the devaluation of money but also to the fall of the "price moral," strengthening the black market. Even during the war, Germans desperately sought to covert money to material assets, which resulted in hording and, in turn, shortages. Cigarettes, food, and other exchangeable goods functioned as currency substitutes. Through 1944, black market trade was limited to the private sphere, taking place within the family, neighborhood, and workplace. Public black markets did not emerge until 1945, spurred on by the damage done by Allied bombing, by Germany's collapse toward the war's end, and by the transition

---

[41] Wehler emphasizes the far-reaching psychological effect of the hyperinflation of 1923: it "left a traumatic impairment in the memories of millions of contemporaries, indeed, in the collective memory of the Germans of this generation, even though it by no means always resulted from personal losses and privations. This inflation trauma negatively impacted an anticyclical trade cycle policy from 1929 on, it was reinforced by the second inflation and the second currency reform, and since then – deeply anchored in affective memory – it has come to be an obvious part of the popular economic memory culture of the (Germans)." Wehler, *Deutsche Gesellschaftsgeschichte*, 249.

[42] Deutsche Bundesbank, ed., *Deutsches Geld- und Bankwesen in Zahlen 1876–1975* (Frankfurt, 1976), 14–18, 313; Benz, *Deutschland unter alliierter Besatzung*, 365–6; Gries, *Rationen-Gesellschaft*, 21–8; Prollius, *Wirtschaftsgeschichte*, 24–6; Steiner, *Plan zu Plan*, 52–4; Abelshauser, *Wirtschaftsgeschichte seit 1945*, 120–3; Adam Tooze, *The Wages of Destruction: The Making and Breaking of the Nazi Economy* (London, 2006), 642–8.

to Allied occupation. The proliferation of black market activity in all four zones laid bare the tremendous inflation and the scope of the crisis that the Nazis had managed to hide for the most part. The black market economy was a brutal system of distribution, deeply privileging those with money and goods and blatantly discriminating against wage and salary earners.[43]

Immediately after the war, illegal barter and trade systems and official rationing systems existed side by side in all four occupation zones. The official rationing systems were supposed to ensure basic, subsistence-level provisions, but the scarcity of raw materials and the poor state of the transportation system and of production facilities made that impossible. Consequently, the underground economy was the basis of economic life, and everyone – individuals as well as companies and retailers – made use of it on a grand scale. Companies often avoided official sales channels and sold their products on the black market, which offered greater opportunities for profit, or bartered them for raw materials or semifinished goods that they needed for their own production. It was estimated that only about half of the industrial output in the Soviet zone was traded legally in 1948 and that one-quarter of the zone's gross national product was transacted on the black market or through barter. During the war and occupation, the black market network extended through all levels of society. All four of the occupying powers realized that they could remedy the situation and establish better conditions for reconstruction only if they combated the illegal markets or made them disappear; otherwise, they would hardly be able to normalize economic and social relations. A necessary first step would be currency reform.[44]

CORNERSTONES OF ECONOMIC REGULATION

The Soviets' first step toward transforming the economy of their zone was to expropriate the property of the Third Reich's agricultural and industrial elites. In September 1945, a land reform initiative was carried out within the framework of the Soviets' denazification program. Large estates were broken up, property redistributed, and refugees and displaced persons were offered a new livelihood as farmers. The land reform did away with centuries-old agrarian structures, replacing large estates with numerous small-scale farm

---

[43] Sven Reichardt and Malte Zierenberg, *Damals nach dem Krieg. Eine Geschichte Deutschlands 1945 bis 1949* (Munich, 2008), 93–7; Wehler, *Deutsche Gesellschaftsgeschichte*, 951–4; Prollius, *Wirtschaftsgeschichte*, 25–7; Zierenberg, *Stadt der Schieber*, 199.

[44] Burghard Ciesla, *"X-Tage." Die Währungsreformen in Deutschland 1948* (Erfurt, Germany, 2008), 13; Gries, *Rationen-Gesellschaft*, 107–12; Benz, *Deutschland unter alliierter Besatzung*, 365–6; Steiner, *Plan zu Plan*, 44–9.

collectives. Poorly equipped and not economically viable, the new farms proved to be a considerable burden on the national economy. Agriculture slid into a permanent state of crisis. In many places, the land reform wiped out the agricultural self-sufficiency that had existed at the war's end.[45]

Soviet troops began to seize property and assets as they marched into Germany, and the Soviet Union issued decrees concerning the seizure and expropriation of Nazi wealth in the summer and early fall of 1945. Binding orders did not follow, however, until October 1945. SMAD Orders No. 124 and No. 126 (October 30 and 31, 1945) officially sequestered all the property and assets of the German state, the Nazi Party, and elite Nazi functionaries as well as abandoned property. These orders were in accord with the agreements the Allies had made at the Potsdam Conference. In carrying them out, the SMAD seized not only all large companies but also numerous mid-sized firms as well. These seizures were the first step toward the establishment of "people's property" (*Volkseigentum*) in the Soviet zone/GDR.[46]

The Soviet Union soon controlled the greater part of its zone's economy. The most important of the sequestered firms were operating as Soviet corporations and producing for reparations deliveries. In 1947, the Soviet Union began to transfer these corporations to German ownership; by 1954, it had either sold them to the East German state sector or turned them over free of charge. An exception was the uranium mine of the Wismut AG, which continued as a Soviet-German corporation until the end of the GDR. The remaining part of the seized industry became the people's property – by referendum in the industrialized state of Saxony on June 30, 1946, and by decree in the states in the Soviet zone shortly thereafter. SMAD Order No. 64 put an official stop to expropriations on April 17, 1948. By the end of 1948, nearly two-thirds of the Soviet zone economy was under the control of German authorities or Soviet corporations; the state sector and Soviet corporations together accounted for more than 60 percent of industrial production. The change in ownership structure, which was intended to marginalize private property by the end of the 1950s, was associated with a shift in the company elites. Workers and newcomers often took over management. Some skilled laborers with Nazi pasts remained in

---

[45] Buchheim, *Folgelasten*, 295–322; Judt, *DDR-Geschichte in Dokumenten*, 90–1; Steiner, *Plan zu Plan*, 38–40; Jens Schöne, *Frühling auf dem Lande? Die Kollektivierung der DDR-Landwirtschaft* (Berlin, 2005), 57–64.

[46] Werner Matschke, *Die industrielle Entwicklung in der sowjetischen Besatzungszone Deutschlands (SBZ) 1945–1948* (Berlin, 1988), 142–59; Tilman Bezzenberger, "Wie das Volkseigentum geschaffen wurde. Die Unternehmens-Enteignungen in der Sowjetischen Besatzungszone 1945–1948," *ZNR – Zeitschrift für Neuere Rechtsgeschichte* 3–4 (1997): 210–48; Steiner, *Plan zu Plan*, 40–4.

their positions because they could not be replaced easily. The shift of elites reinforced the restructuring of property, generating considerable social and political cohesion within the new order.[47]

Behind this new order lay the Russian and German communists' concept of common good – including a comprehensive restructuring of property relations – based on Marxist-Leninist doctrine. That concept, as André Steiner has explained, with its claim to "freedom from crisis, full employment, and basic social security on the basis of socialized – which really meant state – property, was aimed at the economy and required the ex ante steering of the national economy, or rather the state sector." Steiner notes further,

Plans were no longer to be made and realized only on the company level but also on the level of branches, economic sectors, and the national economy. In this respect, the ex ante coordination of economic activities on the micro level was to be transferred via the planned economy to the macro level, thus internalizing external costs, eliminating inefficiencies of the national economy resulting from the pursuit of microeconomically rational goals, and finally implementing their own concept of the common good.[48]

Economic activity in the Soviet zone and later in the GDR was to be carried out within this regulatory framework.

ON THE WAY TO THE CENTRALLY PLANNED ECONOMY

To better understand Soviet influence in the establishment of the centrally planned economy in the Soviet zone/GDR, it is necessary, first of all, to briefly describe the economic policy ideas of the political parties active in the early postwar years. On account of the Soviet occupation, the Communists played a salient role in the Soviet zone. They saw economic planning as an integral part of a new political order. The Social Democrats were also in favor of economic planning, as were the Christian Democrats, with limitations. Only the Liberals continued to favor a market economy.[49]

---

[47] Rainer Karlsch, "'Ein Staat im Staate.' Der Uranbergbau der Wismut AG in Sachsen und Thüringen," *Aus Politik und Zeitgeschichte* 43 (1993): 14–23; Karlsch and Bähr, "Die Sowjetischen Aktiengesellschaften," 214–55; Winfrid Halder, "'Prüfstein . . . für die politische Lauterbarkeit der Führenden?' Der Volksentscheid zur "Enteignung der Kriegs- und Naziverbrecher' in Sachsen im Juni 1946," *Geschichte und Gesellschaft* 25 (1999): 589–612; André Steiner, "Das Gemeinwohl-Konzept als Element der Wirtschaftsordnungen des Nationalsozialismus und der DDR," in *Öffentliches und privates Wirtschaften in sich wandelnden Wirtschaftsordnungen (Vierteljahrschrift für Sozial- und Wirtschaftsgeschichte*, Beiheft 156), ed. Jürgen Schneider (Stuttgart, 2001), 227–42, here p. 234; Steiner, *Plan zu Plan*, 41–4.

[48] Steiner, "Gemeinwohl-Konzept," 238.

[49] Steininger, *Deutsche Geschichte*, 1:119; Steiner, *Plan zu Plan*, 35–8.

Doubts about free market economics and support for planning were not products of the end of the war. Such views had been expressed years earlier. Noting the failure of democracies and the advance of dictatorships in a February 1940 diary entry, Andre Gide remarked, "One must prepare for the fact that, after the war, even if we are the victors, we will sink into such a swamp that only a firmly committed dictatorship will be able to pull us out."[50] In 1942, Joseph Schumpeter published a critique of capitalism in which he declared that capitalism created the conditions that would bring about its downfall. The alternative, he maintained, was socialism.[51] Schumpeter voiced what many were thinking. On account of the world economic crisis, widespread poverty and suffering, and the radicalization of public opinion, the prospects for capitalism looked bleak. An "anticapitalist yearning" was evident across the political spectrum. Economic planning and socialism seemed to be the wave of the future.[52] Many Europeans thought a socialistically oriented system of comprehensive state control would be necessary to lift society out of the postwar economic crisis.[53] Many looked hopefully to the Soviet Union, which had won worldwide respect and admiration during the war. The Soviet rise from a seemingly hopeless situation to victory over the Wehrmacht was taken as proof that the Soviet system had precisely the potential needed for future economic growth and prosperity. Advocates and critics of economic planning alike thought communism and a leading role for the Soviets would be an inevitable part of Europe's future.[54]

The Soviets directed economic policy in their occupation zone with their own benefit in mind, however. Moscow's principle motivation in restarting the economy there was to enable production for its own needs. Its unclear ideas on policy toward Germany at the end of the war gave rise to extremely contradictory economic policies. The emerging Cold War and the Western powers' efforts to form a nation in their occupation zones, however, prompted leaders in the Kremlin to move decisively toward an economic policy aimed at bringing about the socioeconomic transformation of the Soviet zone. A SMAD report of December 1946 gave an early indication of this direction, declaring that "the economically and politically divided existence of the four occupation zones led to growth in the economic independence of the zones as well as the states and provinces within the zones.

---

[50] Quoted in Harold James, *Der Rückfall. Die neue Weltwirtschaftskrise* (Munich, 2005), 287.

[51] Joseph A. Schumpeter, *Capitalism, Socialism and Democracy* (New York, 1975).

[52] Steininger, *Deutsche Geschichte*, 1:116–21.

[53] Dieter Grosser, ed., *Der Staat in der Wirtschaft der Bundesrepublik* (Opladen, 1985), 18–21.

[54] John Kenneth Galbraith, *Die Geschichte der Wirtschaft im 20. Jahrhundert. Ein Augenzeuge berichtet* (Hamburg, 1995), 174.

The available stores of raw materials allowed for a separate existence of the zones without visible economic disruptions."[55]

In light of the difficult economic situation, it very swiftly became clear that the economy of the Soviet zone could only be controlled operatively. Managing the economy proved especially difficult. German agencies worked against one another, and the Soviet occupation authorities' non-transparent production orders made it difficult for the Germans to keep track of reparations deliveries. On July 22, 1945, the SMAD established a Central Administration for Industry (Deutsche Zentralverwaltung für Industrie, or DZVI) with eleven central administrations for various economic sectors. Yet this body had hardly any authority or control rights in consequence of Soviet self-interest and German mistrust. Thus the states in the Soviet zone were able to develop a high degree of independence, which, in turn, resulted in a sort of state selfishness.[56] Different states, for example, developed industries for processing their own raw materials while capacities in other Soviet zone states went unutilized: "Self-confidently, the states not only guarded their independence from Berlin but also sealed themselves off from one another. The lack of a unified rationing system within the zones made this easier for them."[57]

In response to the creation of an economic council for the British–American bizone in late May 1947 and to the deterioration of the economic situation in the Soviet zone, Moscow established the German Economic Commission (Deutsche Wirtschaftskommission, or DWK) on June 4, 1947. Its task was to better coordinate economic activities in the Soviet zone. Up to that point, planners had worked on a quarter-by-quarter basis and had relied upon the German rationing system and wartime price controls. However, the dismantling and growing strain of reparations repeatedly undermined such planning, which, ironically, was supposed to ensure that reparations deliveries would be made.

The DWK initially did little to improve the situation. Its authority was too restricted to resolve the conflict between the states and the central agency or to prevent them from imposing contradictory decisions. Soviet policy shifted decisively in the wake of the Allied foreign ministers conference in

---

[55] Jan Foitzik, "Über die Frage, inwieweit die selbstständige Existenz der sowjetischen Zone zweckmäßig ist, muss schnellstmöglich entschieden werden." Gutachten aus der Sowjetischen Militäradministration in Deutschland vom Dezember 1946 mit Bearbeitungsvermerken von Marschall Sokolowski. *Deutschland Archiv* 36 (2003): 435.

[56] André Steiner, "Zwischen Länderpartikularismus und Zentralismus. Zur Wirtschaftslenkung in der SBZ bis zur Bildung der Deutschen Wirtschaftskommission im Juni 1947," *Aus Politik und Zeitgeschichte* 43.49–50 (1993): 32–9.

[57] Buchheim, *Folgelasten*, 249.

late November 1947. No longer seeking to establish a unified Germany, the Western Allies intended to found a German government for the three Western zones in the very near future. Moscow responded in February 1948 with SMAD Order No. 32, which expanded the authority of the DWK. It was given the right to issue binding directives and to integrate the relatively unsuccessful central administrations of the DZVI into it. With this step, Moscow laid the foundations for an East German government. By the summer of 1948, the DWK had established a new economic order in the Soviet zone. The DWK first revoked the economic policy authority of the states, thus eliminating state sectionalism. It thereafter handled all planning and had sole decision-making authority. With the permission of the SMAD, the DWK drafted a six-month plan for the second half of 1948 under the banner of "reconstructing and developing the peace economy." It built upon that plan by preparing a two-year plan for 1949 and 1950. From the outset, the decisive positions of authority within the DWK were filled by the SED. The establishment of a Soviet-style planned economy thereby became the main goal of economic policy, and the other political parties were forced to adapt to this course.[58]

Probably one of Moscow's most important economic measures was the currency reform in the Soviet zone announced on June 23, 1948. Coming just three days after the currency reform in the Western zones, it might appear at first glance that the Western move had forced Moscow's hand. Washington and Moscow had in fact each begun secret preparations for currency reforms nearly simultaneously back in the late summer and fall of 1947. After June 1948, it was apparent that the two currency reforms were completely different in kind. The Western zones coupled currency reform with other economic measures that, for the most part, lifted price regulations and rationing. The reforms in the Soviet zone, by contrast, merely reduced the money supply. The rationing system remained in place and would serve as the foundation for building a planned economy in the Soviet mold.

Germany's racially motivated war of extermination pushed the Soviet Union into an existential crisis – a crisis that took an enormous toll on the Soviet economy. Germany was therefore to contribute decisively to the country's rebuilding. The Soviet Union initially intended, accordingly, to impose a hard peace on Germany. Moscow, wanting to receive the reparations it was due as quickly as possible, proceeded with great severity and ruthlessness.

---

[58] Steiner, *Plan zu Plan*, 52–62.

In practice, however, the Soviets had to take a more pragmatic approach during the occupation. The policy of economic disarmament nearly paralyzed the zone's economy. The rapid pace of dismantling and reparations practically wiped out the domestic market in the two years following the war. Soviet occupation policy gradually changed in response to the resulting crisis. Economic disarmament was abandoned in favor of the more pragmatic policy of utilizing their occupation zone's resources locally for their own advantage. At the same time, worsening relations with the Western Allies prompted the Soviet occupation regime to begin developing a unified central economic plan for the zone. The process of socioeconomic transformation gained momentum in 1948. The establishment and restructuring of the DWK, the tightening of controls to increase the efficiency of economic planning, and the currency reform of June 1948 – economic measures all enacted under Soviet influence – were reactions to developments in the Western zones and also steps toward the creation of a Soviet-style planned economy. By this point in time, the two parts of Germany were clearly on diametrically opposed paths of development.

4

National Socialist Autarky Projects and the Postwar Industrial Landscape

RAINER KARLSCH

Autarky describes the ability of economic subjects to produce or manufacture everything they consume from their own resources. The economic theorist Friedrich List first formulated the idea of autarky as a macroeconomic theory at the beginning of the nineteenth century. After World War I, economists such as Werner Sombart took up the concept of a closed national economic area in clear opposition to the ideas of economic liberalism. Hitler's economic advisor Wilhelm Keppler and other influential National Socialist officials later picked up on this idea. Even before the emergence of the Third Reich, the Soviet Union, feeling besieged, had moved toward autarky under Stalin. Autarky was at the center of the concept of "socialism in one country" Stalin put forward in 1924, and it was later incorporated in the theory of "socialist industrialization."

As a socialist state under Soviet domination, the German Democratic Republic (GDR) was profoundly influenced by the idea of autarky. Embargos and trade discrimination by Western states prompted the GDR to maintain the old autarky structures created by the Nazis and to begin new autarky projects of its own. The GDR's socialist leaders and the Nazis had fundamentally different intentions in promoting autarky projects, however. Whereas the Nazis had aimed to facilitate the war effort, the GDR's Socialist Unity Party (Sozialistische Einheitspartei Deutschlands, or SED) considered autarky projects part of the "genetic code" of the socialist system.[1]

This difference in intentions notwithstanding, the autarky structures the Nazis left behind or that had been in place since World War I provided the framework for autarky projects in the Soviet occupation zone/GDR. GDR autarky industries thus, in many respects, continued prewar and

---

[1] See Janos Kornai, *Das sozialitische System. Die politische Ökonomie des Kommunismus* (Baden-Baden, 1995), 189, 380–6, 416.

Table 1. *Synthetic Fuel Plants (IG Technology) in Eastern Germany*

Plant	Owner	Initial Construction	Highest Capacity
Leuna	IG	1926/33	625,000 t
Böhlen	BRABAG	1934	252,000 t
Magdeburg	BRABAG	1935	230,000 t
Zeitz	BRABAG	1937	300,000 t
Luetzkendorf	Wintershall	1936	50,000 t
Sum			1,457,000 t

Source: Compiled from Gottfried Plumpe, *I.G. Farbenindustrie AG,* 284.

wartime practices. The GDR also developed its own autarkic "anti-import production" projects. In this essay, I examine the different influences on and directions taken by these autarky projects, and I conclude by sketching what happened to them after German unification in 1990.

THE LEGACY OF AUTARKY INDUSTRIES IN EASTERN GERMANY[2]

The economic structure of Central Germany experienced lasting changes as a result of autarky projects initiated during the Nazi period. The region had been home to numerous other autarky projects dating from as early as World War I. One was an industrial complex for the production of ammonia and nitric acid in Leuna, a town strategically located far from the front. This complex later became the principal site of IG Farbenindustrie AG.[3] The government facilitated the construction of another large chemical plant, the Piesteritz nitrogen plant at Wittenberg, which became operational in 1915.

World War I taught the Nazi regime an important lesson: it could eliminate shortages of raw materials needed for armaments production not only by increasing imports and domestic production but also by developing substitutes. The production of synthetic fuels was one of the most important Nazi autarky projects. More than half of the Third Reich's synthetic fuel production capacity and approximately one-third of the country's facilities for the conversion of brown coal to gasoline by the Fischer-Tropsch process could be found in Central Germany (Tables 1 and 2).

---

[2] For the sake of consistency, *Eastern Germany* will be used here to refer to the area that comprised the GDR from 1949–90 regardless of the historical period under consideration. Before 1945, the term *East Germany* referred to the territories in the eastern part of the old Reich, especially the rural district of East Prussia, and the area that became the GDR was often called *Central Germany.* It included parts of Prussia, Saxony, and Thuringia without a clear borderline.

[3] See Gottfried Plumpe, *Die IG Farbenindustrie AG. Wirtschaft, Technik und Politik 1904–1945* (Berlin, 1990), 69–82; Werner Abelshauser, ed., *Die BASF. Eine Unternehmensgeschichte* (Munich, 2002), 171–2.

Table 2. *Fischer-Tropsch Facilities in Eastern Germany*

Plant	Owner	Initial Construction	Highest Capacity
Schwarzheide	BRABAG	1935	210,000 t
Lützkendorf	Wintershall	1937	80,000 t
Sum			290,000 t

Source: Compiled from Gottfried Plumpe, *I.G. Farbenindustrie AG*, 284.

Brandenburg, for example, saw the construction of the Braunkohlen-Benzin-Aktiengesellschaft (BRABAG) coal gasification plant in Schwarzheide. It was above all the energy projects launched under the Nazi regime's Four-Year Plan that were to have a lasting influence on the economic development of the GDR.

Although the gas industry, which relied on black coal, was based in the Ruhr region, Central Germany also played a part in the industry, especially once gas could be made from brown coal. Before 1945, Central Germany's long-established gas industry got its hard coal from the Ruhr. Then the Lurgie Company developed a new process for gasifying brown coal in the 1940s. This technology, which was put into use at the state-owned Aktiengesellschaft Sächsische Werke (ASW) in Böhlen, would later prove to be of immense importance to the GDR, which had rich brown coal reserves. From the 1940s onward, gas industry autarky projects in Central Germany relied on the Lurgie process although it was costly and did considerable environmental damage. The projects would not have been undertaken but for state demand and massive state subsidies.

The manufacture of synthetic rubber and the development of a domestic synthetic fiber industry, which aimed to reduce raw material imports, also played a central role in the Nazi war economy and shaped the industrial landscape of Central Germany. For strategic reasons, the first and largest German synthetic rubber plant was built in Schkopau, near Merseburg, in the late 1930s. The rapidly growing synthetic fiber industry had important centers in Saxony, Thuringia, Saxony-Anhalt, and Brandenburg. Domestic production of synthetic fibers allowed the Nazi regime to cut natural fiber imports and thereby conserve foreign exchange for the purchase of strategic raw materials for rearmament.[4] The national fiber program led to the construction of Europe's largest plant for the production of spun rayon. It was built on the premises of the AGFA Filmfabrik Wolfen, which belonged to

[4] See Lotto Zumpe, *Wirtschaft und Staat in Deutschland 1933 bis 1945* (Berlin, 1980), 229.

IG Farben.[5] Another large fiber plant was built with government support in Plauen, and existing plants, such as those in Premnitz and Schwarza, expanded their production.[6]

Two other areas in which the Nazis undertook autarky projects that shaped industry in Central Germany were sulfuric acid production and copper mining. Resuming abandoned experiments in the production of sulfuric acid from the 1920s, the Nazi regime began developing a large gypsum-based sulfuric acid plant at the Farbenfabrik Wolfen and another facility in Coswig in 1936.[7] It also reopened the copper mines in the Mansfeld region, one of Europe's oldest European mining areas, because it needed copper for arms production.[8] Because copper could no longer be produced domestically at competitive prices, the state had to support the Mansfeld AG mining company by investing as a "silent partner."

Contrary to the widely held view, the Nazi regime did not focus its economic policy on creating a self-sufficient national economic area. Even in the case of the most important autarky project, the production of gasoline from coal, Germany remained a long way from achieving self-sufficiency, and the Nazis saw synthetic fuel production as merely a "bridging technology."[9] Ultimately, the regime intended resolve the country's fuel supply problem by seizing control of new resources.[10]

Nazi-era investment in autarky projects nonetheless had a far-reaching impact on the economic structure of Central Germany. The most important was the development of the brown coal-based chemical industry in the region around the cities of Halle and Merseburg. This cluster was the heart of what later became known as the "Chemical Triangle."

EASTERN GERMANY'S STARTING POSITION AFTER WORLD WAR II

After the war, Germany was divided into four occupation zones and lost large parts of its eastern territories to the Soviet Union and Poland. During the negotiations on the occupation, the Allies aimed to make the zones

---

[5] See Constanze Seidel, *Die Entwicklung der Vistra-Produktion von 1932–1939 am Beispiel der Filmfabrik Wolfen* (Jena, Germany, 2005). See also Silke Fengler (Chapter 8) in this volume.

[6] See Herbert Bode, *Chronik der Entwicklung der Chemiefaserindustrie in Deutschland* (Dessau, 2006).

[7] See Fritz Welsch, *Geschichte der chemischen Industrie* (Berlin, 1981), 126.

[8] See Eckhard Traubroth, "Zur wirtschaftlichen Wertung der Bergbau- und Hüttenproduktion," in *Mansfeld. Die Geschichte des Berg- und Hüttenwesens*. Vol. 1, ed. Verein Mansfelder Berg- und Hüttenleute e.V. (Eisleben and Bochum, Germany, 1999), 485–527.

[9] See Rainer Karlsch and Raymond G. Stokes, *Faktor Öl. Die Mineralölwirtschaft in Deutschland 1859–1974* (Munich, 2003), 171–202.

[10] See Dietrich Eichholtz, *Krieg um Öl. Ein Erdölimperium als deutsches Kriegsziel (1938–1943)* (Leipzig, 2006).

Table 3. *Area, Population, and Per Capita Net Production of the Later Occupation Zones*

Zone	Area	Population	Per Capita Net Production
	In % of 1937	In % of 1937	1936 in Reichsmark
British	20.8	28.5	596
Soviet	22.8	21.9	546
American	22.8	20.6	427
France	8.5	7.6	417
Saar	0.5	1.3	500
Berlin	0.2	6.3	697
Eastern parts[a]	24.3	13.8	229
German Reich	100.0	100.0	494

[a] Ceded to Poland and Soviet Union.

Source: See Werner Abelshauser, *Wirtschaftsgeschichte der Bundesrepublik Deutschland 1945–1980* (Frankfurt, 1983), 13.

roughly equal in size in terms of area, population, and per capita production (Table 3).

The figures presented in Table 3 suggest that the Soviet zone was relatively well positioned to rebuild its economy. Its economic potential was comparable to that of the British zone, which included the Ruhr coal, steel, and heavy industry region. Many well-known firms that produced a broad range of sophisticated products – from machine tools and airplanes to typewriters and cameras – were based in the Soviet zone. Most manufacturers in the region were mid-sized. Most were also highly integrated within the German market and oriented toward export sales. Although productivity in Central Germany was high, it lagged a few percentage points behind the rate in the Western parts of Germany because the region had a relatively high proportion old industries, notably the textile industry.[11] The region's economy was also characterized by a high level of trade with other German regions. Central Germany purchased large quantities of hard coal, ore, iron, and timber from other parts of Germany and supplied them in return with goods such as textiles, furniture, cameras, and machine tools.

A rapid recovery of the Soviet zone's economy was hindered by Soviet reparations policy. The division of Germany carried an extraordinary price for Eastern Germany: it had to shoulder the burden of Soviet and Polish reparations demands almost entirely alone. It had to surrender the equivalent of $10 billion in the form of dismantled factories, reparations in kind, and the free transfer of knowledge and patents. In addition, approximately

[11] See Jaap Sleifer, "Planning Ahead and Falling Behind: The East German Economy in Comparison with West Germany, 1936–2002," *Jahrbuch für Wirtschaftsgeschichte*, Beiheft 8 (Berlin, 2006), 69–87.

three thousand scientists and engineers were obligated to work in the Soviet Union for many years. Between 1945 and 1948, more than 3,400 industrial firms were stripped of their machinery and equipment, which reduced the zone's industrial capital to 75 percent of the 1936 level. Comparison with the Western zones shows how severe Soviet reparations policy was. The three Western zones together lost fewer than seven hundred enterprises through dismantling. In 1948, the industrial capital of the British and American zones stood at 111 percent of the prewar level.[12] Soviet dismantling, moreover, was not limited to industrial facilities. The Soviets removed approximately one-third of the railroad track in their zone and also confiscated locomotive engines and railcars. Rolling stock was reduced to 26 percent of the level of 1944. These removals severely undermined the rail network in the Soviet zone and created a huge bottleneck that affected the zone's economy as a whole.[13] It took the GDR more than twenty years to compensate for these losses. All in all, the GDR's starting position was made significantly worse by the extraordinarily heavy reparations it had to make.

It is important to keep in mind that the main aim of the Soviet dismantling program was to destroy Germany's capacity to wage war. That is why the Soviets completely dismantled all weapons, aircraft, and explosives factories. This policy carried over into the GDR era. The Soviet authorities never allowed the arms industry to be rebuilt on a large scale in the GDR and prohibited the production of tanks, fighter jets, guns, submarines, and other military goods.[14]

Within a few years of the war's end, the Soviet occupation zone was turned into a socialist society with a communist-led government. Its economy was largely cut off from its traditional markets, and its trade with the Western zones declined even further after the Western Allies imposed a trade embargo in response to the Soviet blockade of West Berlin in 1948–9. The disintegration of German–German trade – above all, the suspension of coal and steel imports – created many problems for the Soviet zone's economy. All large and mid-sized industrial enterprises were expropriated. The state controlled most of the industry and introduced a planned economy on the Soviet model.

---

[12] See Rainer Karlsch and Jochen Laufer, *Sowjetische Demontagen in Deutschland 1944–1949* (Berlin, 2002). See also the contributions by Burghard Ciesla (Chapter 3) and Ray Stokes (Chapter 7) in this volume.

[13] See Rüdiger Kühr, *Die Reparationspolitik der UdSSR und die Sowjetisierung des Verkehrswesens der SBZ* (Bochum, Germany, 1996).

[14] The only exceptions were Carl Zeiss Jena, which produced optical instruments and microelectronics for military purposes and an enterprise in Dresden, the "Spezialkombinat."

In 1950, productivity in the GDR stood at 75 percent of the West German level. That was the closest the GDR ever came to matching its Western rival. The GDR lagged behind the Federal Republic in economic performance from the outset. The main reasons were the reduction of its industrial capital as a result of Soviet dismantling and removal; the disintegration of its economy; the establishment of a Soviet-style planned economy; and, last but not least, the migration of well-trained scientists, engineers, and workers to the West. The division of Germany and the integration of the German states into rival blocs spurred the continuation of autarky projects in the GDR.

CONTINUATION OF PREWAR AND WARTIME AUTARKY INDUSTRIES

The autarky industries the Nazis had fostered in Central Germany survived the war to varying extents. The Soviet zone/GDR was able to continue operating some of these prewar and wartime autarky industries – notably the synthetic rubber, synthetic fiber, and copper industries – with relatively little change. Other sectors, such as the synthetic gasoline production plants, suffered significant capacity losses from Allied bombing and, to an even greater extent, from Soviet dismantling,[15] though at least half of the 1944 capacity survived.[16]

SYNTHETIC FUEL, RUBBER, AND FIBER PRODUCTION: THE CHEMICAL INDUSTRY

In contrast to the synthetic fuel industry, the synthetic rubber and fiber industries in the Soviet zone survived the war without extensive capacity losses and were well positioned for a quick recovery.[17] Whereas the Western Allies prohibited the production of synthetic rubber and synthetic fuel in their zones until the spring of 1951, the Soviets reorganized the sector and continued production. The Buna synthetic rubber plant in Schkopau and all other large chemical plants in the Soviet zone were put under the control

[15] See Rainer Karlsch and Jochen Laufer, eds., *Soujetische Demontagen in Deutschland 1944–1949. Hintergründe, Ziele und Wirkungen* (Berlin, 2002).

[16] See Rainer Karlsch, "Wie Phönix aus der Asche? Rekonstruktion und Strukturwandel in der chemischen Industrie in beiden deutschen Staaten bis Mitte der sechziger Jahre," in *Deutsch-Deutsche Wirtschaft 1945 bis 1990*, ed. Lothar Baar and Dietmar Petzina (St. Katharinen, Germany, 1999), 268. The completely dismantled hydrogenation plant in Magdeburg was one exception.

[17] See Rainer Karlsch, *Capacity Losses, Reconstruction and Unfinished Modernization: The Chemical Industry in the Soviet Zone of Occupation (SBZ)/GDR 1945–1965* (Berkeley, CA, 1997).

of a Soviet corporation. That gave the region's synthetic rubber industry a head start at the time of reconstruction,[18] although this eventually turned out to be a disadvantage. The Western Allies' prohibitions on synthetic rubber and gasoline production accelerated the Western German chemical industry's departure from autarky industries and forced it to abandon its traditional specialization in acetylene chemistry, which in turn spurred it to seek strategic alliances with British and American oil companies. This shift to petrochemisty was a major stimulus to innovation.[19]

Synthetic fiber production quickly recovered after the war. It was one of the few branches of industry in which East Germany led West Germany in research. The SED's main goal in expanding this branch was much the same as the Nazis' goal, namely, to limit imports of raw materials.

As with most other industries, the reconstruction of the chemical industry in the GDR was not accompanied by technological innovation, and its economic and regional structures barely changed. The two World Wars led to the concentration of the industry in the "chemical triangle." This regional concentration prompted the East German chemical industry to continue after 1945 on the distinctly German path of coal-based production that its West German counterpart reluctantly abandoned. Using the available material resources and human capital, Eastern Germany was able to reconstruct the chemical industry by the mid-1950s. It drew on modern developments and relied on improvements in existing technology. This strategy moved the GDR chemical industry backward rather than forward, however. When reconstruction was completed, the GDR's chemical and synthetic fiber industries were at about the technical level of the 1930s.

COPPER MINING

The GDR was able to continue and even expand the Nazi copper-mining project without interruption. Some twenty thousand miners in the Mansfeld district continued to extract copper ore, which was smelted on-site. The policy of relying on domestic resources so far as possible relieved the GDR's

---

[18] See Rainer Karlsch, "Vom Warm- zum Kaltkautschuk. A Comparative Look at Innovation at the Buna Plants in Schkopau and Hüls," in *Innovationsverhalten und Entscheidungsstrukturen,* ed. Dietmar Petzina and Johannes Bähr (Berlin, 1996), 79–108; idem., "Comparaison de la reconstruction de l'industrie chimique en Allemagne de l'Ouest et de l'Est 1945–1949," *Histoire, économie & société, Programme National Persée* 18.2 (1999): 383–95.

[19] See Raymond G. Stokes, *Opting for Oil: The Political Economy of Technological Change in the West German Chemical Industry, 1945–1961* (New York, 1994).

currency balance. This economic strategy allowed for a significant expansion of copper and iron ore extraction so that domestic production covered more than two-thirds of requirements.[20] Between 1952 and 1968, the GDR was able to maintain stable costs at the Mansfeld copper mine as well as to develop new fields and commission modern facilities. However, costs rose in the early 1970s, ushering in the final period of the Mansfeld copper mine, in which production declined and costs quickly escalated.[21]

Copper mining eventually became untenable. In the early 1980s, the regime considered alternatives to shutting down the mine, but the technology for processing imported copper ore did not exist in the Mansfield district. It later reviewed the option of exploiting copper reserves in Spremberg but took no action. It also discussed the expansion of tin production in the hope of developing export production to earn hard currency,[22] but falling global tin prices in the mid-1980s undermined this plan.

The copper industry suffered from the same basic problem that afflicted all of the Nazi autarky projects maintained by the GDR. Like the different branches of the chemical industry, the copper industry failed to invest in innovation and to keep up with technological advances developed in other countries. It was thus poorly positioned when the East German economy was opened to international competition.

"ANTI-IMPORT PRODUCTION" PROJECTS

Alongside the autarky projects inherited from the Nazis, the GDR launched several of its own as part of an "anti-import production" campaign. The SED was particularly eager in the 1950s to achieve independence in the production of iron, steel, and coke as well as in the generation of electricity. The same impulse lay behind the projects associated with the *Störfreimachung* (elimination of disruptions) policy initiated in 1958. From the late 1950s through the mid-1960s, the GDR sought to end its dependence on trade with the Federal Republic by revamping its photochemical industry,[23] expanding Rostock's harbor, intensifying the search for domestic sources of petroleum and natural gas, and developing a microelectronics industry.

---

[20] See Wolfgang Mühlfriedel and Klaus Wießner, *Die Geschichte der Industrie der DDR* (Berlin, 1989), 217.

[21] See Traubroth, "Zur wirtschaftlichen Wertung der Bergbau- und Hüttenproduktion," 515.

[22] See Beratung bei Günter Mittag zu Fragen der weiteren Entwicklung der Rohstoffwirtschaft der DDR am 28.5.1984, BArch Berlin-Lichterfeld, DY 30/IV 2/2.101/107.

[23] On the photochemical industry, see Silke Fengler (Chapter 8) in this volume.

"ANTI-IMPORT PRODUCTION" OF IRON AND STEEL IN THE 1950s

During the first decade of the GDR's existence, coal, iron, and steel formed the backbone of its economy and took center stage in economic policy. Like the other Eastern bloc countries, the GDR pursued the Stalinist "iron concept" – that is, the rapid expansion of coal, iron, and steel production – and redoubled its efforts during the Korean War (1950–3). Both theoretical dogma and military considerations influenced the way they executed this idea. Whether the GDR's adoption of this model was a good or wasteful use of resources has been the subject of debate. Many scholars argue that the SED leadership did not need to copy the Soviet model of industrialization and therefore misdirected economic resources.[24]

The more basic question, however, was whether the GDR had any alternative to pouring resources into the expansion of its iron and steel industry. The GDR was home to only about 7 percent of the German iron-based industry. It held a little less than 3 percent of German black coal reserves and accounted for approximately 5 percent of German iron ore mining activities.[25] The two-year plan for 1949–50 and the first five-year plan (1951–5) thus followed an internal logic. The position of officials who demanded an end to reliance on West German iron and steel was bolstered when the FRG halted deliveries in the early 1950s. Another important factor shaping GDR policy was the fact that the GDR was not initially a preferred trading partner of the other Eastern bloc countries. The Soviet Union and Poland were not willing to deliver iron and steel to East Germans because of their own needs and understandable resentments. This dire situation pushed cost considerations into the background. Consequently, the most important investment project of the first five-year plan was the construction of a new steelworks, the Eisenhüttenkombinats Ost (EKO).

The EKO was a successful enterprise but was also not without its problems in both the short and long runs. Anti-import production of iron reduced the proportion of imported raw iron the GDR used from 42 to 15 percent between 1950 and 1955.[26] That show of strength ensured the survival of the GDR. At the same time, however, a number of planning errors

---

[24] See Helga Schultz, "Die sozialistische Industrialisierung – toter Hund oder Erkenntnismittel? [Discussion]," *Jahrbuch für Wirtschaftsgeschichte* 1999, pt. 2: 105–13.

[25] See Horst Barthel, *Die wirtschaftlichen Ausgangsbedingungen der DDR* (Berlin, 1978).

[26] See Jörg Roesler, "Eisen für den Frieden." Das Eisenhüttenkombinat Ost in der Wirtschaft der DDR," in *Aufbau West- Aufbau Ost. Die Planstädte Wolfsburg und Eisenhüttenstadt in der Nachkriegszeit,* ed. Rosemarie Beier (Berlin, 1997), 149–58.

significantly increased construction costs. The EKO works was to remain unfinished, and the goal of developing a completely integrated metallurgical cycle, including a rolling mill, was never realized. Moreover, long reliance on established technology inhibited innovation: up to the mid-1970s, 75 percent of steel produced in the GDR was based on nineteenth-century Siemens-Martin technology.[27]

Clearly, the GDR had no alternative to establishing the EKO. However, it could have taken another path in the further development of its steel industry. It might have adopted new methods, such as the oxygen process of steelmaking, for example; expanded the secondary processing stage; or reduced production capacity and expanded imports.

Another material that GDR industries urgently needed was coke. This solid fuel was traditionally produced from black coal, which the GDR obtained either from difficult to work mines in Zwickau or by import from Poland and the Soviet Union. East German planners considered black coal too expensive, however, for coke and gas generation, especially as the quantities needed would increase every year. The GDR solved this problem with one of its few technological innovations; it produced high-temperature coke from brown coal. The State Planning Commission responded to this invention with uncharacteristic speed. In 1951, it decided to build a large coking plant at Lauchhammer, which then supplied the newly constructed low-pit furnace plant in Calbe exclusively with high-temperature coke.

The GDR's most important and by far most expensive energy project was the construction of the Schwarze Pumpe Combine near Senftenberg,[28] which produced high-temperature coke, tar, and gas and also generated electricity. Schwarze Pumpe became the symbol of an outmoded energy policy based on brown coal. Developed in the 1930s, the technology employed was already out of date when the plant became operational after a fifteen-year construction period. It also typified the heavy burden East German industry put on the environment. The plan relied on makeshift measures such as settling ponds for tar and landfills for tar sludge that led to extensive soil and water contamination.

---

[27] See Stefan Unger, "Innovationsprobleme in der Schwarzmetallurgie der DDR: Die Einführung des Stranggießens," in *Deutsch-Deutsche Wirtschaft 1945 bis 1990. Strukturveränderungen, Innovationen und regionaler Wandel. Ein Vergleich*, ed. Lothar Baar and Dietmar Petzina (St. Katharinen, Germany, 1999), 224–5.

[28] See *ESPAG. Geschichte eines Unternehmens. Vom Gaskombinat zur Aktiengesellschaft* (Bautzen, Germany, 1993); Günter Bayerl, ed., *Braunkohlenveredelung im Niederlausitzer Revier. 50 Jahre Schwarze Pumpe* (Münster, 2009).

THE STÖRFREIMACHUNG PERIOD

In the late 1950s, GDR economic policy entered a phase known as the *Störfreimachung* period, during which political considerations clearly took precedence over economic. The SED leadership used this term to describe its intention of reducing dependence on Western countries for raw materials and spare parts, thus advancing its anti-import production agenda. The *Störfreimachung* policy initially affected only the photochemical industry, but it was soon extended to other areas.

The regime approved the first *Störfreimachung* program in June 1958. The AGFA Group had photochemical production sites in both Eastern and Western Germany before 1945. The division of labor between the sites that had developed persisted after the war: the film works in Wolfen (GDR) depended on the chemical factory in Leverkusen (FRG) for the supply of chemical products, and, in turn, AGFA Leverkusen depended on film deliveries from Wolfen. The purpose of the *Störfreimachung* program was to supply the Wolfen film plant with photo gelatin produced in the GDR.[29] It was also intended to allow the East German firm to get out of a 1956 contract providing for the marketing of both Wolfen's and Leverkusen's products under the well-known AGFA brand name as soon as possible. The GDR authorities were eager to begin selling all of the Wolfen works products under the "ORWO" (Original Wolfen) label. The brand was, however, to meet with little success in the West. The contract with AGFA Leverkusen was finally canceled in March 1963.

The SED leadership extended the *Störfreimachung* program to areas beyond the photochemical industry as new problems in intra-German trade cropped up. The GDR's imports of specialty products from the West dropped accordingly, and export sales to the West, already at a low level generally, stagnated.[30] Not until 1964 did imports from the West increase significantly, when the regime stopped striving to separate the GDR's economy from the West. It coupled all subsequent attempts to modernize industry with technology imports from the West, cautiously at first, toward the end of the 1960s, and then more dramatically in later years.[31]

---

[29] See Rainer Karlsch, *Von Agfa zu ORWO. Die Folgen der deutschen Teilung für die Filmfabrik Wolfen* (Berlin, 1992); Silke Fengler, *Entwickelt und fixiert. Zur Unternehmens- und Technikgeschichte der deutschen Fotoindustrie, dargestellt am Beispiel der Agfa AG Leverkusen und des VEB Filmfabrik Wolfen (1945–1995).* Bochumer Schriften zur Unternehmens- und Industriegeschichte 18 (Essen, 2009).

[30] See André Steiner, *Von Plan zu Plan. Eine Wirtschaftsgeschichte der DDR* (Munich, 2004), 126.

[31] See Ralf Ahrens, "Die Außenhandelspolitik der DDR im Bereich des Rates für gegenseitige Wirtschaftshilfe 1963–1976" (PhD diss., Technische Universität Dresden, 1999); Raymond G. Stokes, *Constructing Socialism, Technology and Change in East Germany* (Baltimore, MD, 2000); Dolores

The GDR's decision to build a new harbor in Rostock in the late 1950s also marked an effort to reduce dependence on Western countries, West Germany in particular. Before 1945 and into the early years of the GDR, most goods produced in Central Germany for export were shipped from Hamburg. Smaller ports on the Baltic were of only local importance. The port of Rostock, which had been active since the Middle Ages, specialized in the trade of grain, wood, and coal, and it could not compete with the much larger ports of Hamburg, Bremen, and Lübeck. Fearing that the GDR's dependence on Hamburg could seriously impede its foreign trade if political tensions between West and East worsened, SED leaders decided to expand the port of Rostock to accommodate large oceangoing vessels. Opened in the spring of 1960, the new port of Rostock was a success.[32] The volume of goods shipped through the port grew steadily until 1989.

THE SEARCH FOR CRUDE OIL AND NATURAL GAS

The GDR needed Soviet oil and natural gas to bring about a structural change of its economy. During discussions with high-ranking Soviet economic officials in Berlin on January 30, 1964, SED First Secretary Walter Ulbricht pointed to West Germany's advantages in crude oil production. Whereas West Germany processed forty-five million tons of crude oil in 1963, the GDR processed only 3.5 million tons, making it difficult for it to compete with its capitalist counterpart. Ulbricht went on to emphasize the GDR's need for "the right raw materials" for "profitable production."[33] The Soviets did not provide oil and gas in the quantities that the GDR sought. The GDR, consequently, could not change its energy policy and had to increase brown coal production to meet its energy needs.

The GDR never gave up searching for crude oil and natural gas within its borders. The discovery of crude oil and natural gas in the north of the Federal Republic spurred hopes for similar finds in the GDR, as well as an exhaustive search, but it was not fruitful.[34] Geologists looking for natural gas close to Salzwedel (Altmark) near the West German border in the late 1960s were more successful. Salzwedel's natural gas had a low methane

---

L. Augustine, *Red Prometheus: Engineering and Dictatorship in East Germany, 1945–1990* (Cambridge, MA, 2007).

[32] See Ralf Witthohn, "Rostock: Viel mehr als Berlins Kreuzlinerport," *Deutsche Seeschifffahrt* 5 (2010): 24–7.

[33] Stenographische Niederschrift der Aussprache des Genossen Walter Ulbricht mit einer sowjetischen Expertendelegation im Hause des ZK am 30.1.1964, BArch, Berlin-Lichterfelde, DY 30, Nr. 3716.

[34] See Rainer Karlsch, "Der Traum vom Öl – zu den Hintergründen der Erdölsuche in der DDR," *Vierteljahrsschrift für Sozial- und Wirtschaftsgeschichte* 80 (1993): 63–87.

content and a lower calorific value than gas from foreign countries, but it was nevertheless important to the GDR economy. Developing the GDR's natural gas industry cost more than 25 billion marks. Sales of the roughly 178 billion cubic meters of gas generated brought in approximately 22.1 billion marks.[35] Although costs thus exceeded revenues, the GDR was able to sell natural gas abroad for urgently needed hard currency. In addition, the substitution of brown coal had significant macroeconomic effects. The GDR saved money that it otherwise would have had to spend for increased oil and gas imports from the Soviet Union, and it was also able to limit the inefficient production of grid gas.

THE MICROELECTRONICS INDUSTRY

In June 1977, the GDR embarked on an initiative to develop a microelectronics industry. This initiative was aimed at catching up with other industrial nations and was not strictly speaking an autarky program, but it quickly became clear that the GDR had no choice but to act on its own. Advanced technology could not be legally imported from the West because of the Western embargo. Cooperation within the Council for Mutual Economic Assistance (COMECON) was not an option on account of the Soviet military–industrial complex's refusal to cooperate. As no Western European company or government was prepared to conclude a technology licensing agreement with the GDR, the microelectronics program eventually became a de facto autarky project.

The GDR invested a tremendous amount of capital and effort in creating a new industry from scratch, but, without the necessary technology transfer, it was in over its head.[36] Approximately 20 billion East German marks and 4 billion West German D–Marks were spent on the microelectronics program between 1981 and 1988.[37] The three state holding companies involved in microelectronics – Robotron Dresden, Carl Zeiss Jena, and Mikroelektronik Erfurt – were among the five largest state holding companies measured by workforce.[38] The GDR's advances in microelectronics depended heavily

---

[35] See Rainer Karlsch, *Vom Licht zur Wärme. Geschichte der ostdeutschen Gaswirtschaft 1855–2008* (Berlin, 2008), 144–8.

[36] See Friedrich Naumann, "Vom Tastenfeld zum Mikrochip – Computerindustrie und Informatik im 'Schrittmaß' des Sozialismus," in *Naturwissenschaft und Technik in der DDR*, ed. Dieter Hoffmann and Kristie Macrakis (Berlin, 1997), 261–81.

[37] See Hans-Hermann Hertle, "Diskussion der ökonomischen Krisen in der Führungsspitze der SED," in *Der Plan als Befehl und Fiktion. Wirtschaftsführung in der DDR. Gespräche und Analysen*, ed. Theo Pirker, M. R. Lepsius, and Reiner Weinert (Opladen, 1995), 335–6.

[38] See Olaf Klenke, *Ist die DDR an der Globalisierung gescheitert? Autarke Wirtschaftspolitik versus internationale Weltwirtschaft – Das Beispiel Mikroelektronik* (Frankfurt, 2001), 84.

on illegal technology transfer through spying.[39] Still, espionage could not take the place of conventional technology transfer, and production numbers were too low to be profitable. The GDR failed to develop a successful computer industry, as this sector was global from the beginning. With its nationally aligned industrial policy, the GDR was unable to hold its ground in an increasingly internationally organized and global economy.

Like the heritage autarky industries, the autarky projects the GDR developed on its own were shaped in large part by their isolation and the limited resources that resulted from this. Some were able to succeed within the context of a divided Germany, like the port of Rostock and EKO. Others, like the microelectronics and computer industries, suffered from the absence of knowledge transfer. It was clear that none of them could survive unchanged after the end of the GDR.

TECHNOLOGY IMPORTS

Autarky projects no longer played a dominant role in the SED's economic policy during the 1970s and 1980s, but they still had a part to play. The GDR's foreign debt crisis became critical in 1981–2, threatening the state with bankruptcy.[40] The SED leadership responded with a policy of *Export um jeden Preis* (export at any price) to Western countries. New technologies were also supposed to help overcome the debt crisis. A program for the synthetic fibers industry, for example, was launched in May 1983.[41] It encompassed nineteen individual projects to increase fiber production and three projects for the production of hitherto imported raw materials. This ambitious program failed in the late 1980s. The fiber industry was not able to significantly reduce its raw materials imports, and nor could it produce polyurethane fibers of high enough quality to be competitive in international markets.

The SED tried to modernize the steel industry by importing equipment from the West. It declined, however, to shut down even a single obsolete steel mill. After several years of massive investment, very modern and very old technologies stood side by side in steel mills like the giant Eisenhüttenstadt works (Table 4).

---

[39] See Jörg Roesler, "Industrieinnovation und Industriespionage in der DDR," *Deutschland Archiv* 27, no. 10 (1994): 1026–40.

[40] Steiner, *Von Plan zu Plan*, 198–203.

[41] See "Maßnahmen zur Ablösung von NSW-Importen an Faserstoffen sowie textilen Halbfabrikaten und Fertigerzeugnissen für die Leichtindustrie," May 24, 1983, Bundesarchiv Berlin-Lichterfelde, DY 30/17696.

Table 4. *Structure of GDR's Steel Production in 1960 to 1989 (in %)*

Product	1960	1970	1980	1989
Siemens–Martin steel	75	75	62	39
Converter steel	–	–	9	31
Electro steel	13	16	27	30
Other	12	9	2	–

Source: Based on information reported in the annual *Statistisches Jahrbuch der DDR.*

The GDR paid for this partway modernization by export sales of cheap bulk steel. East German exports of steel products to Western countries climbed from 0.3 million tons in 1970 to more than 3.3 million tons in 1985.[42] By way of comparison, the Federal Republic exported approximately 5.7 million tons of steel products in 1985.[43] On a per capita basis, in other words, the GDR had become a larger steel exporter than the Federal Republic. From a country plagued by chronic bottlenecks in steel supply during the 1950s, it had become a major European steel exporter. Exporting large quantities at dumping prices partially alleviated the country's foreign debt problems, but that strategy could not work in the long run because of the high production costs East German steelmakers faced.

WHAT HAPPENED TO AUTARKY PRODUCTION SITES AFTER 1990?

Although both German states had inherited Nazi-era autarky projects, they handled them very differently. The synthetic fuel plants, for example, continued operating, with the help of government subsidies, in both states until the mid-1960s. To reduce its black coal purchases from West Germany, the GDR converted gas production from black to brown coal in the1950s. West Germany closed its synthetic fuel plants in the mid-1960s and relied almost entirely on petroleum and natural gas while the GDR pursued a different route.

When the East and West German economies were merged as part of the unification process in 1990, the protection and isolation that had helped many of the GDR's autarky projects to survive came to an end. Many of these projects had no future when exposed to international market conditions because of their uncompetitively high production costs and prices.

---

[42] Helmut Kinne, *Geschichte der Stahlindustrie der Deutschen Demokratischen Republik* (Düsseldorf, 2002), appendix, 11.
[43] Helmut Wienert, *Die Stahlindustrie in der DDR* (Berlin, 1992), 102.

Some survived by finding new functions or by modernizing and adapting to new conditions, while still others were essentially replaced by Western firms. All in all, although many of the sites of GDR autarky projects continue to house industries today, little besides the location is the same.

The rusty landscapes at the Leuna factory and the ash–gray miasma over the chemical plants in Bitterfeld left no doubt that the chemical industry in the GDR had lost its ability to compete on the world markets long before the revolution of 1989–90. More than €20 billion, of which more than €15 billion came from the government, was invested in rescuing and modernizing the Chemical Triangle between 1990 and 1998. The private sector moved in during this period, led by Elf Aquitaine and Dow Chemical.[44] At the old Leuna site, Elf Aquitaine opened the Mitteldeutsche Erdöl–Raffinerie (MIDER) in 1997. After the old facilities were entirely dismantled, dozens of Belgian, French, and German firms opened new plants on the premises. Today, Leuna is home to completely new plants that have nothing to do with the old technologies and autarky projects. It is a success story of structural changes in chemical production.

The story is much the same at other former GDR chemical sites. In Piesteritz, the majority of the old nitrogen plants were demolished and new facilities were constructed in 1997. The plant has become one of Europe's major producers of ammonia. The Dow Chemical Company took over the Schkopau and Böhlen sites in the spring of 1995 and integrated them, along with parts of the Leuna complex, within its global operations. One of the first tasks after the plans were privatized was to overcome the historically rooted disadvantages of the site. A raw materials pipeline was constructed to link Böhlen with Rostock, and the raw material basis of the plants' operations was completely transformed. These plants, which have been successful, are completely new: all they share with their predecessors is location.

The copper-mining operations at Mansfeld did not survive German unification. The Mansfeld Combine was liquidated, and mining was terminated as early as 1990. As the twentieth anniversary of unification approached, there were plans to start copper production at Spremberg. The future of copper mining in Eastern Germany remains dependent, however, on price trends for raw materials and developments in mining technology.

The steel industry sites handled the transformation process well. EKO Stahl AG was sold to the Belgian firm Cockerill–Sambre in 1993. Following

---

[44] See Rainer Karlsch and Raymond Stokes, *Die Chemie muss stimmen. Bilanz des Wandels 1990–2000* (Leipzig, 2000).

approval by the European Commission, the steelworks was modernized using public funds. EKO, with more than three thousand employees, remains the largest employer in the region. Other once-large steel enterprises in Brandenburg, Hennigsdorf, and Riesa were sold to Italian firms. The new owners closed most of the older facilities and modernized the others.

As for the energy production sites like the antiquated Schwarze Pumpe Combine, production on the basis of expensive domestic raw materials, with the exception of brown coal, was no longer possible after 1990. The successors of the Schwarze Pumpe Combine commissioned a modern brown coal power plant in 1997.[45] The production of gas from coal ended in 1995 after the plants were converted, comparatively quickly, from gas to natural gas. Domestic natural gas production at Salzwedel was continued, though output declined rapidly. Production on a limited scale continues, as does exploration.

The port of Rostock harbor was able to grow only in the context of Germany's division. After unification, the port lost its role in the transshipment of goods but was able to survive as a ferry port for service to Scandinavia, Poland, Russia, and the Baltic States.

The microelectronics industry, the last of the GDR's autarky projects, has been one of Eastern Germany's greatest successes since unification. Although the GDR's uncompetitive state holding companies were quickly liquidated, the sector's well-educated workforce provided the basis for a new start. Aided by massive governmental subsidies, several large electronics firms opened plants in Saxoy. By jobs, sales, and exports, microelectronics ranks as the second-largest industry in Saxony.

---

[45] See Jörg Roesler and Dagmar Semmelmann, *Vom Kombinat zur Aktiengesellschaft. Ostdeutsche Energiewirtschaft im Umbruch in den 1980er und 1990er Jahren* (Bonn, 2005).

5

Innovation and Ideology

Werner Hartmann and the Failure of the East German Electronics Industry

DOLORES L. AUGUSTINE

In March 1961, the leadership of the German Democratic Republic (GDR) put an industrial physicist, Werner Hartmann, in charge of the development of integrated circuits in East Germany. A U.S. company, Fairchild Semiconductor, had only recently brought the first commercially produced integrated circuits on the market in the United States. Hartmann, a student of Nobel Prize winner Gustav Hertz and semiconductor pioneer Walter Schottky, had the scientific background, international reputation, contacts, and managerial talent to successfully see through the founding and consolidation of the East German microelectronics industry. But despite very hopeful beginnings, the institute headed by Hartmann was never given the sort of state support that it would have needed to truly thrive. He fought hard for his institute, which succeeded in developing integrated circuits and building equipment for microelectronics production. Hartmann, however, ran afoul of the authorities, was persecuted by the secret police, fired, shamed, broken, and driven to despair. Microelectronics were neglected for years in the GDR. When the Socialist Unity Party (Sozialistische Einheitspartei Deutschlands, or SED) finally rediscovered the importance of microelectronics, it was too late. Only very expensive copying of Western technologies was possible, and the GDR was condemned to perpetually straggle years behind world developments in the field.

What could the GDR have achieved if it had put a major effort into microelectronics in the early 1960s? We will never know with certainty what the potential of East Germany's high-tech sector was. However, an exploration of Hartmann's story can open up new perspectives on East German history. It demonstrates that in its handling of microelectronics development, the SED committed fundamental errors that arose as a consequence of tightening secret police control over industry as well as of a lack of commitment to microelectronics on the part of Erich Honecker, GDR

95

leader from 1971 to 1989. The functioning of vital information networks was partially disrupted in the 1960s (under Walter Ulbricht, GDR leader from 1949 to 1971), but widespread paralysis set in only in the Honecker era. This essay will explore this profound shift in the relationship between the SED and the subordinated technical elite, dominated up through the 1960s by industrial administrators whose loyalties were primarily professional. What this historical approach to the subject has to offer is a greater appreciation of the importance of contingency in the economic history of the GDR.[1]

After a discussion of the high-tech sector in the East German economy, this essay will outline Hartmann's biography and then turn to the evolution of his ideas about how to innovate in the communist system, his application of these ideas to his building of the Arbeitsstelle für Molekularelektronik (Facility for Molecular Electronics, AME) in Dresden, the problems he encountered, and his crisis and demise. A brief comparison with the situation at Carl Zeiss Jena will be used to buttress my argument.

THE HIGH-TECH SECTOR IN THE EAST GERMAN ECONOMY

Attempts to explain the decline and fall of the East German economy often rely on the idea that the socialist system was doomed from the start. Certainly there was much about the state socialist economy that made it highly inefficient. The high-tech sector was greatly hampered by a planning system that generally expressed output in quantitative terms, thus providing no incentives to make technological improvements, or in terms of weight, thus encouraging the use of technologies that were literally heavy. Attempts were made to encourage technological advances, particularly in the self-proclaimed era of "scientific-technological progress" in the 1960s. However, layers of bureaucracy and the lack of effective incentives conspired to undermine research and development (R&D). For example, it took far longer for new or improved products and methods to make it onto the assembly line in the GDR than in the West. The GDR was also politically hamstrung by the fallout from the 1953 uprising: the SED feared that placing too great demands on the workers could lead to insurrection.[2] This consideration made the SED very reluctant to move workers from less efficient to

---

[1] On the role of historical contingency in the economic history and history of technology of the GDR, see Raymond Stokes, *Constructing Socialism: Technology and Change in East Germany, 1945–1990* (Baltimore, MD, 2000).

[2] See Jeffrey Kopstein, *The Politics of Economic Decline in East Germany, 1945–1989* (Chapel Hill, NC, 1997).

more efficient factories or sectors.[3] The close relationship with the Soviet Union was also on the whole detrimental to technological development. Rainer Karlsch has argued that the Soviet removal of German factories and technical personnel after World War II, harmful though it was to the economy of the Soviet occupation zone, had less of a negative impact than the distortions caused by the redirecting of East German trade to the technologically backward Eastern bloc.[4] Moreover, the Soviet Union discouraged East German progress in key high-tech areas, both because of deep-seated distrust of Germans, even if they were Communists, and because of a sense of economic rivalry with the GDR.[5] Lastly, the lack of cooperation among Warsaw Pact nations forced a kind of autarky on the GDR, which was too small a country to develop many large-scale technology projects efficiently or economically on its own.[6]

Despite these disadvantages, many of them attributable to the state socialist system, the GDR had a high-tech sector that in some phases performed surprisingly well. In the early decades, the GDR built jets, atomic reactors (with some Soviet assistance), lasers, and machinery good enough to be exported to the West. Most scholars would agree that dictatorships from Nazi Germany to Stalin's Soviet Union to later dictatorships such as North Korea have demonstrated considerable technological and scientific prowess, though the significance of their achievements remains controversial.[7] Why did the GDR emphasize high-tech industry? East Germany drew on German traditions of science-based engineering and professionalization among technical specialists as well as on cutting-edge Nazi-era research programs that were military in nature but highly relevant to civilian uses as well. Stalin validated this Nazi-era research establishment by forcing its most prominent representatives to migrate to the Soviet Union to work on the Soviet atomic bomb program and other research programs, conferring

---

[3] See Olaf Klenke, *Ist die DDR an der Globalisierung gescheitert?* (Frankfurt, 2001), 106–7.

[4] See Rainer Karlsch, *Allein bezahlt? Die Reparationsleistungen der SBZ/DDR 1945–1953* (Berlin, 1993).

[5] On the first point, see Jörg Roesler, "Industrieinnovation und Industriespionage in der DDR: Der Staatssicherheitsdienst in den Innovationsgeschichte der DDR," *Deutschland Archiv* 27 (1994): 1032; Jörg Roesler, "Wirtschaftspolitik der DDR – Autarkie versus internationale Arbeitsteilung," *Dresdner Beiträge zur Geschichte der Technikwissenschaften* 25 (1998): 2–14.

[6] On the problems impeding R&D and the technology sector in the GDR, see my book, *Red Prometheus: Engineering and Dictatorship in East Germany, 1945–1990* (Cambridge, MA, 2007), esp. 85–90.

[7] Important contributions to the very extensive literature include Loren Graham, *Science in Russia and the Soviet Union* (Cambridge, 1993); Alexei Kojevnikov, *Stalin's Great Science: The Times and Adventures of Soviet Physicists* (London, 2004); Mark Walker, *Nazi Science* (Cambridge, 1994); and Mitchell Ash and Alfons Söllner, *Forced Migration and Scientific Change: Emigré German-Speaking Scientists after 1933* (Cambridge, 1996). See also the studies on the Kaiser Wilhelm Institute during the Nazi era published by the Max Planck Institute, Berlin: http://www.mpiwg-berlin.mpg.de/KWG/publications.htm (accessed April 26, 2013).

honors and privileges on them and allowing them to return to positions of power and prestige in the GDR. The GDR's scientific and technical "stars" published and attended conferences in the West and maintained close ties with former colleagues who had moved to West Germany after the war or after Soviet captivity. In doing so, they brought about a much-needed transfer of technology from the West.[8]

In the GDR's early years, the SED leadership saw the activities of this technical elite as highly beneficial to the country. These scientists and engineers were able to win over the communist leadership to a vision of the GDR as a high-tech nation because such a conception was very much in accord with Marxist-Leninist-Stalinist notions of the central role of technology in societal progress. East German leader Walter Ulbricht was a great believer in the transformative power of technology. He was on close personal terms with many engineers and scientists, who brought technological developments in the West to his attention. With the Khrushchev-era thaw and the launching of Sputnik (1957), technocratic ideas came to the fore in the Soviet Union and the GDR. Popular enthusiasm for technology was high in this period. The belief in high tech as a kind of peacetime *Wunderwaffe* (miracle weapon) was to have a long-lasting impact on the GDR. Even Honecker, who initially accorded the expansion of the social state a higher priority than technology, soon returned to his predecessor's strategy of promoting high-tech industry. In the final crisis of the GDR, he treated microelectronics as a kind of silver bullet that would somehow dramatically transform hopelessly outdated infrastructure and innovative capabilities choked by bureaucracy and oppression. For the GDR, the high-tech strategy pursued over the entire course of its history had both advantages and disadvantages, the worst being that it took resources away from consumer goods production and many other sectors of East German industry, and eventually bankrupted the state. Nonetheless, high-tech industries could potentially have become the locomotive for growth in the GDR.[9] How much was achieved? Are the failures of high-tech industry in the GDR to be understood as the inevitable consequences of a doomed system, or were there missed opportunities?

The 1960s were a crucial era of transition in the GDR. However, the nature of this transition is unclear. Many historians see it as a period in which the SED began to loosen the reins of power, responding to popular needs and desires to a greater extent, and, in a sense, learning to trust

---

[8] See Augustine, *Red Prometheus*, 19, 162.
[9] Ibid., 350.

society in new ways. Peter Christian Ludz postulated that the reforms of the 1960s – the "New Economic System of Planning and Management of the Economy" (*Neues Ökonomisches System der Plannung und Leitung der Volkswirtschaft*) and the "Economic System of Socialism" (*Ökonomisches System des Sozialismus*) – brought about a transition from totalitarianism to a system of "consultative authoritarianism," opening the way for "welfare totalitarianism."[10] For economic historians and historians of technology, the reform era is generally thought of as an attempt at devolution of decision-making powers to the base (i.e., consumers and individual enterprises) – an attempt that did not go far enough. Opinions vary as to whether the GDR system had the capacity to change enough to stop the economic and technological slide that was well under way by the 1960s. In particular, scholars disagree as to whether or not the SED had the will to go through with reforms that would have seriously weakened its position. André Steiner believes that it did not.[11] With regard to industrial research, the entire narrative of failed decentralization appears questionable.

WERNER HARTMANN AS SCIENTIST AND BUSINESSMAN IN EAST GERMAN INDUSTRY

The career of Werner Hartmann illustrates the deleterious effects of SED attempts to exert greater control over high-tech research.[12] Hartmann makes a good case study because, first, such rich material is available from different sources: his voluminous, handwritten, unpublished memoirs; his letters and reports housed in the enterprise archive in the Saxon State Archives in Dresden; state and party documents at the Bundesarchiv in Berlin; secret police records; and the personal testimonies of his colleagues and wife. This – at times conflicting – primary source material allows a level of critical evaluation often not possible for the GDR. Second, Hartmann is interesting because his career spanned the Weimar, Nazi, and Communist eras. His career illustrates the very dramatic pitfalls of working as a noncommunist for the SED. But most importantly of all for our purposes here, his professional life allows an analysis of crucial cultural divides and cultural shifts over time

---

[10] Peter Christian Ludz, *Parteieliten im Wandel* (Cologne, 1968), 35–7.

[11] See André Steiner, *Die DDR-Wirtschaftsreform der sechziger Jahre* (Berlin, 1999); Jörg Roesler, *Zwischen Plan und Markt: Die Wirtschaftsreform in der DDR zwischen 1963 und 1970* (Berlin, 1990); Kopstein, *The Politics of Economic Decline*, 41–72; Stokes, *Constructing Socialism*, 142–52.

[12] A fuller account of the development of the East German microelectronics industry and of Hartmann's career can be found in my book *Red Prometheus*. In this chapter, I refine that analysis, focusing on changing power relations in industry and making use of newly released documents from the Federal Commissioner for the Stasi records (*Bundesbeauftragter für die Stasi-Unterlagen*, or BStU).

in East German economic life. This shift in the culture of technological innovation in the 1960s eventually undermined the economic viability of the GDR economy.

Who was Hartmann? Born in 1912 in Berlin to a family of modest means, Hartmann studied under Gustav Hertz and Walter Schottky and completed a doctoral degree in physics, with a specialization in solid-state physics, in 1936. An important phase of his professional socialization took place during the Nazi era, when he was involved in industrial research, particularly work on early television. Not a Nazi, Hartmann retreated into what he saw as an apolitical (though nationalistic) stance. It was his belief that scientists who loyally served the Fatherland would be allowed the freedom to do their work. He had no qualms in working on research with military applications. He became disillusioned with the Nazis when it became clear that they had brought ruin upon Germany. In 1945, soon after the end of the war, he decided to accompany his former mentor, Gustav Hertz, to the Soviet Union. As one of many privileged but closely controlled German researchers, he found working on the Soviet atomic program at the institute in Agudseri on the whole quite satisfying. He took his criticism of those restrictions that impinged upon the Germans' scientific work to the top. In one memorable incident, he pounded on the desk of the deputy minister of the interior of the USSR. They drank together, and in the end Hartmann got what he wanted. Hartmann became convinced that "The Soviets give greater recognition to contradiction than to constant servility and fearful compliance – naturally without openly saying so." He took this understanding of the pact between the dictatorial state and the apolitical scientist home with him when he returned to East Germany in 1954. Like many German scientists and engineers who had gone to the Soviet Union, he did not believe in democracy and was happy to accept the privileges, honors, and positions offered by the SED.[13]

Hartmann believed that as long as he promoted the interests of the GDR through his work, he would enjoy much of the professional freedoms of his counterparts in the West. Throughout his career, he resisted joining the SED, though he knew when to follow orders. He headed Vakutronik, an industrial institute that manufactured equipment for the atomic industry, from 1955 to 1961. His most important role was as founder and head (from 1961 to 1974) of the AME.[14] Having maintained ties with colleagues from

---

[13] Technische Sammlung Dresden (hereafter referred to as TSD), Nachlaß Hartmann, vol. F; quotation on p. 56.

[14] Arbeitsstelle für Molekularelektronic (Facility for Molecular Electronics). The institute's acronym was changed to AMD in the late 1960s, but for simplicity's sake the acronym AME will be used in this essay.

the pre-1945 era, Hartmann had many contacts and even close friends in West Germany and the United States. A professor at the Technical University of Dresden, he made a name for himself in the international scientific and technical community through his numerous publications and conference appearances. He was well aware of the invention of the integrated circuit in the United States in 1959. His efforts to improve the semiconductor/electronics industry led to the founding of the AME as an industrial research institute for microelectronics in 1961.[15]

Hartmann recognized the significance of solid-state electronics more clearly than did others. The Academy of Sciences and Research Council failed here, as did key figures in the politico-scientific elite such as Robert Rompe, a member of the Central Committee and a high official of the Academy of Sciences. They thought that microelectronics was an exotic, expensive novelty that could only realistically be used in the space program. The received wisdom in the GDR was that some sort of hybrid technology would be more affordable and a better choice for the GDR. This involved combining the old transistor technology with some degree of integration, for example spraying passive elements onto glass or ceramic wafers and then attaching transistors individually, as in micromodule technology. A more sophisticated approach was a thin-film technique that involved spraying *all* electronic components onto ceramic wafers. Unfortunately, this technique didn't work, and a good deal of time and effort was wasted pursuing it. Hartmann oversaw experiments in thin-film technique, but knew from his observations of what was going on in the world that solid-state electronics was a much better bet. He argued in numerous articles and speeches that the costs would come down over time. These arguments had little impact in top SED circles. AME was severely underfunded and neglected by officialdom, making its expansion very difficult. Rompe prevented AME from becoming part of the Academy of Sciences. According to Hartmann, the SED elite did not become convinced of the importance of microelectronics until the mid-1970s, when West Germany began high-profile programs in the area.[16]

Nonetheless, AME was able to achieve a fair amount. AME was able to create clean rooms with the necessary specifications, and it produced a good deal of equipment for the production of microelectronics. By 1968,

---

[15] TSD, Nachlaß Hartmann, vol. H. BStU MfS AP444/87 (file Werner Hartmann), 202–4 ("Bereitstellung von Bauelementen für die Elektronik," dated December 14, 1960).

[16] See Bernd Wenzel, "Ein Beitrag zur Geschichte der Mikroelektronik unterbesonderer Berücksichtigung der Entwicklung der Halbleiter- und Mikroelektronik in der DDR," (Diss. B, Technical University of Dresden, 1989). SAPMO/BArch DY 30/IV A 2/6.07, Nr. 171, transcript of meeting on February 1, 1965 at State Secretariat for Research and Technology. Landesarchiv Berlin, Rep. 404, Nr. 525, Darlegung zur Perspektivplankonzeption der VVB RFT Bauelemente und Vakuumtechnik, dated April 4, 1966.

AME had successfully copied a Texas Instruments integrated circuit, and it succeeded in reproducing an integrated circuit for pocket calculators that used bipolar technology in 1972–4. AME also produced custom-made integrated circuits for Robotron, the computer maker.[17]

AME would not have become such a successful research installation had it not been for Hartmann's abilities as manager, scientist, engineer, and – if the term may be used here – businessman. Hartmann's professional ethos, values, and behavior were precommunist in origin. As a scientist, he strove to maintain his international reputation and connections, and he saw Western science as the worldwide trendsetter. He was critical both of the GDR scientific establishment, which neglected the production process, and of East German industry, which did not make consistent use of scientific methods. For example, he wrote of the semiconductor industry:

Everywhere I went I encountered the good will of technical people. But what was almost completely lacking was scientifically grounded work, technological discipline and qualified personnel. . . . People continued to use the "formula of the master craftsman," who had been working this way since before the war.

The result, he contended, was that time and resources were wasted on "one-day wonders."[18]

Hartmann had a degree of authority at AME that was unusual for the GDR. His understanding of his role there was much influenced by older, presocialist models, particularly those of research institute director and enterprise director. He essentially handpicked all his employees, bypassing a complicit cadre office (which in most enterprises assured SED control over hirings). He also preferred to promote AME employees rather than recruit outsiders to fill top positions at AME. Hartmann believed that as a result, he was able to inculcate his employees with a stringent work ethic. A very communicative person, he also emphasized the importance of communication and cooperation. He was a tough taskmaster but also a charismatic leader who motivated his underlings to a high level of achievement, despite the difficult conditions of the early years. He was effective in winning his employees' loyalty to the institute. He believed that his position of authority was necessitated by the complexity of scientific procedures and the inexperience of most of the research staff at AME as well as by the need for a spokesman on behalf of the institute. By contrast, he promoted socialist ideology only in a pro forma way. SED members were not favored when it came to promotions. He was a traditional German patriarch in many ways.

---

[17] TSD, Nachlaß Hartmann, vol. H, 142, 148, 197–8.
[18] Ibid., vol. G, 96; quotation on p. 95.

He had distinctly unenlightened attitudes toward women. He thought that it was a waste of resources to recruit young women into engineering studies because he thought them unlikely to succeed. His politeness toward women revealed very conventional attitudes.[19]

As a businessman he developed considerable abilities in negotiating the system and "organizing" scarce resources. For example, he paid bribes to secure construction crews needed for work on AME, the physical building of which took years.[20]

None of this necessarily put Hartmann at odds with the SED system. In the early years, he certainly believed that socialism was the superior system, better suited to the development of technologies, such as microelectronics, that required a good deal of expensive exploratory research to get off the ground. He also hoped that it would be possible to foster collaboration and exchange of research results between enterprises within a sort of organization only possible under socialism. The later *Kombinate* (socialist combines) were not as effective in this task as he had hoped. Hartmann played by the rules as far as cooperation with SED organizations and the secret police were concerned.[21]

HARTMANN'S QUEST FOR TECHNOLOGY

Over the years, Hartmann became increasingly frustrated with what he saw as the massive inefficiency of the economic bureaucracy. We know of these frustrations in some detail because of the almost unbelievable number of letters and memoranda that he wrote to people in positions of power. In the early years, he protested the neglect of AME, particularly its lack of resources, in writing and in meetings. As a result, he incurred the wrath of top economic official Günther Mittag. He also won the support of Erich Apel, whose suicide in 1965 robbed AME of its most powerful ally.[22]

By the mid-1960s, Hartmann's (and AME's) most pressing problem was the lack of access to information on how to produce microelectronics. Microelectronics research was very costly and very vulnerable to technical glitches. In the United States, microelectronics research and development was fueled by personal exchange of information, particularly by employees who changed jobs, moving from one company to another. Hartmann

---

[19] Ibid., vol. H. Hartmann's account confirmed in: SächsHStA Bestand Zentrum für Mikroelektronik, 1903/1, report dated September 23, 1964.

[20] TSD, Nachlaß Hartmann, vol. H, 129.

[21] Author's interview with Hans Becker, July 2000; TSD, Nachlaß Hartmann, vol. H, 173.

[22] TSD, Nachlaß Hartmann, vol. H, 36, 61–3; SächsHStA Bestand Zentrum für Mikroelektronik, 2158, memorandum L-Nr. 108/62, dated September 14, 1962.

had often relied on personal contacts to glean vital insights into technical processes. Around 1965 he hit a wall. The Berlin Wall played a role in his difficulties, but the story is more complicated than that. Some scientists were allowed to travel to the West for conferences and the like even after the building of the Berlin Wall.[23]

Trips to the West provided Hartmann and his employees with much useful information on microelectronics production. They learned a good deal about clean rooms on a trip to West Germany in 1964 as well as from Soviet sources. Hartmann hoped to visit Fairchild, Texas Instruments, and Motorola to learn more about how to conduct experimental production runs of integrated circuits during a proposed trip to the United States in 1965. That trip and a trip to Japan were called off at the last minute, however. Stasi records seem to indicate that Hartmann's 1964 trip was not approved by GDR officials because U.S. officials refused to provide visas to two men who were presumably Stasi agents and who were supposed to accompany Hartmann to the United States. But the problem was bigger than this. For a few years, no delegations from the microelectronics or semiconductor industries were allowed to go to the United States.[24]

The vise was beginning to tighten around Hartmann and microelectronics research in general, the result of growing concerns about security. There are two possible explanations for increased security. One is that restrictions imposed by the Western powers' Coordinating Committee for Multilateral Export Controls (COCOM) on microelectronics triggered East German countermeasures. East Germany could not produce all its own microelectronic components and could not count on a steady supply from Eastern Europe. Its dependence on Western suppliers made the GDR vulnerable to sudden changes in COCOM embargo lists. The fear in SED circles was that foreign intelligence agencies might identify such vulnerabilities, which could then be exploited by the West. This led to Stasi security crackdowns in high-tech areas of industry, aimed at concealing these weaknesses; this practice has certainly been documented for the 1980s.[25]

But this is not all that was going on. The Stasi's security craze of the 1960s could be interpreted as largely of its own making. It was in the 1960s that the SED, following the Soviet example but also reacting to R&D setbacks, decided that it was not worthwhile conducting independent R&D in many

---

[23] BStU MfS, Archive number 14254/69, vol. 6, 240–66 ("Analyse der operativen Ergebnisse zum Vorgang 'Laser' 1966," dated April 12, 1967).

[24] TSD, Nachlaß Hartmann, vol. H, 84–6.

[25] BStU Zentralarchiv MfS-HA XVIII, Nr. 9110, 8 ("Konzeption zur Beratung beim Stellvertreter Operativ der BV Gera, Gen. Oberst Weigelt, am 4.3.1982, 10.00 Uhr").

high-tech areas. Instead, GDR industry was ordered to start trying to copy Western technologies. GDR industry had always tried to imitate Western technologies but not to copy them exactly. One day in June 1967, the minister for electrical engineering and electronics showed up at Hartmann's institute with a briefcase filled with integrated circuits produced by Texas Instruments and ordered AME to produce copies. This strategy was to cause major problems later because the patent infringement this involved was obvious to buyers of East German machinery and equipment in the West. Its immediate impact was worse, however. In attempting to protect the guilty secrets of East German industry, the SED and the Stasi cracked down not only on East-West contacts that might bring GDR patent violations to light but also on any and all contacts between enterprises and even within enterprises that might reveal what was going on. The basic exchange of information, the passing along of know-how, and practical applications of technology went from being the glue that held together the GDR's R&D infrastructure to being industrial secrets shared only on a need-to-know basis.[26]

Hartmann describes in great detail the very negative impact of these new security regulations on the semiconductor and microelectronic industries. Communication between enterprises and even within AME was blocked. Only top management was allowed to see pilfered manuals and such. AME employees were ordered to maintain silence at meetings of technological centers that were supposed to foster exchange of technological information between enterprises. Cooperation with other East German semiconductor manufacturers and with the Technical University of Dresden had to be broken off. Contact became sporadic between Hartmann's institute and the Halbleiterwerk Frankfurt/Oder (HWF), the factory where AME innovations were mass-produced. The result of enterprise autarky was that each R&D unit had to start from scratch – in a field in which this was not possible. Hartmann described high-tech equipment produced at HWF without AME's help as "catastrophically bad – improvised in a primitive way." Hartmann lamented, "No other institution in the world had to develop microelectronics in such isolation as AME." Not allowed to travel west after 1964, Hartmann decided to become "SU-verpflichtet," that is, to gain a security clearance that allowed him to freely communicate with Soviet institutions. Though he had a fine command of the Russian language and excellent contacts from his days in the Soviet Union, he found that Soviet institutions and ministers, though polite, never gave him or his institute the kind of information they needed. Soviet microelectronics researchers sent to AME

---

[26] TSD, Nachlaß Hartmann, vol. H.

turned out to know far less than AME. AME was not given access to Soviet conferences. But due to his new security clearance, Hartmann was not allowed to travel to the West. Hartmann protested vociferously but to no avail. AME was trapped in a vicious circle. Denied access to the latest technological information, AME came to rely more and more on Stasi-procured Western technologies. But this meant that AME would always be years behind the West. Stasi involvement in the R&D process tremendously increased security paranoia, which cut AME off even more from sources (even internal sources) of information on technological problems.[27]

HARTMANN'S PERSECUTION

It was not until after Honecker took over power that Stasi investigations of Hartmann (which had been going on for years) were stepped up, leading to his ouster in 1974. Hartmann's file grew to fill forty-nine oversized loose-leaf notebooks. He was accused of sabotage and espionage for the other side. The evidence was very flimsy, but that did not stop the Stasi. Was the investigation simply the result of neo-Stalinist paranoia? I do not believe so. A whole range of factors played a role. The first is his courage to speak up when GDR officials neglected or mishandled problems relating to industrial R&D. His honesty won him enemies in high places. Second, once the SED realized the importance of microelectronics – around 1974 – the hunt for scapegoats was on. And, third, who better to blame than someone who was not in the SED and was therefore considered to be politically unreliable? His stubborn refusal to join the party was often commented on by high officials. Moreover, Hartmann had secretly been put on a list of disloyal persons by the Soviets in 1954, when he left the Soviet Union. Fourth, his cosmopolitanism and praise for the West reinforced the assessment of him as "bourgeois" and anticommunist. He was accused of employing "managerial methods of capitalist companies," favoring noncommunists in the hiring and promotion process, and being a tyrannical boss who "suppressed all criticism."[28] He also allegedly spent too much time writing articles for scientific and technical journals.[29]

Yet another factor was at work, and it may have been the decisive one. Honecker was part of a faction that had fought Ulbricht's liberalization attempts from 1963 to 1971 tooth and nail. They were much disturbed by

---

[27] Ibid.; quotations on pp. 140 and 86.
[28] BStU MfS Zentralarchiv MfS-HAXVIII, Nr. 9910, 12 ("Sachstandsbericht" dated May 27, 1974, 12).
[29] BStU MfS AP 444/87, 7 ("Stellungnahme," dated July 5, 1975, 7).

what they saw as the destabilizing impact of these reforms. A subtle critique of Ulbricht-era policies and predilections runs through Hartmann's Stasi file. The thesis here seems to be that in that era, the Communist leadership had allowed the "old intelligentsia," and in particular the "specialists" who had been deported to the Soviet Union, to pull the wool over their eyes. Stasi reports assert that Hartmann was aided and abetted by Ulbricht-era officials and policies. He allegedly used the creation of "scientific industrial enterprises" (*Wissenschaftliche-Industrie-Betriebe*) to undermine planning. Hartmann's negotiations with a Western firm are called "legalized treason" in another document.[30] A more direct attack is aimed at Rompe, a high communist official and central figure in the GDR's research establishment under Ulbricht:

> The presentation of a special bonus to Professor Hartmann "for the establishment and construction of AMD" is completely incomprehensible in light of delays of several years and the continued dysfunctionality of AMD at that point. Ultimately it can only be explained by the "helping hand of the Research Council" and by Professor Rompe's preventing of oversight of work at AMD; otherwise, the shortcomings of Professor Hartmann's work would have been discovered by late 1964 at the latest![31]

The hardliners of the Honecker era considered even an SED stalwart and secret police collaborator like Rompe too independent. His brand of bridge building between the SED and the research establishment was being eclipsed by a more primitive form of SED and secret police control.

It is my contention that historical contingency played a crucial role in the failure of the East German microelectronics program. Two shifts in policy in particular are to blame. The first is the intensification of security measures in connection with stepped-up secret police procurement of Western prototypes that were to be copied as exactly as possible in the GDR using similarly acquired Western technical manuals and other forms of documentation. In a different but related subfield – computers – the Soviet Union made the decision to abandon relatively autonomous research in the 1960s and instead to rely on reverse engineering of Western prototypes procured by Soviet intelligence. The East German computer industry followed suit.[32] In the case of microelectronics, Hartmann's memoirs seem to indicate that in microelectronics, the switch to what he called "slavish

---

[30] BStU MfS AP444/87, 163 ("Betr.: Durcharbeitung des übergebenen Materials," dated September 25, 1974, 21).

[31] Ibid., 160 (p. 18 of document). AMD was a later acronym for AME (see n. 14).

[32] See A. Nitussov and B. N. Malinovskiy, "Economic Changes in the Sixties and the Internationalisation of the Soviet Computing," in *Computing in Russia*, ed. Georg Trogemann, Alexander Y. Nitussov and Wolfgang Ernst (Braunschweig, 2001), 163–7.

imitation" took place, both in the GDR and the Soviet Union, in 1967.[33] Previously, AME had practiced a form of imitation that was widely practiced in smaller countries, even in the West. These incremental innovations built upon the radical or fundamental innovations pioneered in the United States or other countries with a large innovative infrastructure. Given that conformity with international law was not high on the list of priorities of the GDR economy, it is quite possible that even under this older system, some products might not have adhered to international patent law. But they were generated by a system of free experimentation and consideration of alternate technological solutions. Hartmann sought access to Western technologies through legitimate means, particularly professional contacts. He presents compelling arguments in favor of this approach, as opposed to the later system of exactly replicating Western devices illegally obtained by the secret police. Hartmann was quite critical of a strategy of reliance on espionage to procure electronic components that were then copied in Eastern bloc countries. In a memorandum of April 10, 1964, he asserted that such "artificial and rushed development" did not lead to a mastery of new technologies. They condemned the GDR to the role of a laggard that was always years behind other industrial nations. Hartmann asserted that scientific and technical "provincialism" could be avoided through international cooperation.[34] But far worse was the Stasi's reaction, namely a policy of choking off legitimate international and even internal communications that were the life blood of technical research. Honecker's takeover ushered in a second phase, in which an even greater SED and Stasi penetration and redirecting of R&D took place. As an independent-minded professional and scientist, Hartmann was no longer acceptable to the regime.

NEW DYNAMICS AT CARL ZEISS JENA

My archival research and the secondary literature on Carl Zeiss Jena indicate that something similar to what happened in microelectronics research was going on elsewhere as well. At Zeiss, the more independent-minded general director Hugo Schrade (who was the subject of an elaborate Stasi investigation) was replaced by an SED team player, Ernst Gallerach. Scholars such as Reinhard Buthmann and Axel Salheiser have shown that political loyalty became key to careers at Zeiss and more generally in high-tech industry.[35]

---

[33] TSD, Nachlaß Hartmann, vol. H, 121.
[34] SAPMO/Barch DY 30/IV A 2/6.07 171, memorandum L 15/64, dated April 10, 1964.
[35] See Reinhard Buthmann, *Kadersicherung im Kombinat VEB Carl Zeiss Jena* (Berlin, 1997); Axel Salheiser, "'Du und deine Elite!' – Leitungskader im Elektroniksektor der DDR-Industrie zwischen

Zeiss was saturated with Stasi informants. The longtime research director, Paul Görlich, who played a key role in the introduction of lasers into the GDR, was subjected to a Stasi investigation. He seems to have become aware of it and felt intimidated. The only reason that he was not shamed, blamed, and driven mad like Hartmann is that he was lucky enough to be a few years older. He was allowed to retire in peace in 1971, though there had been talk of trying to force him out. What happened once the SED gained fuller control over Zeiss? Militarization; Stasification – in the sense of production of "security" products of various kinds; Sovietization – in the sense of production for the Soviet Union; and the defunding and decline of traditional, export-oriented Zeiss products.[36]

After Hartmann left, AME went into a period of decline, and eventually (in 1986), Zeiss was made the center of microelectronics research and production in the GDR. It was headed by a man, Klaus Mütze, who was not only an SED loyalist but also a Stasi collaborator, as were many managers at Zeiss by this time.[37] Under a baroque security system, Zeiss R&D personnel were forced into purely derivative, unoriginal copying of Western microelectronics, a role that Hartmann had foreseen would condemn the GDR to the role of perpetual straggler. The terrible expenses involved in microelectronic autarky eventually helped bankrupt the GDR.

CONCLUSION

A shift in power relations took place from the mid-1960s to the early 1970s, as the practices of a centrally directed but professionally controlled system of industrial high-tech research were disrupted by SED and Stasi penetrations. The Stasi saw the strangling of communications as a necessary corollary to increased reliance on espionage, espionage necessitated precisely by the cutting off of other forms of technological transfer. This vicious circle was the result of excessive Stasi involvement in industry. In other Eastern bloc countries, microelectronics experts were more frequently allowed to go abroad to hone their expertise and gather information on cutting-edge techniques.[38] However, it was not until Honecker's takeover that important

fachlicher Qualifikation und politischer Loyalität," *Historical Social Research/HistorischeSozialforschung*, Special Issue: *Funktionseliten der DDR* 28, nos. 1–2 (2003): 187–215.

[36] Carl Zeiss Archive (Jena) NG 148, "Beschlußfassung über die Konzeption zur weiteren Konzentration der Forschungs- und Entwicklungskapazitäten"; Carl Zeiss Archive, VA 826, "Aktennotiz," dated November 10, 1970. See Wolfgang Mühlfriedel and Edith Hellmuth, *Carl Zeiss in Jena 1945–1990* (Cologne, 2004). See also my analysis in *Red Prometheus*, 157–68.

[37] BStU MfS ASt. Gera XV/1890/77 "Michael," pt. I, vol. 2, 186 ("Verpflichtung," dated January 17, 1977).

[38] TSD, Nachlaß Hartmann, vol. H, 87.

vestiges of professional autonomy in industrial research were destroyed. Honecker and his SED supporters put other policy initiatives (notably the expansion of the social state) first. They failed to understand the inability of the Stasi and the SED to play the central role in the innovative process. And they put control before economic and technological innovativeness. They did not cast aside Hartmann because he was implicated in the Nazi past – Rompe and many, many people in important positions in the Ulbricht period were former Nazis – but because he stood in the way of greater SED control. But by installing a new, subservient elite and a comprehensive system of control, the SED greatly weakened the old innovative system without creating a viable new one. Paradoxically, though, the stabilization of this "fortress economy" seems to have also given them enough of a feeling of security that they embarked on the building of a more responsive social state and on a gradual reduction of East-West tensions through détente policies.

6

East German Workers and the "Dark Side" of Eigensinn

Divisive Shop-Floor Practices and the Failed Revolution of June 17, 1953

ANDREW I. PORT

In the fall of 2007, Alf Lüdtke's friends and colleagues held a symposium in his honor at the University of Michigan in Ann Arbor.[1] What was most striking, after a weekend of intense discussion about his impressive oeuvre and influence, was the lack of any real consensus about the exact meaning of *Eigensinn*, the celebrated concept associated most closely with his name. It is a term that has launched a thousand dissertations, as David Blackbourn once memorably quipped about E. P. Thompson's famous phrase "the enormous condescension of posterity."[2] But it is also one that remains remarkably elusive, which may very well have been the intention of Lüdtke, who emphasizes its "ambiguity" (*Vieldeutigkeit*).[3] *Eigensinn* has nevertheless – or perhaps for that very reason – become one of the most popular concepts used to describe a wide range of behavior in East Germany.[4] And though originally employed by Lüdtke primarily with respect to industrial workers, it has now been applied to almost all social groups in the German Democratic Republic (GDR) – and even to entire regions.[5]

This inflationary use of the term has not led to greater conceptual clarity. Most generally, *Eigensinn* refers to willful conduct – "rebelliousness" (*Widerborstigkeit*), "troublemaking behavior" (*quertreibendes Verhalten*) – that allows

[1] See the conference report by Kathleen Canning, "Practices and Power in the Everyday Life of the Twentieth Century: A Symposium in Honor of Alf Lüdtke," H–Soz–u–Kult, 28.05.2008, http://hsozkult.geschichte.hu–berlin.de/tagungsberichte/id=2112 (accessed April 26, 2013).
[2] David Blackbourn, *A Sense of Place: New Directions in German History* (London, 1999).
[3] Alf Lüdtke, "Geschichte und Eigensinn," in *Alltagskultur, Subjektivität und Geschichte. Zur Theorie und Praxis von Alltagsgeschichte*, ed. Berliner Geschichtswerkstatt (Munster, 1994), 19.
[4] That is especially the case since the publication of Thomas Lindenberger, ed., *Herrschaft und Eigen-Sinn in der Diktatur. Studien zur Gesellschaftsgeschichte der DDR* (Cologne, 1999).
[5] See the perceptive discussion of this term in Christoph Vietzke, *Konfrontation und Kooperation. Funktionäre und Arbeiter in Großbetrieben der DDR vor und nach dem Mauerbau* (Essen, 2008), 26–9.

I am grateful to Sylvia Taschka, who coined the term *dark side* during a spirited private discussion that she and I had with Alf Lüdtke in Ann Arbor in December 2008.

individuals to demarcate a space of their own.[6] Regardless of its meaning, whenever an author doffs his or her cap to Lüdtke by dropping the word *en passant*, the reader has some vague and fuzzy feeling of what is meant. Or at least thinks that is the case. According to Lüdtke, it is an attempt to go beyond the black-and-white, either-or categories of obedience and opposition. Instead, and through no fault of Lüdtke's, it has become a blanket term used to designate almost any type of nonconformist behavior in the GDR – becoming, in a sense, what the term *Resistenz* once was for the Third Reich.[7] This essay is not another attempt to define this slippery concept, for there are already several useful descriptions of a term that seems to defy exact definition. Nor will it propose a new range of helpful scales and spectrums to emphasize and describe the gradations of oppositional behavior in the GDR, similar to the ones previously developed for the Nazi era. Instead, it will focus on an often-neglected aspect of *Eigensinn*: its "dark side."

The term *Eigensinn* has customarily been used in a circumscribed way when it comes to the GDR, namely to describe the behavior of East Germans vis-à-vis authority figures – more specifically, behavior that somehow went against the grain, that indirectly confronted authorities by resisting the demands and expectations of the regime and its leadership. But that is only one aspect of *Eigensinn*, which is more than just "Resistance-Lite." As Lüdtke has pointed out, it refers not only to the "distance" of individuals "vis-à-vis 'superiors' [*oben*] but also vis-à-vis peers [*Gleiche*]," for example, colleagues, neighbors, and friends.[8] This essay explores this other, less prominent aspect of *Eigensinn*. It is especially concerned with the deleterious effects that such behavior could have on the East German economy, largely as a result of the social cleavages it engendered – not only between workers and other social groups but also *among* workers themselves.

At the same time, this essay examines the paradoxical way in which such behavior had a *stabilizing* effect on the regime despite the economic havoc it wrought. To get at this last aspect in particular – at the "conflictual stability" that arguably lay at the root of the GDR's puzzling longevity – it looks in detail at social tensions on the East German shop floor as well as at the events surrounding June 17, 1953, the first mass uprising in the Soviet bloc, when hundreds of thousands of East Germans lay down their tools and took

---

[6] See Alf Lüdtke, *Eigen-Sinn. Fabrikalltag, Arbeitererfahrungen und Politik vom Kaiserreich bis in den Faschismus* (Hamburg, 1993), 10–12, 136–43.

[7] On the concept of *Resistenz*, see Martin Broszat, "Resistenz und Widerstand. Eine Zwischenbilanz des Forschungsprojektes," in *Bayern in der NS – Zeit. Herrschaft und Gesellschaft im Konflikt*, vol. 4, ed. Martin Broszat, Elke Fröhlich, and Anton Grossmann (Munich, 1981), 691–709.

[8] Lüdtke, *Eigen-Sinn*, 10.

to the streets in protest against a series of highly unpopular policies. The latter included an across-the-board hike in production quotas, the diversion of scarce resources to the military, forced agricultural collectivization, as well as a heightening of state-sponsored repression – all of which led to consumer shortages and high prices, which, in turn, prompted widespread anger and discontent as well as mass flight to the West.

The poor performance of the East German economy was clearly one of the most important factors fueling high levels of popular disaffection, both before and after the events of June 1953. Yet the exact reasons for the GDR's many economic shortcomings are less clear and have, as a result, become the subject of fierce debate. Whereas some scholars emphasize the unpropitious starting point after World War II, others blame the structural shortcomings of state socialism along with poor decision making by East German authorities later on. Was the economy doomed from the outset because of wartime destruction, Soviet dismantling, and the adverse effects of national division? Or did it ultimately fail instead because of bureaucratic ineptitude, the inefficiency of rigid centralized planning, and the absence of self-correcting market mechanisms?[9] This essay does not provide an answer to this important question. Instead, it looks at the extent to which the everyday behavior of "ordinary" East German workers served to reinforce and exacerbate whatever problems already plagued the economy – thus undermining its performance even further in what amounted to a vicious circle. Unlike the other contributions in this volume, it takes a social historiographical approach to get at this important, often-neglected reason for and aspect of the GDR's poor economic performance – which was, in the end, more than just the result of the many structural deficiencies associated with central planning and a command economy.

"CONFLICTUAL STABILITY" IN A DIVIDED SOCIETY

Throughout much of the GDR's history, officials waged an uphill battle against the tendency of worker wages to increase at a faster rate than productivity.[10] There were a number of reasons for this trend, many of

---

[9] For an overview of this debate, see Corey Ross, *The East German Dictatorship: Problems and Perspectives in the Interpretation of the GDR* (London, 2002), 69–96; André Steiner, *Von Plan zu Plan: Eine Wirtschaftsgeschichte der DDR* (Munich, 2004), 229–38.

[10] This section summarizes some of the main findings of Andrew I. Port, *Conflict and Stability in the German Democratic Republic* (New York, 2007), 164–94. For other studies of East German workers that deal with these specific issues and that arrive at broadly similar conclusions, see Peter Hübner, *Konsens, Konflikt und Kompromiß. Soziale Arbeiterinteressen und Sozialpolitik in der SBZ/DDR, 1945–1970* (Berlin, 1995); Jeffrey Kopstein, *The Politics of Economic Decline in East Germany, 1945–1989*

which resulted from the willingness of factory personnel and other low-level functionaries to adopt practices aimed at maintaining harmony on the shop floor. This included the liberal distribution of bonuses and premiums regardless of actual achievement, as well as the widespread practice of assigning "soft" norms, or production quotas, that could be easily filled and even overfilled. At a 1958 meeting of metal union officials in one administrative district, the characterization of average fulfillment levels of 125 to 150 percent as "healthy" met with no objections. The head of the union did warn that some norms had to be modified in order to prevent fulfillment rates from rising even further but hastened to add that "it can't look as if staff members are taking home less money. . . ."[11] This gives some indication of the extent to which local officials had capitulated to many workers on this explosive issue, especially after June 1953.

Officials nevertheless adopted a variety of strategies aimed at stimulating worker performance in an attempt to reverse the distorted wage/productivity trend. This included the implementation of innovative "new methods" (*neuere Methoden*) that supposedly encouraged more efficacious and efficient production practices; an "activist movement" modeled on Soviet Stakhanovism; and, last but not least, various forms of "industrial competition" (*Wettbewerb*) that bestowed awards upon those workers or teams of workers ("brigades") who performed best in head-to-head production contests.

These strategies had several features in common. In the first place, their overall economic effects were uneven, not least with respect to a reversal of the wage/productivity trend. Second, they elicited a great deal of resistance on the part of many workers, who feared that these transparent efforts to squeeze more work out of them would only lead to lower earnings. Just as important, they created a great deal of bad blood *among* workers. For example, those who adopted "new methods" or who served as "activists" – workers who received a variety of rewards and privileges in return for voluntarily increasing their output to set an example for the less industrious – often earned the ire of their colleagues, who were now expected, in turn, to increase their own performance. Physical attacks against activists, as well

(Chapel Hill, NC, 1997); Christoph Kleßmann, *Arbeiter im "Arbeiterstaat" DDR. Deutsche Traditionen, sowjetisches Modell, westdeutsches Magnetfeld (1945 bis 1971)* (Berlin, 2007); Sandrine Kott, *Le communisme au quotidien: Les entreprises d'Etat dans la société est-allemande* (Paris, 2001); Peter Alheit and Hanna Haack, *Die vergessene "Autonomie" der Arbeiter. Eine Studie zum frühen Scheitern der DDR am Beispiel der Neptunwerft* (Berlin, 2004); Christoph Vietzke, *Konfrontation und Kooperation. Funktionäre und Arbeiter in Großbetrieben der DDR vor und nach dem Mauerbau* (Essen, 2008); and the essays in Peter Hübner and Klaus Tenfelde, eds., *Arbeiter in der SBZ-DDR* (Essen, 1999).

11 Thüringisches Staatsarchive (hereafter reffered to as ThStA) Rudolstadt, FDGB BV Gera 853/209, Prot. der Sitz. der KV IG Metall Slf, 9.5.58, 12.9.58.

as willful efforts to sabotage the work of those known for their superior performance, were not uncommon. Industrial competition engendered similar frictions that frequently led to behavior equally frowned upon by officials. Besides complaints that more successful competitors had supposedly enjoyed unfair advantages, this included a variety of practices aimed at disadvantaging one's competitors, such as hoarding materials or leaving the workplace in poor condition at the end of a shift – something commonly referred to as "shift selfishness" (*Schichtegoismus*).

A further (and related) source of bad blood among many workers was disparities in income levels resulting from officially sanctioned variations in base wages, norms, and bonuses. These were often regarded as flagrantly unjust, leading to anger at the regime, as well as to mutual resentment among workers. Such frictions were perhaps most pronounced in worker brigades, that is, in small groups, or "collectives," composed, on average, of a dozen individuals working together to accomplish a given task or set of tasks. Officials hoped that such forms of cooperation would lead to greater ties among workers and thus heighten overall performance. Instead, they often had just the opposite effect. The ability to satisfy norms and succeed in industrial competition – both of which ultimately determined one's own wages – depended on the performance of one's immediate coworkers, as well as on that of other brigades and departments within a given factory. Such mutual dependence prompted complaints, and even denunciation, to officials about carelessness, poor work, or laziness on the part of undisciplined or less talented colleagues. Much of this resentment was directed at "shirkers" (*Bummelanten*) and the chronically "sick," that is, those who regularly feigned illness in order to take advantage of the GDR's generous sickness benefits, for example, or to procure scarce consumer goods by not going to work. The anger that such behavior caused led to widespread efforts by workers to discipline the undisciplined themselves, something that local officials actively encouraged. This often involved ad hoc meetings in which workers censured the supposed offenders and demanded that they be sanctioned: that they receive lower bonuses – or none at all.[12]

The East German regime claimed that industrial competition and the brigade movement had led to closer ties and greater cooperation among workers. This was undoubtedly true in many cases, but it was only part of the story. Workers may have felt a greater sense of responsibility for their entire brigade's performance and been loath to perform more poorly

---

[12] The many "sociopolitical" duties of rank-and-file party members were a source of friction as well, especially when this adversely affected performance on the shop floor.

than their rivals in other collectives. But what officials and several scholars have neglected to point out was the way in which this pressure to perform helped undermine worker solidarity: not only by creating tensions within individual collectives and among competing brigades but also by making many workers prone to police their closest colleagues in order to expose perceived inequities as well as behavior that endangered their own income levels. As functionaries at the famous Maxhütte steel mill in Unterwellenborn (Thuringia) admitted, a certain "material incentive" was often necessary to make sure that the workers there "keep close tabs on each other."[13]

There were many other sources of tension and resentment besides the frictions engendered by organized industrial competition and the brigade movement. This included the privileged treatment of certain social groups deemed economically (or socially and politically) more important as well as the daily scramble for limited goods and services. Shortages of materials, tools, machinery, and spare parts led to fights among workers and to accusations of hoarding. The struggle over scarce supplies became even more pronounced after the construction of the Berlin Wall in August 1961, which effectively cut off access to hard-to-find items previously available through clandestine channels in the West. A series of new wage and norm schemes introduced later that decade as part of Walter Ulbricht's New Economic System heightened such tensions by making workers even more dependent on the performance of their immediate colleagues.

The various incentive policies introduced by the regime were clearly intended, first and foremost, to spur productivity and heighten performance through greater cooperation. But such policies could cut both ways: they gave rise to divisive shop-floor practices that certainly proved beneficial to the performance of some workers but that, at the same time, seriously impaired that of their colleagues – thus effectively offsetting any economic gains. The overall economic benefits of these official incentive schemes were, in short, unclear. Such policies nevertheless had other, less tangible benefits for the regime and its leaders, namely the frictions they created – frictions that potentially promoted regime stability by seriously undercutting worker solidarity.

The types of tensions discussed here were only the tip of the iceberg. Laboring women frequently complained about discrimination and harassment by male workers. Older workers of both genders often complained

---

[13] ThStA Rudolstadt Maxhütte, Sozialversicherung (Sammelordner, 1954–9), Protokoll der BGL–Sitzung, 24.9.59.

about the lack of respect and solidarity on the part of their younger colleagues. East German workers living in the provinces complained about
the superior provisioning of other regions, especially the capital Berlin.
There were similar tensions as well in the countryside on the part of those
engaged in the primary sector, where similar schemes aimed at stimulating
production were implemented.

The larger point is that the GDR was a deeply divided society, and it
was those very divisions that effectively prevented the creation of extended
solidarity networks that might have allowed East Germans to present a
united front against authorities, give more effective expression to their
anger and frustration, and bring about desired change. Such frictions help
explain the virtual absence of coordinated protest during most of the GDR's
forty-year history and thus accounted – just as much as, if not more than,
repression – for the instable stability of the regime. After all, the two greatest
challenges to the regime came in the early 1950s, at the height of Stalinism,
and the late 1980s, when the power of the Stasi was at its peak. The
next section demonstrates this argument by looking, paradoxically, at the
tumultuous events of June 17, 1953, the greatest crisis faced by the Socialist
Unity Party (Sozialistische Einheitspartei Deutschlands, or SED) prior to
the mass unrest that brought about the collapse of the regime in the fall of
1989.

EXPLAINING THE "NONEVENT" OF JUNE 17, 1953

For obvious reasons, most investigations of June 1953 have focused on the
factories, towns, and regions where strikes, protests, and demonstrations
actually occurred. But what about those places where *nothing* of note happened? Is the fact that "nothing" happened not *some*thing of note in itself?
An investigation of the "nonevent" on June 17 can be instructive in a number of ways. In the first place, an understanding of why disturbances did not
occur in some places might help to pinpoint more precisely those factors
that led to disturbances in other locales. Second, such an investigation could
reveal underlying tensions and social dynamics that ostensibly had little to
do with the uprising itself but that were at its very root. Finally, it can shed
light on why, and the strategic ways in which, officials in some regions were
able to maintain domestic peace and harmony – all of which could help us
to understand better the longevity of the GDR.

The vast majority of East German cities, towns, and villages did not
experience any demonstrations or strikes whatsoever on June 17. Various forms of protest were reported in only 701 – or approximately

12.5 percent – of the GDR's then 5,585 localities. That said, upheavals were reported in all twenty-four East German cities with a population greater than fifty thousand, and in almost 83 percent of towns with populations between ten thousand and fifty thousand.[14] These are impressive numbers, especially given the fact that approximately half of the East German population lived in towns of this size at the time. But they say little about the *breadth* of involvement, especially in terms of the actual number of participants. According to one estimate, more than 225,000 people went on strike in 332 factories on June 17; that same day, approximately 339,000 took part in 129 demonstrations outside of Berlin.[15] These are obviously high figures, and they alone justify using the term *mass uprising* to characterize the events on and around June 17. But more than eighteen million people lived in the GDR at the time, which means that only a small percentage was involved – even taking only those of working age or only active members of the labor force into consideration.

Gerhard A. Ritter rejects as "nonsensical" the arguments of those who attempt to relativize the significance of the upheaval by emphasizing the fact that only a small minority was involved, "since all known uprisings and revolutions in history have been carried out by only a minority of actively involved persons."[16] That is a valid point, but it still leaves unanswered a whole series of questions related to the failure of most East Germans to participate. Why did only certain groups of workers join in the protest, and why did certain social groups remain largely aloof from the events? Why were there so few examples of concerted strike action? Why did the demonstrations peter out so quickly, and why did some regions experience no disturbances at all?

Strikes and protests took place across all of the GDR, though with differing levels of intensity. Besides East Berlin, where a strike begun on June 16 by construction workers on Stalinallee – the site of a massive building project intended to serve as a showcase of socialism – sparked the statewide uprising that took place the following day, the main centers of activity included the industrial region around Halle, Merseburg, and Bitterfeld, as well as middle-size towns like Jena, Görlitz, and Brandenburg. There were, in contrast, few disturbances in the predominantly agricultural regions of the north, Mecklenburg-Vorpommern in particular. Karl-Marx-Stadt

---

[14] Ilko-Sascha Kowalczuk, *17.6.1953. Volksaufstand in der DDR. Ursachen – Abläufe – Folgen* (Bremen, 2003), 103–4, 284–93.

[15] Volker Koop, *Der 17. Juni 1953. Legende und Wirklichkeit* (Berlin, 2003), 349–50.

[16] Gerhard A. Ritter, "Der '17. Juni 1953'. Eine historische Ortsbestimmung," in *Volkserhebung gegen den SED-Statt. Eine Bestandsaufnahme zum 17. Juni 1953*, ed. Roger Engelmann and Ilko-Sascha Kowalczuk (Stuttgart, 2005), 27.

(Chemnitz) remained relatively quiet as well, unlike the other large Saxon cities of Dresden and Leipzig. As this suggests, there were also important variations within any given region, and as Andrea Herz has observed with respect to Thuringia, the "events, influences, those involved, and the timings were *very different according to locale* during the week of June 17. Some places, factories, and rural areas remained untouched by the events, while in others, huge masses of people quickly agreed on the need for fundamental political change." But, as she also notes, "*The majority of Thuringian factories did not strike.*"[17]

That was certainly true for the southeastern Thuringian district of Saalfeld, where not a single major factory struck that day. Construction workers in the town of Unterwellenborn, the site of the Maxhütte steel mill, did lay down their tools on June 17 and launched a mass demonstration, but they failed to rally other workers to their cause – including the thousands who worked at the steel mill. There were a number of reasons for this failure. In the first place, those employed at the Maxhütte enjoyed a variety of material privileges that their counterparts employed elsewhere could only dream of. This was especially true of the construction workers, who complained about abominable living and working conditions. Because they lived and labored in close proximity to the steel mill – for which they were building apartments and other structures at the time – their indignation and frustration must have been all the greater. Conversely, the superior material position of the steelworkers apparently made them impervious to the overtures of their striking colleagues. Some even threatened to throw the construction workers into the blast furnace if they did not leave the factory compound.[18]

This was perhaps an extreme example of nonexistent solidarity on that fateful day, but it was not an isolated case. In Brandenburg's newly established socialist model city Stalinstadt, steelworkers similarly rejected the overtures of striking construction workers to join them; the latter consequently mocked the former as "*rote Hochöfner*" (red blast furnace operators).[19] In the steel town of Calbe, located south of Magdeburg, many steelworkers did join together with striking construction workers; yet, workers at two of the town's largest state-owned factories – the VEB Soda-Werk (with a

---

[17] Andrea Herz, ed., *Der 17. Juni 1953 in Thüringen. Quellen zur Geschichte Thüringens* (Sömmerda, Germany, 2003), 18–19, 21. Emphasis in original.

[18] See Port, *Conflict and Stability*, 70–94.

[19] Kowalczuk, *Volksaufstand*, 193. Only 2,000 people demonstrated in Stalinstadt and in neighboring Fürstenberg. See Burghard Ciesla, ed., *"Freiheit wollen wir!" Der 17. Juni 1953 in Brandenburg* (Berlin, 2003), 36.

workforce of 1,500) and the Kaliwerk (1,900) – remained on the job: "only individual brigades stopped working."[20] Only a small handful of factories briefly struck in Karl-Marx-Stadt, a city of three hundred thousand.[21] And even though construction workers were usually at the forefront of most protests – ostensibly a sign of solidarity with their striking brethren in East Berlin – only 12 percent of the approximately eleven thousand working in Leipzig laid down their tools.[22] In Halle, one of the main centers of strike activity, miners at the Ammendorf coal mine, one of the largest employers in the city, did not join the demonstrations. According to reports, mining officials there were apparently able to persuade the "mates" (*Kumpel*) not to strike by reminding them of their many "miners' privileges."[23] As at the Maxhütte, this suggested the way authorities could successfully co-opt certain privileged groups, thanks to the preferential treatment of those deemed most essential to the economy.

There were, however, exceptions to that rule. After all, those constructing the Stalinallee were among the most privileged workers in the GDR at the time – and at the forefront of the upheaval. The same was true of the strike movement in Jena, which was initiated by workers at the Zeiss optical firm, who were then joined by colleagues at the Schott glassworks and Jena-Pharm – the small city's three most advantaged firms.[24] And, as Heidi Roth has argued for Saxony, it was the highest-paid and materially most privileged workers who "first and most vehemently rose up against the system" on June 17. Her explanation for this phenomenon is not altogether convincing, however. She argues that because those factories tended to be the largest in the region, their very size made their workers and employees "strong and self-confident" because they knew they were protesting en masse. She suggests, further, that these firms had core workforces (*Stammbelegschaften*) whose members had not only amassed valuable experience, but had also been steeled in the workplace and by the political struggles waged during the Weimar Republic and then against the Nazis.[25] That is possible. One could also add that their knowledge of their importance to the economy

---

[20] Kowalczuk, *Volksaufstand*, 197.

[21] See, e.g., ibid., 175; Ritter, "Der '17. Juni 1953,'" 27; Hubertus Knabe, *17. Juni 1953. Ein deutscher Aufstand* (Munich, 2003), 163–5, 169.

[22] Heidi Roth, "Der 17. Juni 1953 in Sachsen," in *Die abgeschnittene Revolution. Der 17. Juni in der deutschen Geschichte*, ed. Hans-Joachim Veen (Cologne, 2004), 48.

[23] Hans-Peter Löhn, "Der Aufstand im Bezirk Halle – ein Vergleich zweier Aufstandszentrums," in Engelmann and Kowalczuk, *Volkserhebung*, 322.

[24] On the events in Jena, see Herz, *Der 17. Juni 1953 in Thüringen*, 118–30.

[25] Roth, "Der 17. Juni 1953 in Sachsen," 49–50. Also see Heidi Roth, "Leipzig und Görlitz. Die SED zeigt sich hilflos," in *Der 17. Juni 1953. Ein Aufstand für Einheit, Recht und Freiheit*, ed. Ulrich Mählert (Bonn, 2003), 105.

also gave them some backbone. But that fails to explain the many instances in which workers who were in a similar position (i.e., privileged, working in a large factory, and socialized in the 1920s and 1930s) did *not* join in the disturbances – as was the case at the Maxhütte. In any event, all of this clearly suggests the difficulty of making facile generalizations about behavior on that day.

Thanks to the opening of the former East German archives, scholars now know more about the social makeup of those who participated in the Soviet bloc's first statewide uprising. This has changed views about June 17 in at least one important way: the disturbances were not limited to workers, as earlier scholars like Arnulf Baring had erroneously claimed.[26] Individuals from almost all social groups and generational cohorts were involved – even though young industrial workers clearly predominated. To that extent, the term "people's uprising" (*Volksaufstand*) is certainly more accurate than "worker's uprising" (*Arbeiteraufstand*). But the former term is still misleading because it suggests a degree of *intergroup* solidarity that simply did not exist on June 17 – at least not across the board.

The consensus remains that most members of the intelligentsia remained on the sidelines that day. Teachers, architects, lawyers, and professors, Hubertus Knabe writes, "seldom . . . participated."[27] Leading intellectuals, including many artists and academics, not only remained aloof from the protests, but also publicly supported the East German leadership and, more to the point, strongly criticized the protesters. "How Ashamed I Am" (*Wie ich mich schäme*), the title of an article published in the official party newspaper *Neues Deutschland* by Kuba (the pen name of Kurt Barthel), the head of the East German Writers' Union, provides the best known example of such public condemnation.[28] The most important exception to this general trend was the so-called technical intelligentsia employed in larger factories, that is, "technicians, engineers, inventors, and designers," many of whom were members of, or even led, the strike committees formed on June 17.[29]

[26] See Arnulf Baring, *Uprising in East Germany: June 17, 1953*, trans. Gerald Onn (Ithaca, NY, 1972). The first major archivally based study to put a dent in that interpretation was Armin Mitter and Stefan Wolle, *Untergang auf Raten. Unbekannte Kapitel der DDR-Geschichte* (Munich, 1993), 27–162.

[27] Knabe, *17. Juni 1953*, 255.

[28] See John C. Torpey, *Intellectuals, Socialism, and Dissent: The East German Opposition and Its Legacy* (Minneapolis, MN, 1995), 30; Prokop, *Intellektuelle*, 90; Knabe, *17. Juni 1953*, 258; Ritter, "Der 17. Juni 1953," 28.

[29] See Knabe, *17. Juni 1953*, 255–6; Torpey, *Intellectuals*, 26; Heidi Roth, *Der 17. Juni in Sachsen* (Cologne, 1999), 600; Siegfried Prokop, *Intellektuelle im Krisenjahr 1953. Enquete über die Lage der Intelligenz der DDR. Analyse und Dokumentation* (Schkeuditz, Germany, 2003), 87.

What explains the behavior of the intelligentsia that day, especially on the part of those who refused to partake in the disturbances? The many material privileges that the SED granted the intelligentsia in an effort to keep them from fleeing to the West were one factor. Another was the subsequent reversal of discriminatory measures adopted following the Second Party Conference in July 1952, which had first proclaimed the accelerated "construction of socialism" – measures that were highly unpopular among the intelligentsia. Jonathan Sperber speculates that many intellectuals remained aloof from the disturbances because of their tendency to associate mass protest and violence with the fascist era. As the writer Friedrich Wolf wrote in *Neues Deutschland* several days after the upheaval, "I suddenly recalled the Nazi incendiaries [*Brandstifter*] of 1933. . . . " Along similar lines, John Torpey tries to explain the behavior of the intelligentsia by pointing to "the legitimating power of the antifascist credo and the persistence of the hope for a socialist society."[30]

These are valid suppositions. But they leave one important factor out of the equation: the intense animosity felt between large segments of the intelligentsia and the working classes. It is small wonder that highly trained and better educated East Germans stayed off the streets on June 17, given the frequency of demonstrations that day in which industrial workers openly criticized their supposedly higher salaries and other privileges. According to Siegfried Prokop, "The privileges that the intelligentsia enjoyed were, over and over again, the bone of contention [*Stein des Anstoßes*] for the striking workers." A so-called intelligentsia store open only to members of that social group and their families even prompted a protest by working-class women in Schwerin.[31] But working women were also the target of attacks that day – which might help explain why so few were elected to the strike committees that formed during the upheaval.[32] As Sperber notes, the gendered aspect of the uprising has received little attention.[33] But we do know of a number of cases in which male protesters called for lower wages for their female colleagues and even demanded that they leave the labor force: "it would be better," one crane operator in Erfurt opined, "if

---

[30] Jonathan Sperber, "17 June 1953: Revisiting a German Revolution," *German History* 22 (2004): 632; Knabe, *17. Juni 1953*, 260; Torpey, *Intellectuals*, 24, 27–8, 31.

[31] Referring to public comments made by Walter Ulbricht in July 1953 ("The members of the intelligentsia continued to work loyally during the days of the fascist provocation"), Prokop suggests that the SED General Secretary created a legend "that amounted to 'divide and rule' and that was intended to drive a wedge between the workers and the intelligentsia." That may be true, though there is no evidence that this was an intentional policy. Regardless, a "wedge" had already existed before the summer of 1953. See Prokop, *Intellektuelle*, 90–4. Also see Kowalczuk, *Volksaufstand*, 231; and especially Port, *Conflict and Stability*, 73, 240–1.

[32] That was the case in Halle and Bitterfeld, for example. See Löhn, "Der Aufstand im Bezirk Halle," 316. The same was true in Saxony: see Roth, "Der 17. Juni 1953 in Sachsen," 55.

[33] Sperber, "17 June 1953," 632–3.

men earned twice as much and women did not need to work and could [instead] perform activities appropriate to them."[34]

Not all women stood aside during the disturbances, as the example from Schwerin suggests. A courageous group in Jena even blocked the path of Soviet tanks trying to enter the town square.[35] But, as a rule, women played a less active role on and around June 17. Ilko-Sascha Kowalczuk suggests several reasons for this. To begin with, there were fewer of them at the time in the workforce: "In addition, the traditional patriarchal gender hierarchy banned women 'automatically,' for all intents and purposes, from public spaces."[36] Working women were in fact subject to various forms of discrimination by their male colleagues and superiors. This may not have been the main reason why they were less visible during the upheaval, but it certainly did little to foster solidarity between the genders – as openly sexist comments made that day by some of their male counterparts suggested in no uncertain terms. The events of June 17 may have constituted a "people's uprising," then, but one in which only *half* the *Volk* was involved – at least with respect to gender and geography, if not in terms of actual numbers.

Archival discoveries about the active involvement of many East Germans living in the countryside were one of the main reasons why researchers began to distance themselves from the inaccurate term *worker's uprising*. Protests took place in more than two hundred villages between June 17 and 21, leading Knabe to speak of a "peasant revolt" (*Bauernrevolte*).[37] That is not a very high figure, and there were several reasons why so few farmers were involved – besides Knabe's dubious contention that "it is traditionally difficult to involve the rural population in political protest because of its tendency to accept difficult living conditions." Leaving Marxist notions about the political passivity of farmers aside, it is likely that low population density and the fact that strikes are not a typical form of protest in the primary sector were more important factors.[38] Many East German farmers nevertheless did take advantage of the disturbances to vent their anger with the regime and its recent policies. But they usually did so in isolation and not in conjunction with other social groups. Despite isolated instances in which farmers supposedly expressed solidarity with industrial workers striking in Berlin or locally, the two groups in whose name the SED claimed to rule went their own ways on June 17 – even in cases in which they were not

---

[34] See Kowalczuk, *Volksaufstand*, 172, 210.
[35] Thomas Auerbach, "Der 17. Juni 1953 in Thüringen," in Veen, *Die abgeschnittene Revolution*, 77.
[36] Kowalczuk, *Volksaufstand*, 223. On the general lack of participation by predominantly female factories in Thuringia, see Herz, *Der 17. Juni 1953 in Thüringen*, 21.
[37] Knabe, *17. Juni 1953*, 232–3.
[38] Ibid., 32; Herz, *Der 17. Juni 1953 in Thüringen*, 22.

separated geographically. After approximately three thousand farmers held a demonstration in the center of Mühlhausen, for example, they called on industrial workers at the Möwe-Werk, the largest factory in this Thuringian town, to join them – but met with a clear rebuff.[39] It speaks volumes about the degree of solidarity in the GDR, even within a given social group, that the most common form of rural protest at the time was the decision to quit and/or dissolve recently formed collective farms and go off once again on one's own.

That said, there were certainly instances of solidarity during the disturbances. The most visible expressions of this – apart from the strikes and mass demonstrations – were the hundreds of prison stormings that took place across the GDR. Such actions, in which protesters demanded the release of those recently jailed for political reasons, were not limited to industrial workers. Approximately 250 farmers gathered in the central square of Jessen (located between Leipzig and Cottbus), for example, calling for the release of "kulaks" (*Grossbauern*) arrested because of purported "economic crimes."[40] Whether or not they really stood in the tradition of the European "liberation movement" (*Freiheitsbewegung*) that began in the late eighteenth century with the storming of the Bastille, as Ritter suggests, the success of such actions demonstrated that East Germans could act in concert.[41]

Still, the only known cases involving some degree of sustained coordination and cooperation among striking workers employed at different factories took place in the Halle-Merseburg-Bitterfeld industrial triangle, as well as in the Saxon city of Görlitz on the Polish border. Central strike committees were set up there, and their members included white-collar employees as well as members of the intelligentsia, such as teachers, architects, engineers, and other professionals. The latter played a leading role in these committees, which formulated demands, established contact with other strike centers, and coordinated local protest activity while attempting to maintain order and discipline. A twenty-member "urban committee" (*Stadtkomitee*) was even set up in Görlitz, where, Kowalczuk claims, a full-blown "revolution" took place: protesters occupied the most important buildings,

---

[39] See Auerbach, "Der 17. Juni 1953 in Thüringen," 79. Kowalczuk relates the story of a white-collar employee in Weimar who declared at a public rally that the East German government was ruining the farmers, but then adds that "a real solidarity with the farmers [was] not typical." See Kowalczuk, *Volksaufstand*, 219, 222. In Thuringia as a whole, "there was only rudimentary solidarity between workers and farmers," according to Herz, *Der 17. Juni 1953 in Thüringen*, 23. On alleged instances of solidarity elsewhere, see Kowalczuk, *Volksaufstand*, 197; Knabe, *17. Juni 1953*, 232, 235, which refers to "action alliances" (*Aktionsbündnisse*).

[40] For partial statistics on prison stormings, see Koop, *Der 17. Juni 1953*, 351; on the events in Jessen, see Knabe, *17. Juni 1953*, 233–4, and Ciesla, *"Freiheit wollen wir!"* 36.

[41] See Ritter, "Der '17. Juni 1953,'" 30–3; Knabe, *17. Juni 1953*, 313–33.

deposed the local city government, took over administrative duties, and even set up a local citizens' militia (*Bürgerwehr*).[42]

But all of this was the exception that day, not the rule. Despite Heidi Roth's claim that "worker solidarity in the SED state was . . . not yet broken," most shows of unity failed to extend beyond the narrow ranks of a given factory, department, or even brigade.[43] The advice given by one speaker to a large crowd assembled in Görlitz – "Remember the famous oath: be a unified band of brothers [*Volk von Brüdern*] and stick together in danger. For we are only united in a crowd: an individual accomplishes nothing"[44] – largely went unheeded across the GDR, especially when Soviet tanks began rolling in later that day.

This essay has already suggested some of the reasons why there was so little coordinated activity on June 17, pointing in particular to the many divisions within East German society. These were the result of frictions between the genders, for example, of anger and envy over material privileges bestowed upon certain groups and not others, as well as of traditional animosities between different classes (such as blue- and white-collar workers). These tensions not only hindered coordinated action but also contributed to the climate of discontent that had helped spark the uprising in the first place – an important point frequently ignored. There were other reasons for the general lack of coordination: the spontaneous nature of the upheaval, its very brevity, as well as the ability of the East German repressive apparatus – despite its embryonic state at the time, and despite its general incompetence on June 17 – to prevent the formation of sustained and organized opposition during the period leading up to the disturbances.

The instances of actual solidarity require explanation, not least because they potentially throw light on its absence elsewhere. In those areas that experienced serious disturbances, there was usually at least one major factory or large group of workers that served as a "rousing example" or trailblazer of sorts that emboldened others to strike.[45] But this in itself does not explain why so many major factories failed to strike; just as important, the ones that did were not always successful in persuading others to join them. Communal

---

[42] Knabe calls the events in Bitterfeld "revolutionary" as well; Ritter is much more skeptical of this term. See Heidi Roth, *Der 17. Juni in Görlitz* (Bautzen, Germany, 2003); Löhn, "Der Aufstand im Bezirk Halle," 312–13, 317–19, 322; Knabe, *17. Juni 1953*, 201, 206–7, 212–14, 223, 255; Roth, "Der 17. Juni 1953 in Sachsen," 53–4; Roth, "Leipzig und Görlitz," 89; Kowalczuk, *Volksaufstand*, 235–40; Ritter, "Der '17. Juni 1953,'" 29.

[43] Roth, "Der 17. Juni 1953 in Sachsen," 44.

[44] Knabe, *17. Juni 1953*, 222.

[45] Torsten Diedrich, *Der 17. Juni 1953 in der DDR. Bewaffnete Gewalt gegen das Volk* (Berlin, 1991), 97, 112.

living in large quarters – as was often the case with construction workers and miners – seems to have promoted at least rudimentary forms of solidarity. Local traditions played a role as well. The Halle-Merseburg-Bitterfeld region was known as "the red heartland of Germany" ever since the tempestuous industrial unrest that took place there during the early Weimar period. It was a stronghold of the Social Democratic and Communist parties and even after 1923, "a focus over and over again of strikes and other working-class disputes."[46] These were, in short, people who knew how to strike. Other regional "peculiarities" played a role as well. Roth attributes the intensity of the disturbances in Görlitz to the large percentage of refugees from the former eastern territories and to the resulting housing shortages there.[47] But similar circumstances obtained for many other places in the GDR, including the district of Saalfeld, where steelworkers at the Maxhütte did not lose a single hour of production time.[48] This was, once again, the case for the overwhelming majority of factories and villages in the GDR.

The obvious point of all this is that one cannot make facile generalizations about what transpired – or failed to transpire – on June 17. Although the majority of large cities witnessed disturbances, the situation remained surprisingly quiet in major places like Rostock, Potsdam, Karl-Marx-Stadt, Erfurt, and Zwickau.[49] Privileged factories were quiet in some areas but at the forefront of the disturbances in others. While most members of the intelligentsia remained on the sidelines, others were leaders of interfactory strike committees. Some industrial workers and farmers protested collectively, yet most went their own separate ways – or, in the case of those employed in the primary sector, generally stayed put on the farm, only to withdraw in protest from the collective later on.

There were, in short, only isolated cases of "cross-class cohesion" – or even, for that matter, cohesive behavior within a given social group.[50] And whatever solidarity did exist was decidedly short-lived, even if, as we now know, rumblings of protest continued throughout the summer. The unusual show of solidarity between blue- and white-collar workers in the area around Halle and Merseburg was, according to the Stasi, "one of the most important" reasons why opposition and protest continued to flare up there over the next several months.[51] But this was, again, the proverbial exception to the rule. "The lack of an alliance between the working class and the

---

[46] Löhn, "Der Aufstand im Bezirk Halle," 313; also see Ritter, "Der '17. Juni 1953,'" 29.
[47] Roth, "Leipzig und Görlitz," 92–4.
[48] See Port, *Conflict and Stability*, 72–4.
[49] Kowalczuk, *Volksaufstand*, 172–5.
[50] Torpey, *Intellectuals*, 26.
[51] Mitter and Wolle, *Untergang auf Raten*, 38.

intelligentsia against the party . . . ," John Torpey writes, "would in subsequent years become a familiar feature of political opposition to the SED."[52] Along with all of the other social fissures that rent East German society, this absence was one of the main reasons for the surprising longevity of the GDR.

CONCLUSION: THE "DARK SIDE" OF EIGENSINN

What does all of this have to do with the multivalent concept of *Eigensinn* – and especially with what this essay refers to at the outset as its "dark side"?

As we saw in the first section, official strategies aimed at boosting worker productivity and keeping labor costs under control were largely ineffective in the end. This attested to the successful way in which many workers continued to defend their own immediate material interests by successfully resisting many of the shop-floor demands placed upon them by the party and state. The long-term economic effect of such *eigensinnig* behavior was an entirely different matter. By impairing the functioning of the economy, East German workers were ultimately cutting off their noses to spite their faces. One thinks of continuing scarcity, for example, or of the poor quality goods produced in the GDR as a result.[53] Such behavior harmed workers in another way as well: by hurting and thus alienating one's own colleagues and friends, that is, those with whom one could have most effectively attempted to counter unpopular policies and official demands.

Yet, most invocations of the term *Eigensinn* continue to focus on its positive, or "light," side: on the way in which individuals demarcated a space for themselves in response to undesired developments and unwelcome expectations from above. In the ever-expanding growth industry of GDR studies, *Eigensinn* has become synonymous with (some vague notion of) resistance vis-à-vis authority – above all the successful defense of workers' own perceived interests. But that recalcitrance was only one side of the proverbial coin. As Alf Lüdtke has written, "To distance oneself from the demands of one's superiors as well as from workplace operating procedures – without struggling against them directly – could lead not only to individualistic behavior, *but also to hostile disregard of one's own colleagues*."[54] That, in

---

[52] Torpey, *Intellectuals*, 39.

[53] For a more sympathetic account of efforts by East German workers to make "candy out of shit" (*Bonbons aus Dreck*), i.e., to produce quality goods given the modest means at their disposal, see Alf Lüdtke, "'Helden der Arbeit' – Mühen beim Arbeiten. Zur mißmutigen Loyalität von Industriearbeitern in der DDR," in *Sozialgeschichte der DDR*, ed. Hartmut Kaelble, Jürgen Kocka, and Hartmut Zwahr (Stuttgart, 1994), 193–6.

[54] See Lüdtke, *Eigen-Sinn*, 143. Emphasis added.

essence, was the "dark side" of *Eigensinn* in the GDR: the way in which it created social tensions that, in turn, not only hurt the economy but also – as the "nonevents" of June 1953 demonstrated – inadvertently promoted the stability of this highly unpopular regime by hindering the formation of extended solidarity networks. The light and dark sides of *Eigensinn* were intimately linked, then. It is this very ambiguity that makes the term such an attractive, if imperfectly understood, concept.

PART III

Living beyond One's Means

The Long Decline, 1971–1989

7

From Schadenfreude to Going-Out-of-Business Sale

East Germany and the Oil Crises of the 1970s

RAY STOKES

The oil crises of the 1970s wreaked havoc on Western industrialized capitalist economies in the short term. Having moved in the course of the post-1945 period, slowly at first and then in a pell-mell dash, toward overwhelming reliance on petroleum-based liquid fuels by the late 1960s to meet their primary energy needs, these economies felt the effects of the oil price shocks of 1973–4 and 1979–80 inevitably and intensively. The substantial and sudden increase in the cost of oil was not the only factor, but it was a major contributor to the end of the so-called golden age and the high levels of inflation and general economic instability that followed.

The German Democratic Republic (GDR), which in the 1970s still relied on solid fuels (mostly brown coal) to meet its primary energy needs and had other tools at its disposal to control inflation and manipulate the economy than did the capitalist countries, might have been expected to have been less affected by the energy crises during the decade and a half following the onset of the first one. But was the impact as limited as might be expected? This essay explores the short- and long-term economic effects of the oil crises on the GDR through 1989. I start with a brief overview of the development of primary energy usage and petroleum-related foreign trade in the GDR during the 1970s and 1980s. I then try to connect these trends with more general developments in the GDR economy. I will argue that the oil crises did not cause the collapse of the GDR but did contribute to its growing weakness in various ways. What is more, the impact of the oil crises was more than just economic: the GDR's response to them was closely related to a general tendency to mortgage the country's environmental well-being to try to overcome its long-term and ever more serious economic and political problems.

The approach here is drawn primarily from economic history, with particular attention to developments in the role of energy in the GDR

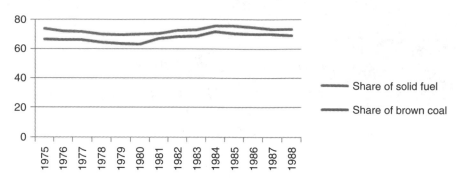

Figure 1. Shares of solid fuel and brown coal in GDR primary energy consumption, 1975–88. *Source: Statistische Jahrbuch der DDR 1989, 153; 1988, 153; 1985, 153; 1982, 143.*

economy and foreign trade in comparison to other industrialized countries. But energy – and oil in particular – can never really be discussed without some reference to politics, so that what follows is an exercise based on an analysis of key developments in the GDR's political economy from the late 1960s until 1989.

THE DEVELOPMENT OF PRIMARY ENERGY USAGE AND
PETROLEUM–RELATED FOREIGN TRADE IN THE GERMAN
DEMOCRATIC REPUBLIC IN THE 1970s AND 1980s

Primary energy usage is a widely used measure for an economy's energy mix, and it includes energy consumed in the form of solid and liquid hydrocarbons, nuclear fuel, other fuels such as natural gas, and from hydropower. Electricity is not included in these statistics because it is a secondary energy source, although nuclear power and hydropower are used almost exclusively for its generation. Unlike many other countries, the GDR did not publish data on primary energy usage before 1975, but it is probably safe to say that things were not much different in the five years before that. As we can see from Figure 1, about three-fourths of primary energy usage was produced using solid fuels, with about two-thirds overall coming from brown coal.

Were earlier figures for the 1950s and 1960s available, they would almost surely show higher levels of reliance on solid fuels at the beginning of the period, with gradually lower levels over time as the GDR, like other industrialized economies, began to rely more heavily on nuclear power and on liquid fuels produced from crude oil. There were, though, two unusual things about the GDR compared to other countries in this trend toward greater use of liquid fuels. For one, the extent of reliance on solid fuels in

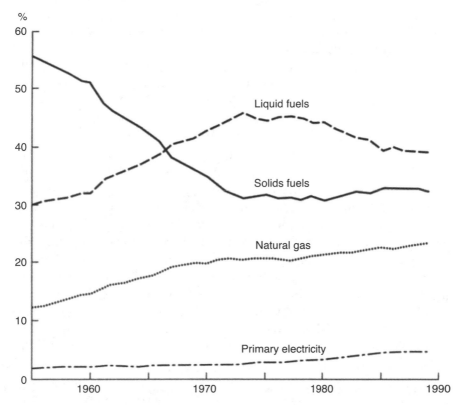

Figure 2. World primary fuel consumption, 1955–89 (percentage shares of different fuel classifications). *Source:* J. E. Hartshorn, *Oil Trade: Politics and Prospects* (Cambridge, 1993), 5.

the GDR remained consistently very high compared to developments over time around the world, which, as we can see from Figure 2, had shifted overwhelmingly toward liquid fuels and natural gas already by the mid-1960s. (Primary electricity in the chart, by the way, is essentially hydropower plus nuclear power.) The primary energy mix in the GDR even in 1975, in contrast, looked very similar to the prevailing pattern in Western European countries in about 1957.[1] The second unusual feature of the GDR was that the movement toward nonsolid fuel sources not only did not continue beyond 1979 but also actually went into reverse, something Rainer Karlsch and I have characterized as a trend "from opting for oil to retreat to coal."[2]

[1] OEEC, *The Coal Industry in Europe: The Situation in 1959 and 1960 and Outlook on Future Trends: A Study by the Coal Committee* (Paris, 1962), 15.
[2] Rainer Karlsch and Raymond G. Stokes, *Faktor Öl. Die Mineralölwirtschaft in Deutschland 1859 bis 1974* (Munich, 2003), 340.

The share of solid fuel in GDR primary energy consumption in 1988 was virtually identical to what it had been in 1975; the share of brown coal in that mix had actually increased.

It is important to underscore, however, that the GDR had actually made great strides during the 1960s and 1970s toward greater use of liquid hydro-carbons. Initial attempts were made to explore the GDR to find oil. During the 1950s, the country shelled out more than 150 million marks in this effort, but the yield was no more than 4,085 tons of crude in total and 110 million cubic meters of natural gas. To put the former figure in perspective, it amounted to less than thirty thousand barrels over ten years, at a cost of around 5,000 marks per barrel.[3] Thus growth in the GDR's oil consumption could only occur on the basis of imports, which grew tenfold between 1960 and 1979. Again, there are two unusual features here. First of all, the GDR relied overwhelmingly on one supplier, the Soviet Union, for its crude oil imports. This level of dependence never fell below 73.5 percent in the period 1960–88, although there were noticeable differences by period. Four can be identified. Between 1960 to 1971, the USSR routinely supplied 90 percent of East German crude imports; in 1972 and 1973, there was a sharp, if short-lived, drop to 75 and 81 percent, respectively; from 1974 to 1979, this rose again to levels of dependence prevailing in the 1960s, that is around 90 percent; and finally during the period from 1980 to 1988 levels were again closer to 80 percent on average (see Figure 3). The second unusual feature here in comparison to other countries was that there was essentially no growth in imports of crude oil to the GDR after 1979: import levels in 1988 were virtually identical to those of the earlier year.[4] We shall return to the reasons for these trends shortly.

There is one further unusual aspect of the GDR's foreign trade in petroleum products. Although East Germany did not produce its own crude oil, importing virtually all of it, it also did not use all of the products of its refining domestically. Instead, there was a substantial export trade in finished petroleum products, including gasoline, diesel fuel, heating oil, paraffin, and petroleum-based waxes. Let us just look at one example in

---

[3] Wolfgang Mühlfriedel and Klaus Wießner, *Die Geschichte der Industrie der DDR bis 1965* (Berlin, 1989), 240. The calculation of barrels equivalent is based on multiplying by 7.3. See Raymond G. Stokes, "The Oil Industry in Nazi Germany," *Business History Review* 59 (1985): 256n3. Walter Ulbricht, in a letter to Nikita Khrushchev in October 1964, underscored the extent of the GDR's effort to find crude within its borders, but also the lack of success and the improbability of this situation changing. Bundesarchiv Berlin-Lichterfelde (hereafter referred to as BAL), SAPMO DY30 IV/2/202/41.

[4] This is based on figures drawn from (and calculations made from) various issues of the *Statistisches Jahrbuch der DDR* (hereafter referred to as *StatJB DDR*): 1989, 243, 245, 259; 1988, 243, 245, 259; 1985, 243, 245, 257; 1982, 232–3, 245; 1980, 236, 247, 249; 1977, 271, 274, 276; 1975, 280; 1974, 297, 300, 303; 1972, 320; 1971, 303, 306, 309; 1965, 392, 397.

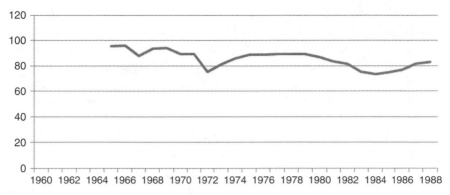

Figure 3. Percentage of crude oil imports to GDR from USSR, 1960–88. *Source: Statistische Jahrbuch der DDR*, 1989, 243, 245, 259; 1988, 243, 245, 259; 1985, 243, 245, 257; 1982, 232–3, 245; 1980, 236, 247, 249; 1977, 271, 274, 276; 1975, 280; 1974, 297, 300, 303; 1972, 320; 1971, 303, 306, 309; 1965, 392, 397.

detail, from 1965. In that year, the GDR imported 5.13 million tons of crude oil, more than 95 percent of it from the Soviet Union. It exported a little more than 1.54 million tons of refined petroleum products. In other words, only a maximum of 70 percent of the GDR's relatively modest refinery output remained in country, a figure that drops to less than two-thirds if typical levels of refinery losses were to be taken into consideration.[5]

This is a very high level of export. To put it in perspective, most Western European countries used everything they refined, although some, such as the Netherlands, were net exporters. West Germany, in stark contrast to all of them, including the GDR, essentially consumed all of what it refined in country plus an additional 25 percent in finished products that it imported.[6] In any case, this practice of exporting a large proportion of refinery output changed dramatically by the early 1970s in the GDR. By 1971, the last year for which we have figures on exports of all of the major refined petroleum products, imports of crude oil had practically doubled over those in 1965 to 10.9 million tons, 89.3 percent of which came from the USSR. With the exception of gasoline, however, exports of refined products had declined markedly, amounting to just 7.8 percent of crude imports by weight (and even less given refinery loss).

---

[5] *StatJB DDR* 1971, 303, 306, 309; refinery losses in 2009 in the United States were about 6.5% on average, and I have used this figure (which must constitute a best case scenario for petroleum refining in the GDR in 1965) in my calculations. For the latter, see Energy Information Administration, "U.S. Refinery Yield," June 2009, available at http://tonto.eia.doe.gov/dnav/pet/pet_pnp_pct_dc_nus_pct_m.htm (accessed July 23, 2009).

[6] Willem Molle and Egbert Wever, *Oil Refineries and Petrochemical Industries in Europe: Buoyant Past, Uncertain Future* (Aldershot, UK, 1984), 45.

It is probably no accident that heating oil exports were dropped from official published statistics in 1972, for it appears that GDR petroleum policy changed across the board along with many other policies after Erich Honecker replaced Walter Ulbricht. In line with Honecker's new emphasis on social policy and satisfying consumer demand, imports of petroleum increased steadily, practically doubling between 1971 and 1980. Initially, in 1972 and 1973, it is clear that increased imports came from other suppliers besides the Soviets because the proportion from the USSR dropped sharply (see Figure 3). Again, this may well have been part of Honecker's concerted attempt to improve consumer provision, reflecting, too, a willingness to go into hard currency debt to fund it. In 1974, and even more so in the five years that followed, however, the proportion of crude oil imports drawn from the USSR rebounded to historic levels of about 90 percent. There is not much doubt that this was owing to opportunism by GDR authorities in exploiting, at least in the short term, a peculiarity in the Soviet bloc's price system: the price for oil, as was the case also with other commodities within the Council for Mutual Economic Assistance (COMECON), was set using a price based on the international (i.e., Western world) price of the previous five years and fixed for a subsequent five-year period.[7] COMECON had put this system in place during the 1950s owing to the fact that prices within and between COMECON countries had little meaning on their own and also owing to the desire to smooth fluctuations in prices to enable more accurate and stable planning. The timing was also in line with the five-year plans that were the norm in the Soviet bloc.

Let us keep in mind, though, that, in this particular context, the average international price of a ton of oil in 1970 was $13; in 1975, $77; in 1980 (in the midst of the second oil crisis), $144; and in 1982, $272. COMECON (and especially the Soviet Union) tried to react to the impact of these unprecedented and sharp price increases on its price-setting system in January 1975 by changing prices to a five-year rolling average that changed annually. The effect was that "oil supplied by the Soviet Union to its partners ... more than doubled."[8] But even this measure did not really address the issue entirely. Regardless of the move toward five-year rolling average pricing and annual price changes, the full – and startling – implications of these figures were drawn out clearly in a 1993 interview with the former

[7] Hans-Hermann Hertle and Franz-Otto Gilles, "Struktur, Entwicklung und Probleme der chemischen Industrie in der DDR. Ein Rückblick. Gespräch mit Dr. Friedrich Goetz, ehem. Stellv. Des Vors. der SPK für die Grundstoffindustrie," *Berliner Arbeitshefte und Berichte zur sozialwissenschaftliche Forschung* Nr. 81 (April 1993): 12–13; Marie Lavigne, "Some Studies of COMECON Trade, Pricing, and Integration," *Soviet Studies* 27 (1975): 648–54, esp. 648.

[8] Lavigne, "Some Studies," 648.

deputy chairman of the GDR state planning commission for basic industry, Dr. Friedrich Götz: "By virtue of the time delay and the cushioning effect of average price formation [after 1975], the GDR imported its oil from the USSR at substantially more favorable conditions than if the country had, for instance, bought it on the Rotterdam spot market."[9]

The natural reaction of the GDR leadership to this situation – both before and after the change in pricing policy – was to take advantage of it, importing as much crude as was allowed from the Soviet Union at essentially precrisis prices and selling refined products at current market rates to capitalist countries in exchange for much-needed hard currency. We do not know the exact level of those exports, given the aforementioned lack of data on heating oil after 1971 and also, after 1974, on paraffin and wax. These may well have been removed from publication owing to a desire to conceal an upsurge in heating oil exports. But it is nonetheless possible to make some rough, conservative estimates based on a few simple assumptions. First of all, we know that the output of the Schwedt refinery, by far the largest and most modern in the GDR, was about 20 percent each for gasoline and diesel fuel, and about 50 percent for heating oil. If we assume that heating oil exports were in proportion to the relative output of motor fuels, we can simply multiply the export figures for one of those fuels by 2.5. To err on the conservative side, I have chosen gasoline, the smaller of the two motor fuels in terms of export. We can also safely assume that amount of export of paraffin and wax would be no lower than it had been on average for the period 1967–74, that is ca. sixty thousand tons in total per year. If we add these estimated figures to the actual ones and divide the total by crude oil imports, we get the following graph (see Figure 4).

It is worth noting several things here. First of all, the relationship between exports and imports was not as high during the entire Honecker period as it had been in the mid-1960s, but it was consistently higher than it had been in 1971. Second, the proportion of refined goods exported to crude oil imported dropped steadily over the period from 1972 to 1981. Third, at the same time, the foreign currency yield of that total would have increased dramatically, not just because of price increases for the goods sold but also because of relatively lower prices paid for the crude oil used to make them. Finally, there was a higher proportion of exports after 1982, when world prices for crude and finished products declined substantially even as the

---

[9] Dollar prices drawn from Friedrich-Wilhelm Matschke, "Die Entwicklung der Mineralölindustrie der DDR" (unpublished typescript, ca. 1989/90), 34; quotation from Hertle and Gilles, "Struktur, Entwicklung und Probleme," 13.

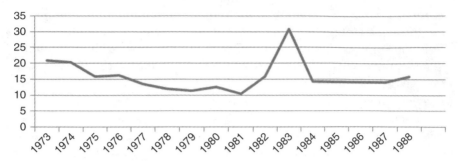

Figure 4. Estimated GDR refinery exports as percent of crude oil imports, 1973–88. *Source: Statistische Jahrbuch der DDR*, 1989, 243, 245, 259; 1988, 243, 245, 259; 1985, 243, 245, 257; 1982, 232–3, 245; 1980, 236, 247, 249; 1977, 271, 274, 276; 1975, 280; 1974, 297, 300, 303; 1972, 320; 1971, 303, 306, 309; 1965, 392, 397; and own estimates of exports of heating oil, paraffin, and waxes.

price for imported Soviet oil, owing to the price-fixing system, became and for some time remained relatively high.

THE IMPACT OF THE ENERGY CRISES ON THE EAST GERMAN ECONOMY

But what did all of this mean? When the first oil crisis hit with full force in 1973, its effects seemed to be uniformly positive for the GDR, an occasion not just for *Freude* but also for *Schadenfreude*. After all, archrival West Germany seem to be on its knees, which revived (even if fleetingly) the dream of East Germany winning the battle of the two systems. What is more, supplies of crude to the GDR were largely unaffected because they came for the most part from the Soviet Union, and, as an added bonus, the country was raking in foreign exchange by exporting finished products. But any celebrations that may have been prompted by the turn of events soon proved themselves to be overly hasty.

First of all, if the GDR's taking advantage of the situation in which it found itself was entirely natural and understandable, it was also short-termism taken to an extreme. It did not require an abundance of imagination to anticipate that the five-year moving average might – and did – eventually cause prices of crude oil imports from the Soviets to be higher rather than lower than world market rates, with the prices that could be fetched for finished products correspondingly lower than had been the case before. The price scissors were acting in reverse now. More seriously, the East German action was bound to provoke an incensed reaction from the Soviets when they realized what was happening. As has been mentioned, the Soviets already in 1975 pioneered a change in COMECON intercountry pricing that allowed for a five-year moving average price that fluctuated each year rather than a price set for five years, which resulted in a doubling of prices (and of income to the Soviet Union) paid by their fellow Soviet bloc customers.[10] But even this measure did not solve the problem of generalized underpricing of Soviet crude relative to the world market, at least in the short term as oil prices continued to rise. Soviet anger about this situation combined in 1980 with the USSR leadership's increasing desperation with its economic plight (and that of the bloc it dominated) to provoke cutbacks in promised deliveries of crude oil to the GDR. Soviet exports of petroleum to East Germany peaked in 1981. Thereafter, the level fell by more than 20 percent, where it remained with astonishingly little fluctuation for the remainder of East Germany's existence.

Günter Mittag, the GDR's top economic functionary during the 1970s and 1980s, recalled the chain of events that led to this in an interview in the mid-1990s. A member the central committee of the Soviet communist party who was responsible for relations with the communist parties in the other Soviet bloc countries, Konstantin Russakov, came to the GDR in 1980 at the behest of Leonid Brezhnev to deliver bad news. The current state of the Soviet Union, Russakov told his German allies, "is like just before [the Treaty of] Brest-Litovsk."[11] It was the second part of Russakov's message, however, that was of more concern for the GDR leadership. Owing to the fragile economic state of the Soviet Union, he told them, the superpower would have to sell additional quantities of petroleum for hard currency, which meant that it would be necessary to cut the promised twenty million ton per year Soviet delivery of crude by two million tons. This would be devastating, and as a result, Honecker appealed directly to Brezhnev, making it clear that "petroleum was the existential question for us, . . . and . . . that the very existence of the GDR is bound up with it." Unlike the response of the Soviet leadership to earlier entreaties by the GDR's leadership in 1964 in the face of threatened cutbacks in Soviet supplies of crude oil, however, this time no concessions were made. Russakov reportedly wept as he handed Honecker the letter from Brezhnev officially notifying him of the cuts, which remained at the level that had been threatened. The Soviet communist party general secretaries who followed – through Mikhail Gorbachev – repeatedly promised to increase deliveries. But there was never

---

[10] Lavigne, "Some Studies," 648.
[11] Interview with Günter Mittag in Theo Pirker, M. Rainer Lepsius, Rainer Weinert, and Hans-Hermann Hertle, *Der Plan als Befehl und Fiktion. Wirtschaftsführung in der DDR* (Opladen, 1995), 26.

any action taken to fulfill the promise. Mittag claims that the GDR sought an alternative supplier for the shortfall in crude, noting Iran in particular, but it was all in vain, not least because of the GDR's own escalating foreign currency problems.[12]

The response to the crisis involved drastic measures. Already in early 1981, a paper prepared for Mittag entitled "On the Structural Change in the GDR Economy in Relation to Deployment of Fuel" ("Zum Struktur-wandel in der Volkswirtschaft der DDR beim Einsatz von Brennstoffen") declared that: "The substitute [for imports of hard coal and crude oil] can and must take place through brown coal. *This amounts to a fundamental and permanent orientation of economic strategy.*"[13] As part of its plan to cut back on the consumption of oil products, the country's leadership decided on a policy of "Heizölablösung," that is, a retreat from the use of heating oil in houses, offices, and factories and in electricity generation. It foresaw a reduction in the use of heating oil from more than seven million tons in 1980[14] to just 1.2 million tons in 1989. Thus the cutbacks were deeper than the shortfall of Soviet supplies (i.e., two million tons of crude per year) would have indicated, and this was for two reasons. One was that the projected growth in demand for petrochemical feedstocks for the chemical industry would have to come through more intensive refining of crude, which would result in less heating oil being available for other purposes. But the other reason for the deeper than expected cutbacks in domestic heating oil consumption arose from the need of the GDR to earn vast quantities of foreign exchange in order to stave off bankruptcy: a substantial part of what had previously been consumed domestically would now be sold in foreign markets.[15]

This selling of oil on foreign markets – along with the other aspects of the "retreat from heating oil" program – became a matter of life and death for the GDR as it sought to avoid bankruptcy. By the 1980s, sales of oil products constituted the largest single earner for GDR foreign trade, and Alexander Schalk-Golodowski, who controlled both the sales and the resulting foreign

---

[12] Mittag in Pirker et al., *Der Plan als Befehl und Fiktion*, 26.

[13] Ehrensperger to Mittag, Hausmitteilung, March 10, 1981, and attached paper, BAL DY30/6474, quotation from page one of attached paper. Emphasis in original.

[14] This figure, by the way, indicates that my estimate for heating oil exports for 1980 is probably far too low. If half of total refinery output were heating oil, this would make for ca. 10.5 million tons of heating oil. Seven million tons were used domestically in that year, while estimated exports were just one million, leaving 2.5 million tons unaccounted for.

[15] Rainer Karlsch, "Das Chemieprogramm DDR von 1958 – Hintergründe, Ziele, Resultate" (part of unpublished series), "Beiträge zur Geschichte der chemischen Industrie der DDR" (typescript, Berlin, 1990), 124; Hertle and Gilles, "Struktur, Entwicklung und Probleme"; Matschke, "Die Entwicklung der Mineralölindustrie der DDR," 80. See also p. 142.

exchange in his capacity as head of the Commercial Coordination agency (Bereich Kommerzielle Koordinierung, commonly referred to as KoKo), became ever more important and influential as a result. But this all came at a cost, both economic and environmental. The "deep cracking" processes to achieve a greater yield of higher fractions of petroleum were expensive to operate (and therefore not used in many other places in the world): their cost amounted to an estimated 6 to 7 billion eastern marks in all. The heating oil program was even more expensive, costing between 12 and 15 billion marks for investment to replace and/or retrofit electric power generation plants using oil with brown coal. The products freed up by this were sold on the open market for between DM 1.0 and 1.5 billion in hard currency, which kept the GDR solvent. But the relationship between the added costs of intensive cracking and the investments in retrofitting or newly outfitting equipment for brown coal, on the one hand, and the hard currency income from the sale of finished petroleum products, on the other, was a poor one, amounting to just ca. 15 to 20 east marks outlay for each D-Mark in hard currency. Thus, with a yield of as low as DM .05 per east mark expended, this would appear to have been even worse business than usual.[16] What is more, the strategy had negative structural effects on the GDR economy, and established a pattern of cumulative self-destruction. Related to this, it was attained at the cost of enormous environmental damage and led eventually to political crisis.

CONCLUSIONS

But to what extent were the GDR's economic problems of the 1980s the result of the oil crises? On one level, it can be argued that these broader economic difficulties were not caused by the crises at all but rather by chronic

---

[16] Siegfrid Wenzel, *Plan und Wirklichkeit* (St. Katharinen, Germany, 1998), 76ff; Harm Schröter, "Öl-Krisen und Reaktionen in der chemischen Industrie beider deutscher Staaten. Ein Beitrag zur Erklärung wirtschaftlicher Leistungsdifferenzen," in *Innovationsverahlten und Entscheidungsstrukturen. Vergleichende Studien zur wirtschaftlichen Entwicklung im geteilten Deutschland*, ed. Johannes Bähr and Dietmar Petzina (Berlin, 1996), 119, 122; Rainer Karlsch and Raymond G. Stokes, *Die Chemie muss stimmen. Bilanz des Wandels 1990–2000* (Leipzig, 2000), esp. 40–1. The effective income from exports overall was 0.4 Valuta (foreign exchange) marks per eastern mark spent on raw materials and production of the product in 1980 and by 1988 stood at just 0.25 Valuta marks income per eastern mark expended. The income from exports of oil may have involved better yields at times depending on the price paid to the USSR and the prices commanded on the world market for finished goods, but even here there is no question that export was a losing proposition. For overall figures, see André Steiner, "Ausgangsbedingungen für die Transformation der DDR-Wirtschaft: Kombinate als künftige Marktunternehmen?" *Zeitschrift für Unternehmensgeschichte* 54, no. 2 (2009): 139–57, esp. 155–6.

and long-standing problems associated with the nature of the planned economy; being cut off from full participation in world markets and technological development; and dependence on the Soviet Union, which had its own
deep-seated problems.[17] In this reading, the oil crises had little to do with
causing the difficulties. It might even be argued that the GDR's response to
the crises and their longer-term effects was a symptom rather than a cause
of these underlying economic problems.

The hypothesis that there was a lack of a causal connection between the
oil crises and economic difficulties is supported by other evidence. The use
of exports of refinery products to earn foreign exchange was something that
had been a feature of GDR economic policy even in the 1960s. Although
this practice was diminishing by the late 1960s and early 1970s, the pattern
of trying to balance the GDR's foreign currency books with exports of
refined products appears to have resumed in 1972, that is, before the onset
of the first oil crisis but in line with the newfound commitment of the
Honecker regime to satisfying consumer desires, and it continued until
the country's demise, despite the attenuation of oil price rises (and price
decreases for oil products on the world market).

Still, I would argue that oil – and the oil crises – played a pivotal role in
the GDR's economic development. After all, although exports of refinery
products were used previously, the sheer scale of this was different starting in
1972. What is more, the easy money earned during the oil crises created a
level of dependence on this particular source of hard currency revenue that
was difficult to shake even when Soviet imports were eventually curtailed,
hard currency for imports from other countries was unavailable, and prices
for finished products declined markedly. In the end, the oil crises led in
the short term to increased hard currency earnings, and thus arguably made
Honecker's spending programs appear viable for a brief time, but this also
created a pattern of behavior and a level of dependency that exacerbated
the GDR's economic problems of the 1980s.

When confronted with the twin problems of declining supplies of crude
oil from the Soviet Union (while prices for imported crude increased, at least
for a while) and declining prices for refined oil products on world markets,
the GDR leadership simply intensified exports, which in turn required
more intensive reliance on domestic energy supplies, that is, brown coal.
The mortgaging of the GDR's land and environmental well-being that this
entailed was part of a broader tendency, evident as well for instance in the

---

[17] See, e.g., André Steiner, *Vom Plan zu Plan. Eine Wirtschaftsgeschichte der DDR* (Munich, 2004), esp.
225–6.

GDR's growing foreign trade in solid waste disposal services for capitalist countries.[18] Such measures were surely unsustainable in the longer term, but they arguably enabled the increasingly unviable economy and society to last longer than they might have done otherwise.

[18] E.g., "Ministerrat der DDR (gez. Mittag), Betr.: Beschluß über die Sicherung der erforderlichen Voraussetzungen für die Durchführung des 20-Jahres-Vertrages über die Verbringung Westberliner Abfallstoffe und ihre Beseitigung in der Deutschen Demokratischen Republik," February 13, 1975, Mimeograph, stamped "VVS," in BAL, DK/5/1615.

8

Innovation in a Centrally Planned Economy

The Case of the Filmfabrik Wolfen

SILKE FENGLER

The history of the German Democratic Republic's (GDR's) largest manufacturer of photochemical products, the state-owned Filmfabrik Wolfen, can be read as a history of continuous failure. The enterprise is said to have lived off resources developed before the socialist era, neglected technological innovation, and produced poor quality products. Sealed off from Western competition, the Filmfabrik Wolfen barely survived the 1980s and died shortly after the political and economic collapse of the GDR. Business and economic historians usually explain this story with the help of a monocausal theory. An integral part of an ineffective system, the enterprise was doomed to fail.[1] The Filmfabrik Wolfen, a successor of the powerful chemical trust IG Farben/Agfa, can thus be seen as a victim of East Germany's centrally planned economy.

This essay challenges that view by considering the history of the Filmfabrik Wolfen from a transnational perspective. Selling up to 70 percent of its film products abroad, the film works was among the most export-oriented enterprises in the GDR.[2] I argue that although system-related influences certainly hindered the film work's development in the long term, its ultimate demise was due to the interplay of several other factors.

---

[1] See, e.g., Janos Kornai, *The Socialist System: The Political Economy of Socialism* (Oxford, 1992), 71–4. For a comparison of the economic and technological performance of selected East and West German industrial branches, see Lothar Baar and Dietmar Petzina, eds., *Deutsch-deutsche Wirtschaft 1945 bis 1990: Strukturveränderungen, Innovationen und regionaler Wandel: Ein Vergleich* (St. Katharinen, Germany, 1999).

[2] During the 1960s, the film works was the seventh-largest export enterprise in the GDR. Volker Wenda, Elvira Wenda, and Harald Zschiedrich, *Analyse der internationalen Kooperation und Spezialisierung der Produktion des Fotochemischen Kombinats VEB Filmfabrik Wolfen mit der fotochemischen Industrie der anderen RGW-Staaten: Schlussfolgerungen für die Durchsetzung der ökonomischen Gesetze des Sozialismus bei der sozialistischen ökonomischen Integration* (Dissertation A, Hochschule für Ökonomie, Berlin, 1972), 40.

The study of the GDR's economic and technological performance benefits from taking the country's far-reaching international integration – in both the Council for Mutual Economic Assistance (COMECON) system and, to a more limited extent, Western markets – into account.[3] Earlier scholarship on transnational economic integration in Central and Eastern Europe pointed to the economic and technological disequilibrium between the Soviet Union and its so-called satellite states.[4] Although the East German economy as a whole seems to have profited in the short and medium term from favorable energy and raw material prices, intra-COMECON trade led some industries into a dead end, both technologically and commercially.[5] The "lack of incentive to rationalize and innovate" inherent in the COMECON barter system was responsible for the member states' loss of industrial competitiveness because it freed them from the necessity of facing international market competition.[6]

This essay argues that cooperation and competition within COMECON fundamentally affected the East German photochemical industry's technological capabilities and productivity. The negotiations on the technological course of the German and Soviet photochemical industries offer insight into economic and political relations within the multilateral framework of COMECON and at the bilateral level. They also shed light on the economic nationalism of the COMECON members and its role in undermining closer cooperation. But the example of the photochemical industry also shows that the consequences of the GDR's transnational involvement are far more complex. The photochemical industry generally and the Filmfabrik Wolfen, the largest manufacturer in Central Germany before and after the

---

[3] COMECON was founded in January 1949 at the behest of the Soviet Union. With economic integration and specialization of the Eastern and Central European countries as its guiding principles, parallel investments and industrial autarchy were to be eliminated, without violating the sovereignty of its member states (Bulgaria, Czechoslovakia, Hungary, Poland, and Romania; Albania and the GDR were admitted later). On the institutional history of COMECON, see Michael Charles Kaser, *Comecon: Integration Problems of the Planned Economies*, 2d ed. (London, 1967).

[4] Randall W. Stone, *Satellites and Commissars: Strategy and Conflict in the Politics of Soviet-Bloc Trade* (Princeton, NJ, 1996), 5.

[5] See, e.g., Ralf Ahrens, "Spezialisierungsinteresse und Integrationsaversion im Rat für Gegenseitige Wirtschaftshilfe: Der DDR-Werkzeugmaschinenbau in den 1970er Jahren," *Jahrbuch für Wirtschaftsgeschichte* 2 (2008): 73–92; Simon Donig, "'As for East European Producers, East Germany Provided the Only Success Story': Die Computerindustrie in den Jahren 1967–1973 als Beispiel für eine transnationale Wirtschaftsgeschichte der ehemaligen DDR," in *Historische Erinnerung im Wandel: Neuere Forschungen zur deutschen Zeitgeschichte unter besonderer Berücksichtigung der DDR-Forschung*, ed. Heiner Timmermann (Berlin, 2007), 135–66.

[6] This argument is put forward, e.g., by Christoph Buchheim, "Dreimal Integration in Europa nach 1945: Weltmarktintegration – kleineuropäische Integration – Integration der sozialistischen Volkswirtschaften im RGW," in *Wirtschaftliche und soziale Integration in historischer Sicht*, ed. Eckart Schremmer (Stuttgart, 1996), 362–3.

war, faced a unique set of circumstances that impeded their growth and development. Some of those circumstances were nonsystemic and "external" in the sense that they affected the photographic industry worldwide. These include technological changes in film processing that put Eastman Kodak's competitors at a sharp disadvantage and rising prices on international markets for important basic commodities such as silver.

I begin by briefly sketching the situation of the Wolfen film works during the interwar period and structural developments in those years that influenced the firm's later course. The main focus of the essay, however, is the 1970s and 1980s. I discuss the causes that lay behind the Filmfabrik Wolfen's long reliance on a particular course and the consequences of that reliance for its economic viability in the long term.

LAYING THE GROUND FOR COOPERATION

The Agfa corporation of Berlin had been a major European photochemical company before World War I, and it flourished during the interwar years.[7] In 1925, Agfa became part of Germany's largest chemical trust, IG Farben.[8] The plant in Wolfen, a small town in Central Germany, soon became the largest film factory in Europe. The company concentrated production of film, developing chemicals, and other photochemical products there along with research and development.[9] Vertical integration put IG Farben/Agfa in a position to become the main supplier of raw film and other intermediate products to the German photochemical industry. Thanks to a series of cartel agreements and informal marketing arrangements, the company also controlled almost 60 percent of the German film market.[10] Its share of the market for photographic paper reached 45 percent.[11] During the 1930s, economic difficulties elsewhere in Europe took a toll on IG Farben/Agfa's exports. European sales dropped from 33.8 percent of the company's total sales in 1934 to 25 percent in 1937. Exports beyond Europe fell during the same time from 18.4 percent of sales to 10 percent.[12]

---

[7] Lutz Alt, "The Photochemical Industry: Historical Essays in Strategy and Internationalization" (PhD diss., MIT School of Management, 1986).

[8] Peter F. Hayes, *Industry and Ideology: IG Farben in the Nazi Era*, 2d ed. (Cambridge, 2001), 16.

[9] Ulrich Marsch, "Strategies for Success: Research Organization in German Chemical Companies and I.G. Farben until 1936," *History and Technology* 12 (1994): 53.

[10] W. H. Dimsdale, "The Photographic Industry in Germany during the Period 1939–1945," *British Intelligence Objectives Sub-Committee Overall Report* 19 (London, 1949): 5.

[11] The Bavarian State Archives Munich (hereafter referred to as BSA) OMGBY13/84–1/1, p. 60, Special Report on Agfa Photographic Activities, December 1945.

[12] Bundesarchiv Berlin (hereafter referred to as BA) R8128/AW4377, Branch Table, Total [Total-Branchen-Aufstellungen], 1933–7.

During World War II, the company capitalized on the German Reich's expansionist policies. Export sales in Europe doubled between 1939 and 1943, accounting for nearly 40 percent of the company's total turnover.[13] Cut off from foreign suppliers, the German movie industry and amateur photographers alike had to rely on Agfa film. Booming export and domestic sales allowed IG Farben/Agfa to run Wolfen film works at capacity, and even then the company could not fully meet the growing demand for its products.

The Soviet occupation of Eastern Germany after 1945 created the foundation for shared knowledge and technology in the Eastern bloc's photochemical industry. Innovative color film products that IG Farben had developed at Wolfen in the 1930s and sold under the brand name Agfacolor were at the center of a comprehensive technology transfer to Eastern Europe.[14] The Soviet Union had a significant photographic equipment and supplies industry of its own as well as large photochemical research laboratories that had been working on color film technology before 1945. Moscow hoped that an evaluation of the Agfacolor patents and procedures could provide a decisive technological boost to the Soviet photochemical industry. Representatives of the Soviet photographic industry studied East German industrial documentation with the help of German experts. At the same time, several institutes and laboratories in Moscow and film works elsewhere in the Soviet Union received equipment taken from Wolfen. Although the Soviets removed 60 percent of its equipment, the Wolfen works still had a slightly larger production capacity during the occupation than it had in the mid-1930s. In 1946, the KGB forced a number of Agfa employees to participate in the reconstruction of a film works in Schostka, Ukraine. In 1947–8, the Schostka works began production of color negative films technically identical to the Agfacolor films. The photographic industries in Czechoslovakia, Hungary, and Poland soon began their own research on color film technology.

The Filmfabrik Wolfen was integrated into the SAG Photoplenka in 1946. The new enterprise's status as a so-called Soviet corporation – which meant it was the property of the Soviet state – helped preserve the established structures of the photochemical industry in Eastern Germany. Thanks to that status, Wolfen benefited from increased allocations of electricity and supplies, from financial assistance from the GDR's state budget to recruit

---

[13] BSA OMGBY13/84–1/1, p. 53: Special Report on Agfa Photographic Activities, December 1945.
[14] Brian Coe, "The Rollfilm Revolution," in *The Story of Popular Photography*, ed. Colin Ford (London, 1989), 81–4.

labor, and from barter trade with other Soviet corporations not provided by the GDR's planning system.[15] In 1950, the Wolfen works, the SAG Photoplenka's largest facility, accounted for 60 percent of the GDR's film production.[16] Because of the division of labor between the German photochemical and chemical industries before World War II, a number of intermediate products necessary for producing film were not available in the GDR.[17] Others were locally available but were of poor quality or could not be supplied in the quantities needed. Thanks to an agreement with former IG Farben chemical plants in West Germany, however, the Wolfen film works could trade raw film for the locally unavailable chemical products it needed.[18] Such barter arrangements were common in several industries during the early 1950s as the two German states were rebuilding their economies.[19] Barter agreements allowed the Wolfen film works to circumnavigate the shortage of raw materials better than other East German photochemical manufacturers could. Able to draw on technological developments of the interwar years, the Wolfen works caught up to the industry's world leaders in the early 1950s. During this period, it was able to market its color film products successfully in West Germany and other capitalist countries.

The cornerstone of Wolfen's close economic ties to the other COMECON states was laid during the Soviet occupation of East Germany.[20] The reparations payments the Soviets demanded slowly gave way to regular export contracts. Wolfen's growing exports to Western countries notwithstanding, it sent as much as three-quarters of its film output to the USSR between 1951 and 1954. In 1954, the film works was transferred to the ownership of the East German state, but it continued to export almost

---

[15] BA DY30/IVA2/6.03/123: Minutes of the debate with executive members of the intelligentsia at the Wolfen film works [Niederschrift über eine Aussprache mit leitenden Angehörigen der Intelligenz der Filmfabrik Wolfen], December 2, 1963.

[16] Rainer Karlsch, "Capacity Losses, Reconstruction, and Unfinished Modernization: The Chemical Industry in the Soviet Zone of Occupation (SBZ)/GDR, 1945–1965," in *The German Chemical Industry in the Twentieth Century*, ed. John E. Lesch (Dordrecht, The Netherlands, 2000), 388–9.

[17] Industrie- und Filmmuseum Wolfen Archives (hereafter referred to as AIFM) Office of the Chairman [Büro Vorstandsvorsitzender] No. 2354: Science and Technology Center, On the scientific and technological state of film production in the GDR [Wissenschaftlich-technisches Zentrum, Über den wissenschaftlichen und technischen Stand der Filmproduktion in der DDR], January 3, 1963.

[18] AIFM Office of the Works Management [Sekretariat Werkleitung] No. 380: Commercial Director, Disposition [Disposition des Kaufmännischen Direktors], September 4, 1956.

[19] Peter E. Fässler, *Durch den "Eisernen Vorhang": Die deutsch-deutschen Wirtschaftsbeziehungen, 1949–1969* (Cologne, 2006), 41.

[20] For the debate on the economic sovietization of the satellite states in the heyday of stalinism, see E. A. Rees, "The Sovietization of Eastern Europe," in *The Sovietization of Eastern Europe: New Perspectives on the Postwar Period*, ed. Balázs Apor and Péter Apor and E. A. Rees (Washington, DC, 2008), 1–28.

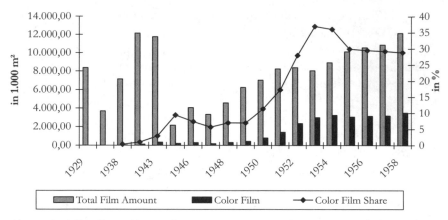

Figure 5. Wolfen film works, production of color film in relation to total film production, 1929–58 (in 1.000 m²).

80 percent of its output to Central and Eastern Europe.[21] The Soviet Union needed copy film above all on account of the rapid multiplication of movie theaters across the country. The Wolfen works was well positioned to meet that demand with the product line it had developed over the years (see Figure 5).[22]

Already in 1929, cinematographic recording and copying film made up almost 70 percent of the Wolfen work's film production; by 1960, the figure had reached 75.9 percent. Photographic film, by contrast, accounted for a continuously declining share of its production, dropping from 18.9 to 10.9 percent between 1929 and 1960.[23] In response to Soviet demand, the Wolfen film works increased production of high-quality color films rather than of black-and-white films. The export of industrial products such as film financed the GDR's imports of petroleum and other raw materials from the Soviet Union.

Beginning in the mid-1950s, the Filmfabrik Wolfen repeatedly failed to meet planning targets, both quantitative and qualitative, because its production facilities were worn out, it was understaffed, and it lacked funding

---

[21] BA DG2/CHII/476/13: Prospective Planning R&D Wolfen film works [VEB Filmfabrik Agfa Wolfen, Perspektiv-Planung Forschung und Entwicklung], June 20, 1955.

[22] Harald Michel, ed., *Die Filmfabrik Wolfen. Unternehmens- und sozialpolitische Streiflichter* (Berlin, 2007), 137.

[23] BA DE4/VS1729: Ministry of Chemical Industry, Economic position and assignment for the film industry [Ministerium für Chemische Industrie, Volkswirtschaftliche Stellung und Aufgabe des Industriezweiges Film], undated [1959].

for investment. It was nonetheless able to continue to export its products to the other COMECON states thanks to long-term trade agreements.[24] The East German photochemical industry continued to be dependent on West German raw materials and intermediate products, and GDR authorities considered the intra-German trade as a makeshift solution. In the 1950s, several attempts were made to establish industrial facilities in the GDR for the production of photochemical intermediates: most failed.[25] In the spring of 1958, leaders of the ruling Socialist Unity Party (Sozialistische Einheitspartei Deutschlands, or SED) decided to make the photochemical industry permanently independent of West German suppliers.[26] The decision was part of a larger program "to overtake" the booming West German economy "without catching up" (*überholen ohne einzuholen*). Before long, the East German film industry was using seventy-seven domestically produced intermediate products that had previously been imported.[27] To retain its monopoly of power in economic matters, the SED forbade intra-German cooperation at the company level. Henceforth, raw materials and intermediate products were to be supplied by other COMECON member states, primarily the Soviet Union.[28] The initiative to expand the East German–Soviet trade in chemicals was part of the *Störfreimachung* (elimination of disruptions) program intended to end the GDR's reliance on West German suppliers. The GDR committed itself to delivering processed chemical goods, such as plastics, pesticides, and film, in exchange for steel, wood, and chemical raw materials from the Soviet Union. Soviet deliveries, however, fell short of the photochemical industry's needs, both in scale and quality.[29] The forced reliance on domestic raw materials resulted in a rapid decline in the quality of the Wolfen work's film products. Not only

---

[24] AIFM Office of the Works Management [Sekretariat Werkleitung] No. 404: Sales Department Photo, Account [Bericht der Abteilung Absatz Photo], September 10, 1956.

[25] BA DY30/IV2/2.029/37: State Planning Commission of the GDR to Walter Ulbricht [Staatliche Plankommission an Walter Ulbricht], May 3, 1958.

[26] BA DY30/IV2/2.029/37: Politburo decision to make the photochemical industry independent from deliveries of the Federal Republic of Germany [Politbüro des ZK der SED, Beschluss zur Unabhängigmachung der fotochemischen Industrie von Zulieferungen aus der BRD], April 3, 1958.

[27] BA DG11/647/162: Directive on futher activities for the advancement in quality of photochemical products [Direktive über weitere Maßnahmen zur Weiterentwicklung der Qualität der fotochemischen Erzeugnisse], June 20, 1961.

[28] BA DE1/2465: State Planning Commission of the GDR, Decision on the safeguarding of the GDR economy against arbitrary perturbations [Beschluss der Staatlichen Plankommission über die Sicherung der Wirtschaft der DDR gegen willkürliche Störmaßnahmen], January 4, 1961.

[29] AIFM Office of the Works Management [Sekretariat Werkleitung] No. 634: Minutes of the 77th R&D Conference [Protokoll der 77. FE-Besprechung], November 16, 1961.

did sales in Western markets collapse, but several COMECON states also temporarily dispensed with deliveries from Wolfen.[30]

THE EFFECTS OF COOPERATION AND COMPETITION WITHIN COMECON

The production crisis caused a sharp decline in color film output in the early 1960s. Although the Wolfen film works was able to reverse the decline by the mid-1960s, it nonetheless continued to lose ground in international markets.[31] Its quality problems were compounded by a structural problem: television was gradually displacing movies. Many Western photochemical firms responded to this shift by turning more and more to the photographic film business. Eastman Kodak, the market leader, made a major push to improve the quality of its photographic films and of its developing services. Lab services – to quote Hughes – became a reverse salient, or technological bottleneck, for the expansion of the color film business.[32] The two leading color film procedures worldwide, Agfacolor – produced by Wolfen's Western counterpart in Leverkusen and most of the European and Japanese photochemical companies – and Kodak's Ektachrome technology could not be processed with the same developing equipment. Owners of fully automated processing labs had to choose one of the two procedures to achieve as high a load factor as possible.[33] Processing Wolfen-made film took twice as long as that produced by Western suppliers, and they were not compatible with Kodak's high-temperature processes, which became the most common lab processes worldwide during the 1960s. Relying on Agfa Leverkusen to process Wolfen film products was no longer an option after the formal cancellation of their collaboration agreement in 1964.[34] The Wolfen works

[30] BA DC20/I/4/694: Council of Ministers of the GDR, Report on the safeguarding of photochemical products exports of the Wolfen film works [Ministerrat der DDR, Bericht über die Sicherung des Exportes der fotochemischen Erzeugnisse des VEB Filmfabrik Wolfen], March 15, 1963.

[31] Ladislaus A. Mannheim, *Perspective World Report of the Photographic Industries, Technologies, and Science* (London, 1968), 40.

[32] Thomas P. Hughes, *Networks of Power: Electrification in Western Society, 1880–1930* (Baltimore, MD, 1993), 79.

[33] Peter L. M. Rockwell and Peter W. Knaack, *Out of the Darkroom: A Short History of the Photofinishing Industry* (London, 2006), 93. To compete with Kodak, the majority of European and Asian photochemical companies made their film material compatible to Kodak processes during the 1960s. See Ch. Gehret, "Epitome of Progress: Color Photography," *The British Journal of Photography Annual* (1972): 167.

[34] Based on a formal contract of 1956, which had been renewed several times, the cooperation included the barter of Leverkusen's photochemical intermediates against Wolfen's raw film as well as a shared use of the brand name Agfacolor. See BA DC20/I/4/877: Council of Ministers of the GDR, Decision on further activities for the safeguarding of export of photochemical products by the Wolfen film works [Ministerrat der DDR, Beschluss über weitere Maßnahmen zur Sicherung des Exportes von fotochemischen Erzeugnissen des VEB Filmfabrik Wolfen], January 9, 1964.

and other East German photo firms had only marginal success in making up for the loss of access to Western partners by building up a network of developing facilities in nonsocialist countries.[35]

Against this background, the Filmfabrik Wolfen sought to expand its position as the main supplier of color film in the COMECON. The number of movie theaters in the Soviet Union was still on the rise, and demand for cinematographic recording and copying materials was growing accordingly.[36] However, the Soviet Union and several of the smaller COMECON states had begun to build up their own color film capacities in the late 1950s to become independent of the Wolfen film works' inferior quality products.[37] As resources in the GDR were limited, the East German photographic industry had a vital interest in a division of labor in research, development, and production. The Soviet Union had research capacities at its disposal equaled only by Eastman Kodak.[38] Although Orwocolor, as Agfacolor was renamed in 1964,[39] remained the standard technology in the Eastern bloc, the signs did not bode well for a multilateral division of labor. A COMECON photochemical industry task force established in 1958 was to decide on production plans and draft proposals for the development of the film industry. The East German delegation insisted that research and production at Wolfen be narrowly specialized. As a 1972 study noted, that move would have put photochemical producers in the other COMECON states at a considerable disadvantage. The East Germans wanted to transfer the production of technically outmoded and unprofitable film products to enterprises outside the GDR and to turn the Wolfen works into a highly efficient, technologically advanced producer that could compete in international markets.[40]

The Soviet Union was not prepared to give up production of the complete range of photochemical products. It changed its position only in the mid-1960s, but nonetheless continued to expand its photochemical

---

[35] BA DC20/I/4/877: Council of Ministers of the GDR, Decision on further activities for the safeguarding of export of photochemical products by the Wolfen film works [Ministerrat der DDR, Beschluss über weitere Maßnahmen zur Sicherung des Exportes von fotochemischen Erzeugnissen des VEB Filmfabrik Wolfen], January 9, 1964.

[36] "Die filmtechnische Wissenschaft und die Filmtechnik der UdSSR zum 50. Jahrestag der Oktoberrevolution," *Bild und Ton* 20, no. 11 (1967): 325.

[37] BA DC20/I/4/877: Committee of the Workers' and Peasants' Inspection, Report on the fulfillment of the export plan concerning film material [Komitee der Arbeiter- und Bauern-Inspektion, Bericht zur Erfüllung des Exportplanes von Filmmaterial], September 19, 1963.

[38] "Die Arbeitsperspektiven des NIKFI," *Bild und Ton* 18, no. 5 (1965): 133–6.

[39] The brand name Agafacolor was changed to Orwocolor in 1964 as a result of the termination of the collaboration between Agfa Leverkusen and the Wolfen film works.

[40] Wenda et al., *Analyse der internationalen Kooperation*, 79.

Table 5. *Exports of Photochemical Products by the Wolfen Film Works, 1960–9 (in 1.000 marks, convertible currency)*

Year	USSR	CSSR	Poland	Hungary	Rumania	Bulgaria	India	UAR	Brazil
1960	67.589	25.469	12.726	11.617	6.091	5.433	9.620	1.090	1.021
1965	60.758	23.928	19.131	13.568	11.825	8.514	17.472	4.738	2.299
1966	46.703	25.218	22.063	12.080	12.704	10.400	17.580	4.086	2.558
1967	55.207	27.515	23.100	12.205	13.653	11.786	13.580	2.602	2.793
1968	66.651	37.224	19.324	13.246	13.053	13.431	5.015	2.474	4.307
1969	63.399	35.092	19.052	10.293	16.102	14.425	12.313	7.085	3.641

Source: Wenda, Wenda, and Zschiedrich, *Analyse der internationalen Kooperation*, 123–4.

production capacities.[41] The Soviet share of photochemical production in COMECON rose from 51.1 (1966) to 56.3 percent (1970). In the same period, the GDR's share sank from 32.8 to 29.2 percent.[42] The Hungarian photo industry refused to agree to any sort of specialization and would accept only barter deals for the exchange of goods. The division of labor went furthest with the Czechoslovakian photochemical industry. In 1967, it took on the production of color photo paper, a product on which the Wolfen works' research and development department had made little progress.[43] Wolfen's exports to the smaller COMECON states grew steadily in the 1960s, but its sales to the Soviet Union increased only late in the decade (Table 5).

Encouraged by ongoing reforms within the framework of the New Economic System (NES) introduced by SED leader Walter Ulbricht in 1963, the Filmfabrik Wolfen's management attempted to reorient the firm's product range more strongly toward photographic film.[44] In cooperation

[41] AIFM Office of the Works Management [Sekretariat Werkleitung] No. 888: Abridged report on a meeting with the deputy head of the German delegation in the Standing Commission for the Chemical Industries of the COMECON [Kurzbericht über eine Besprechung bei dem Stellvertretenden Leiter der deutschen Delegation in der Ständigen Kommission für Chemische Industrie des RGW], January 7, 1965. On the failed attempt of mutual economic cooperation within the COMECON, see Nigel Swain, "Socialist Atarky and Failed Socialist Internationalism: Comecon and 'Perverse Successes' of the Hungarian Computer Industry," in *National Borders and Economic Disintegration in Modern East Central Europe*, ed. Uwe Müller and Helga Schultz (Berlin, 2002), 210–15.

[42] Wenda et al., *Analyse der internationalen Kooperation*, 6.

[43] AIFM Office of the Works Management [Sekretariat Werkleitung] No. 79: Bilateral Cooperation with the USSR, the CSSR, and the People's Republic of Poland [Zweiseitige Zusammenarbeit mit SU, CSSR, VRP], May 2, 1967.

[44] These reforms aimed at rationalizing industrial production, introducing a new, dynamic price system and thus stimulating innovation. Hubert Laitko, "The Reform Package of the 1960s: The Policy Finale of the Ulbricht Era," in *Science under Socialism: East Germany in Comparative Perspective*, ed. Dieter Hoffmann and Kristie Macrakis (Cambridge, MA, 1999), 49–52.

with the Soviet and the Czechoslovak photographic industries, it developed still and motion picture systems that were conceived as alternatives to the products offered by Western suppliers. This initiative did not succeed, however. Exports beyond COMECON were prevented by patent constraints. Moreover, technical progress was impeded by a lack of cooperation at the enterprise level.[45]

This effort to move beyond the tried-and-true field of cinematographic film production soon came to an end. Ulbricht's fall from power in 1971 marked the abandonment of the NES. That same year, the State Planning Commission presented a plan under which the GDR was, for political, strategic, and economic reasons, to receive raw materials primarily from the Soviet Union.[46] The GDR's position in international trade worsened severely two years later following the first oil price shock. The Council of Ministers hoped that the "long-term provision of bulk petroleum chemicals from the USSR in exchange for highly refined chemical products from the GDR" would put a stop to that negative trend.[47] One of these highly refined chemical products was the color cinematographic film produced in Wolfen. The film works – part of a combine since 1970[48] – thus had to continue along the path it had set out upon in the immediate aftermath of the war. Cinematographic color film accounted for almost 90 percent of the Wolfen works' film exports in the mid-1970s.[49] This development also gave new impetus to the bilateral division of labor in research and development within COMECON, which had until then been carried out rather informally at the local level. In 1973, the umbrella organization

[45] AIFM Office of the Chairman [Büro Vorstandsvorsitzender] No. 2357: Script of a speech held by Brunhilde Jaeger, managing director of the Photochemical Combine Wolfen, on the occasion of a visit of the Politburo chairman to the Photochemical Combine Wolfen [Vortragsmanuskript Brunhilde Jaeger anlässlich des Besuches des Vorsitzenden des Politbüros im Fotochemischen Kombinat Wolfen], May 31, 1979.

[46] BA DY30/J/IV/2.2A/1.511: State Planning Commission of the GDR, Draft of a concept for the long-term safeguarding of raw materials [Staatliche Plankommission der DDR, Entwurf der Konzeption zur langfristigen Rohstoffsicherung], April 24, 1971. On the comprehensive program for socialist economic integration, see Stone, *Satellites and Commissars*, 35–6.

[47] BA DC20/I/4/3075: Council of Ministers of the GDR, Decision on outcomes and experiences of the chemical industry in developing the socialist economic integration with the USSR, and conclusions for further activities [Ministerrat der DDR, Beschluss über Ergebnisse und Erfahrungen der chemischen Industrie bei der Entwicklung der sozialistischen ökonomischen Integration mit der UdSSR und Schlussfolgerungen für die weitere Arbeit], May 23, 1974.

[48] The creation of large combines went along with the recentralization of research and development in twelve major research institutions. Raymond G. Stokes, *Constructing Socialism in Eastern Germany: Technology in the German Democratic Republic, 1945–1990* (Stanford, CA, 1999), 149–52.

[49] BA DC20/I/4/3711: Horst Sölle (Minister of Foreign and Intra-German Trade) to Günther Wyschowsky (Minister for the Chemical Industry), November 10, 1976.

Assofoto was created to unite the Soviet and East German photochemical industries' research efforts.[50] At the Soviets' insistence, Assofoto's research and development work focused on cinematographic films. Wolfen was given responsibility for research on bulk color positive film.[51]

As it became increasingly integrated in COMECON's structures for division of labor, the Wolfen film works saw its room for maneuver in the area of color film technology shrink. At the start of the 1970s, representatives of the Eastern bloc photochemical industries increasingly called into question Orwocolor's standing as the industry standard in the region. Qualitatively, the procedure, which dated from the 1930s, could not be substantially improved. Orwocolor films were unmarketable in hard currency countries, nor did they find favor with consumers within COMECON. Nevertheless, there were good reasons for holding onto the Orwocolor technology. The procedures were technologically mature and therefore less research and development intensive, and the raw materials for the product line were available within COMECON. What was not available, however, was the technical know-how to adapt Kodak's color film technology. To change to the Kodak procedure would require not only fundamental procedural development, but also an additional processing step. Finally, the network of developing facilities in the COMECON was not equipped to process Western films.[52] Going it alone in color film technology, in short, was out of the question for the East German photo industry. In the end, the Soviets decided that the change to a new color film technology would be carried out by 1985. The shift to a new technology was to coincide with an overhaul of the East German photochemical combine's dilapidated production facilities. How this ambitious program was to be realized – or financed – remained a subject of dispute among GDR officials. The estimated budget for the project was equal to annual investment budget for the East German chemical industry as a whole.[53]

---

[50] BA DC20/16904: Report on the 14th meeting of the Standing Sub-Committee for the Cooperation in Science and Engineering of the GRD and the USSR [Bericht über die 14. Tagung der Ständigen Unterkommission für wissenschaftlich-technische Zusammenarbeit zwischen der DDR und der UdSSR], May 18, 1973.

[51] Color positive film was used for copying movies. These copies were applied in a vast number of cinemas throughout the Soviet Union and the COMECON states.

[52] BA DC20/I/4/3500: Council of Ministers of the GDR, Decision on the advancement of the camera industry, including the photo- and cinematographic industry, toward an improvement of supply and the fulfillment of export plans [Ministerrat der DDR, Beschluss über die Entwicklung der Kameraindustrie einschließlich der Foto-Kino-Industrie zur Verbesserung der Versorgung der Bevölkerung und zur Erfüllung der Exportaufgaben], February 5, 1976.

[53] The photochemical combine's director of R&D estimated the costs of the project at 3 billion marks. AIFM Office of the Chairman [Büro Vorstandsvorsitzender] No. 2358: Verbal report on the state of working out a R&D strategy and the government order on color film materials respectively

The GDR photographic industry soon faced a serious dilemma on account of its dependence on sales to the Soviet Union. The rising price of silver on international markets cut deeply into the Wolfen works' profits from its copy film. Each year, the East German photochemical industry lost forty-five tons of silver because the Soviet Union returned none of the precious metal reclaimed in the development process. But the GDR did not try to renegotiate the prices of photochemical products, "lest it lead to corresponding activities on the part of the Soviet partner with imports in other areas."[54] The situation grew more critical in 1979 as silver prices rose by more than 300 percent within a year. Because it was obliged by long-term contracts to deliver a predetermined quantity of film to the Soviet Union each year, the GDR temporarily stopped its film exports to India and Brazil.[55] The GDR price-regulation authorities passed the drastic price increase for silver on to the photochemical industry in a 1981 reform of industrial prices.[56]

Meanwhile, the Soviet Union continued to expand capacity in color film production, largely by purchasing technology and know-how from nonsocialist countries. Uncertain whether the GDR would benefit from this transfer of knowledge, East German planning officials urged the Wolfen works to expand the range of its photographic film products through the purchase of Western technology. Because most Western photo companies refused to sell closed product lines for fear of additional competition, the GDR had to make the shift to a new color film technology compatible with Kodak lab processes on its own. The decision to do so came, however, at a point when the GDR found itself in a general economic crisis.[57] Considerable money went into research on new color film technology, but research could not be translated into new products because of the lack of investment in plant construction.[58]

[Fachdirektor Forschung und Entwicklung, Mündlicher Bericht über den Stand der Erarbeitung der FE-Strategie bzw. des Staatsauftrages Colormaterialien], April 27, 1982.

[54] BA DY30/2705: The Office of Günter Mittag, Report on the debate with Brunhilde Jaeger [Büro Günter Mittag, Bericht über die Aussprache mit Brunhilde Jaeger], May 29, 1979.

[55] BA DL2/VA2209: State Planning Commission of the GDR, Proposals for production and export of recording materials containing silver in the year 1980 [Staatliche Plankommission der DDR, Vorschläge zur Produktion und zum Export silberhaltiger Aufzeichnungsmaterialien im Jahr 1980], December 14, 1979.

[56] AIFM Office of the Chairman [Büro Vorstandsvorsitzender] No. 2355: Price Agency [Amt für Preise] to Brunhilde Jaeger, June 28, 1983.

[57] AIFM Office of the Director General [Büro Generaldirektor] No. 1683: The Socialist Party's In-Plant Organisation Wolfen [SED-Betriebsparteiorganisation] to Brunhilde Jaeger, April 10, 1980.

[58] AIFM Office of the Chairman [Büro Vorstandsvorsitzender] No. 2247: Statement on a letter by the director R&D [Stellungnahme zum Schreiben des Leiters der Abteilung Forschung und technische Entwicklung], August 23, 1988.

The changeover was complicated by difficulties in the Wolfen works' cooperation with other combines and its Soviet partners. A Council of Ministers decision of September 1983 provided the formal framework for concerted action on the part of different branches of industry.[59] Plans to provide the photochemical industry with domestically made intermediate products, for example, was made part of the strategy to revamp the chemical industry.[60] The development of the necessary capacities fell far behind schedule, however, or had to be abandoned for lack of funding.[61] A contract with the Soviet Union for the division of labor in the development and production of intermediate products for the new color film product line did little to improve the situation. By the mid-1980s, the Soviet photochemical industry was providing only three of the thirty chemicals needed.[62]

Cooperation in the design and production of equipment for the manufacture of film likewise did not progress far beyond the planning stage. For example, the GDR's largest producer of photographic equipment, Pentacon Dresden, was to produce high-performance equipment for developing Kodak-compatible photographic and cinematographic film. By order of the Council of Ministers, the GDR's network of dilapidated developing labs was to be revamped by the addition of nine new facilities that, together, would be capable of developing one hundred million color photos annually. Although the new equipment was supposed to be developed in cooperation with Soviet and Czechoslovak partners, Pentacon refused to participate in the project on the grounds that it lacked the necessary personnel and financial resources.[63] Because its Soviet trading partners fulfilled their contractual obligations ever more infrequently, the GDR was forced to continue to

---

[59] BA DC20/I/4/5258: Council of Ministers of the GDR, Decision on the information regarding the scrutiny to reduce the silver consumption in photochemical products [Ministerrat der DDR, Beschluss zur Information über die Überprüfung zur Senkung des Silberverbrauches bei fotochemischen Erzeugnissen], September 22, 1983.

[60] BA DG11/3565/4: Ministry of Chemical Industry, Safeguarding of raw materials and intermediate products for the new color films and silver-free recording materials [Ministerium für Chemische Industrie, Sicherung der Ausgangs- und Zwischenprodukte für die neuen Colorfilme und silberfreie Aufzeichnungsmaterialien], May 21, 1981.

[61] AIFM Office of the Chairman [Büro Vorstandsvorsitzender] No. 2355: Director R&D, Preparatory material regarding the complex "safeguarding of intermediate products for the new color film system" [Fachdirektorat Forschung und Entwicklung, Vorbereitungsmaterial zum Komplex Zwischenproduktsicherung für das neue Colorsystem], August 29, 1984.

[62] AIFM Office of the Director General [Büro Generaldirektor] No. 2061: Speech on the state of fulfillment of the agreement on cooperation with the USSR in the field of new color cinematographic and photographic film materials [Vortrag über den Erfüllungsstand der Zusammenarbeit auf dem Gebiet der neuen Color-Kine- und Fotomaterialien], undated [1985].

[63] AIFM Office of the Chairman [Büro Vorstandsvorsitzender] No. 2355: Herward Pietsch (director R&D) to Brunhilde Jaeger, June 9, 1986.

import intermediate products, lab equipment, and production facilities – and to pay for them in hard currencies.[64]

In December 1985, representatives of the COMECON photographic industries undertook a new attempt to improve scientific and technical cooperation in color film research. Soviet experts decided, however, that COMECON's long-standing system of exchange – raw materials for finished products – had no future.[65] In light of changes in international markets and in the terms of trade within COMECON, GDR officials decided to limit future photochemical research and development to color photographic film, leaving the cinematographic film product line to the Soviet Union. In the meantime, research on the rest of the range of film products had stagnated.[66] This shift in policy did nothing to change the basic pattern of the Wolfen works' business: in 1989, 70.2 percent of its profits still came from bulk cinematographic films, and higher-priced photographic films contributed only 15.2 percent.[67]

The management of the Wolfen film works hoped that a new series of color photographic films and long-standing contacts in Eastern European markets would enable the firm to survive the economic transformation of Eastern Germany after 1989. Following the dissolution of the combine in July 1990, the film works were transformed into a stock corporation under the sole ownership of the agency entrusted with the privatization of onetime GDR state enterprises, the Treuhandanstalt. Its attempt to gain a foothold in the Western photo market met with no success, however. Dependence on sales in the Soviet market proved fatal: the East German photo industry's strength within the COMECON became a weakness as Eastern European demand for Wolfen's products dwindled in the early 1990s.[68] After a failed attempt to privatize the company, the Treuhandanstalt decided to liquidate the Wolfen works in 1994 and gradually stopped production. The company's name was deleted from the trade register in June 1998, putting an end to the nine-decade history of the Wolfen film works.

[64] BA DC20/I/4/6498: Council of Ministers of the GDR, Information on the realization of activities to achieve the advanced international quality level in color films, and of the agreement with the USSR in this field [Ministerrat der DDR, Information über die Realisierung der Maßnahmen zur Erreichung des fortgeschrittenen internationalen Qualitätsniveaus bei Colorfilmen sowie des auf diesem Gebiet bestehenden Regierungsabkommens mit der UdSSR], August 17, 1989.

[65] Stone, *Satellites and Commissars*, 205.

[66] AIFM Office of the Chairman [Büro Vorstandsvorsitzender] No. 2251: Director Development, State and continuation of R&D in black-and-white film materials [Bereichsdirektion Erzeugnisentwicklung, Stand und Weiterführung der FE-Arbeiten zu Schwarzweiß-Materialien], April 21, 1989.

[67] AIFM Inspectorate Combine Development [Hauptabteilung Kombinatsentwicklung] Nr. BA10471: Production development, 1990–2000 [Mengenentwicklung 1990–2000], undated [October 1989].

[68] Franz-Otto Gilles, *Am Ende blieb nur die Verpackung: Die Restrukturierung und Privatisierung der Filmfabrik Wolfen* (Berlin, 1998), 21–30.

CONCLUSION

The story of the Wolfen film works and the East German photochemical
industry touches on issues at the heart of the GDR's economic, technological, and political development. It therefore also touches on the causes
and consequences of the country's economic failure in the long term. The
evidence presented here makes clear that the GDR's increasing economic
integration into the COMECON system affected at least some industries'
ability to innovate and to increase productivity. The East German photochemical industry's decoupling from the intra-German division of labor was
the first step on the path that led to its falling behind the rest of the industry
technologically and economically. Cooperation with Western partners was
restricted for political reasons, but the partners available in Eastern Europe
were not their equal. It was for economic reasons that the GDR officials
sought to strengthen ties with the other COMECON countries, and the
Soviet photochemical industry in particular. They hoped to gain access to
the Soviet Union's large photochemical research infrastructure, and bulk
copy film was an important offering in the barter trade for Soviet raw materials, especially oil. By focusing its capacities on this trade, the GDR became
ever more dependent on its Eastern European trade allies, which limited its
freedom to move away from established technologies. The photochemical
industry's continuing dependence on silver, which the GDR had to procure on the world market, added to the country's general economic crisis
of the early 1980s, and that in turn further diminished its opportunities
for autonomous action. In the end, it was not one single factor – such as
integration within COMECON – but the interaction of several factors over
time that prevented the East German photochemical industry from catching
up with international technological standards.

9

Debt, Cooperation, and Collapse

East German Foreign Trade in the Honecker Years

RALF AHRENS

For a relatively small industrialized country like the German Democratic Republic (GDR), foreign trade was of vital interest. Trade was necessary not only to obtain scarce raw materials but also to improve the efficiency of the allocation of production factors and to promote technological progress as a precondition for intensive economic growth. The structure of East Germany's foreign trade changed radically with the country's integration into the Soviet bloc. The planned economies of Eastern Europe and the USSR became its largest trading partners.[1] This politically preferred trade with the less industrialized member states of the Council for Mutual Economic Assistance (COMECON) had a number of advantages. For one, it helped stabilize the East German economy. For the GDR, the other COMECON countries were a seller's market in which goods not competitive in the West could be sold. The Soviet Union purchased GDR exports at relatively high prices while, at least in the period from the mid-1960s to the mid-1980s, selling its raw materials below world market prices. Leaving aside the methodological problems of making precise calculations, it is safe to say that these implicit subsidies varied over time as a result of changes in the composition of Soviet–East German trade. Nevertheless, the GDR and other COMECON exporters of manufactured goods obviously profited from a principal-agent relation: the Soviet Union, although the politically hegemonic power, was long unable to enforce price relations according to those on the "capitalist world market" – whether for political

[1] See the early study by Heinz Köhler, *Economic Integration in the Soviet Bloc: With an East German Case Study* (New York, 1965); on the history of COMECON and, in particular, the negotiations on trade and integration policy since the 1960s as well as the position of the USSR as a "weak dictator," see Randall W. Stone, *Satellites and Commissars: Strategy and Conflict in the Politics of Soviet-Bloc Trade* (Princeton, NJ, 1996).

reasons or because of the asymmetrical distribution of information in barter negotiations.[2]

Carrying on most of its foreign trade within COMECON also had disadvantages for the GDR. Above all, it limited the country's chances of using foreign trade as a stimulus for innovation and economic growth. The GDR therefore increasingly imported capital goods from the capitalist economies of the West. The result was a rapidly growing trade deficit. The regime was thus confronted with escalating hard currency debts. Attempts to intensify industrial cooperation within COMECON seemed initially to offer a partial solution to this problem, but the deficits of "socialist economic integration" became increasingly obvious in the 1960s. During the 1970s and 1980s, the dilemma was aggravated by a policy of consumer pacification and by the massive rise in prices for raw materials, especially oil, on international markets, which led to deterioration in East Germany's terms of trade with even the USSR. This dilemma was not resolved before the dissolution of the GDR, but a variety of economic policies were enacted in attempts to confront it.

This essay analyzes political responses to these problems during the 1970s and 1980s and the economic consequences of those responses. Viewing the history of economic policy from a macroeconomic perspective, it argues that there was a basic economic continuity despite the change of political leadership when Erich Honecker supplanted Walter Ulbricht and despite the termination of economic reforms in 1970–1. A closer look at the microlevel of industrial combines and foreign trade enterprises is beyond the scope of this essay, although it could certainly illuminate the different strategies and conflicting interests at the various levels of the planned economy's hierarchy.

BASIC DATA: THE SHIFT TO THE WEST

Foreign trade in Soviet-style planned economies was a highly political task because the dependence on foreign markets always carried an implicit risk of undermining national macroeconomic plans. Autarky was not an option for industrialized economies, especially not for a small country poorly supplied with raw materials like the GDR. COMECON, founded in 1949 mainly as a response to the Marshall Plan, seemed to offer a solution to this dilemma. It was officially designed as an organization of equal partners who shared

---

[2] For a brief discussion of relevant literature, see Ralf Ahrens, *Gegenseitige Wirtschaftshilfe? Die DDR im RGW – Strukturen und handelspolitische Strategien 1963–1976* (Cologne, 2000), 81–3. The second argument is extensively illustrated by Stone, *Satellites*.

the goals of increasing trade and stimulating the economic development of the member countries through the division of labor. In theory, disruptive foreign influences on national planning were to be eliminated by coordinating the member states' investment, production, and trade. Economic and political objectives seemed to be in accord as COMECON also facilitated the Eastern bloc countries' independence from the capitalist West.[3]

According to the official data published in the GDR's statistical yearbooks and internal compilations, the COMECON countries' share of East German foreign trade increased sharply after the economic division of Germany in the 1940s and steadily accounted for about two-thirds of the country's total trade volume. These figures were based, however, on economically unrealistic exchange rates between the GDR mark and Western currencies. The GDR mark was increasingly overvalued over time, whereas the conversion coefficients for intra-COMECON trade remained more realistic.[4] The ultimate reason for this disparity was the political dogma of a 1:1 parity between the East and West German marks, which was an expression of the GDR's pretension to cast itself as an equal competitor to the West German class enemy. Further distortions resulted from incomplete adjustments to exchange-rate revisions in the Western currency system. Consequently, the relative importance of East German trade with the Eastern bloc countries was increasingly overestimated. A revaluation of the GDR's foreign trade based on the real efforts of East German production units for export and the real cost of imports in GDR marks demonstrates that trade with nonsocialist countries accounted for an increasing share of the country's foreign trade from at least the mid-1960s (Table 6).[5]

These figures include the Federal Republic of Germany (FRG) among the GDRs nonsocialist trade partners, ignoring the legal peculiarities of so-called inner-German trade in order to give an economically realistic picture. Even after revaluation, the USSR stands as by far the largest import and export market with shares fluctuating around one-quarter of East German foreign trade in the 1980s.[6] The coefficients for revaluing the trade volumes

---

[3] For an extensive analysis of the basic economic mechanisms of COMECON as well as an historical overview, see Jozef M. van Brabant, *Economic Integration in Eastern Europe: A Handbook* (New York, 1989).

[4] Armin Volze, "Die gespaltene Valutamark. Anmerkungen zur Währungspolitik und Außenhandelsstatistik der DDR," *Deutschland Archiv* 32 (1999): 232–41. See also Oskar Schwarzer, "'Die Währung der DDR beruht [. . .] auf der gesunden Grundlage der sozialistischen Gesellschaftsordnung'. Wechselkurse zwischen Mark der DDR und D-Mark," in *Wirtschaftsordnung und Wirtschaftspolitik in Deutschland (1933–1993)*, ed. Jürgen Schneider and Wolfgang Harbrecht (Stuttgart, 1996), 173–205.

[5] Ahrens, *Gegenseitige Wirtschaftshilfe*, 60–8. This trend probably started in the late 1950s: there is no data of a comparable quality, however, to document it.

[6] On the recalculation of individual countries' shares, see ibid., 70.

Table 6. *Regional Shares of East German Exports and Imports (%), Based on Real Efforts of East German Production Units for Exports and the Real Cost of Imports in GDR Mark*

Exports	COMECON Countries	Other Socialist Countries	Non-Socialist Countries	Imports	COMECON Countries	Other Socialist Countries	Non-Socialist Countries
1965	66,4	3,7	29,9	1965	63,3	4,6	32,1
1966	64,4	5,2	30,3	1966	62,7	4,0	33,3
1967	65,6	4,8	29,5	1967	64,0	4,2	31,9
1968	63,2	4,6	32,2	1968	63,0	3,4	33,6
1969	59,2	4,4	36,4	1969	60,1	2,7	37,2
1970	61,1	4,7	34,2	1970	57,8	2,9	39,3
1971	59,5	4,5	36,0	1971	58,3	3,2	38,5
1972	61,4	3,1	35,5	1972	58,2	2,6	39,2
1973	60,2	2,8	37,0	1973	59,6	2,3	38,1
1974	59,8	3,3	36,9	1974	60,3	2,8	36,9
1975	60,2	3,4	36,5	1975	63,7	3,1	33,3
1976	57,3	3,2	39,5	1976	60,3	2,6	37,0
1977	58,9	3,4	37,6	1977	62,0	2,9	35,1
1980	56,1	2,8	41,1	1980	56,4	2,9	40,6
1985	40,5	1,2	58,2	1985	50,2	1,6	48,2
1988	43,9	1,6	54,5	1988	47,0	1,8	51,0

The figures presented here are recalculations of the data reported in *Statistisches Jahrbuch Außenhandel* (1989/I, 10–11; 1981/I, 10–11; 1978/I, S. 12–13; 1970, S. 8–9) using the coefficients put forward by Volze, "Die gespaltene Valutamark," 237–8. For methodological details, see Ahrens, *Gegenseitige Wirtschaftshilfe*, 65.

since 1971 are based on the average efforts of the various industrial branches and thus more or less come up to macroeconomic unit value ratios; for the earlier years, politically determined coefficients (*Richtungskoeffizienten*) can be used as a very rough approximation to purchasing-power relations. One methodological weakness in these calculations is the reliance on East German prices in measuring trade; those prices usually bore little relation to prices on world markets. Moreover, the rising share of Western countries in East German trade especially during the 1980s mainly reflects the loss of GDR industry's competitiveness on international markets – consequently, an integration of these figures into a calculation of gross domestic product would show sharply rising export shares, which normally stand as a positive indicator of a country's performance on international markets but in this case reflect the diminishing purchasing power of East German goods.[7] Nonetheless, the recalculated figures are more realistic than the older figures

---

[7] For calculations of the GDR's gross domestic product that are based on a roughly similar approach to that used in in revaluing its foreign trade, see Udo Ludwig and Reiner Stäglin, "Das Bruttoinlandsprodukt in der DDR und in der Bundesrepublik Deutschland von 1980 bis 1989 – Quellen,

in that they allow for a rough comparison of the GDR's trade with socialist and nonsocialist countries over a long time period. These "least bad figures" also reflect accurately the shift in East Berlin's political interest toward the latter during the closing years of the Ulbricht era and especially in the Honecker years. They thus also serve as evidence of the fact that the change in political leadership in 1970–1 did not bring about a fundamental and sustained change in regional trade policy.

Only at first glance does it seem astonishing that a trend toward disproportionate trade with the class enemy developed in parallel with a permanent loss of competitiveness of East German products. The East German metal-working and electrical industries' exports to the West, for example, had to be subsidized already in the early years of the GDR's existence, and both branches saw their traditionally high shares in international markets decline.[8] Consequently, the balance of trade with capitalist countries was "chronically negative" even during the 1950s, as GDR experts observed at the end of that decade.[9] Trade with the West nevertheless was a necessary evil to obtain goods that could not be produced domestically or obtained from the Eastern partners by barter and coordinated planning. But it was easier to manage exports to Eastern Europe, a seller's market for the GDR, than to the more competitive West. The disproportionate growth of trade with nonsocialist countries thus is to be explained as a result of an "import hunger" for high-quality goods meeting international technological standards that could not be satisfied by the less industrialized COMECON countries. This "hunger" was inherent to a centrally planned economy short of incentives to efficiency and innovation.[10] In short, East Germany's claims that it was following its own self-contained path of development and that it would outperform the West "without catching up" fell victim to economic necessity. Political efforts to escape the foreign trade dilemma – dependence on imports from the West while lacking competitive exports to pay for them – failed in the long run on account of structural economic reasons, as the following sections will demonstrate.

Methoden und Daten," in *Deutsch-deutsche Wirtschaft 1945 bis 1990. Strukturveränderungen, Innovationen und regionaler Wandel: Ein Vergleich*, ed. Lothar Baar and Dietmar Petzina (St. Katharinen, Germany, 1999), 530–81, esp. 546–51; Gerhard Heske, "Die gesamtwirtschaftliche Entwicklung in Ostdeutschland 1970 bis 2000 – Neue Ergebnisse einer volkswirtschaftlichen Gesamtrechnung," *Historical Social Research* 30, no. 2 (2005): 238–328, esp. 320.

[8] For an insightful case study, see Johannes Bähr, *Industrie im geteilten Berlin (1945–1990). Die elektrotechnische Industrie und der Maschinenbau im Ost-West-Vergleich: Branchenentwicklung, Technologien und Handlungsstrukturen* (Munich, 2001), esp. 151–3, 356, 463–4.

[9] Staatliche Plankommission (hereafter referred to as SPK), Abt. Außenhandel und Innerdeutscher Handel, Analysen der Entwicklung des Außenhandels 1951–1958, 18.1.1960, Bundesarchiv Berlin (hereafter referred to as BAB), DE 1/21212.

[10] János Kornai, *The Socialist System: The Political Economy of Communism* (Princeton, NJ, 1992), 346–8.

FOREIGN TRADE AND THE ECONOMIC REFORMS OF THE 1960s

It was not the case that, as one historian has recently argued, only "[a]fter the failures of Ulbricht's reforms, SED [Sozialistische Einheitspartei Deutschlands] leaders concluded that the key to economic growth lay outside the planned economy – in technology transfers from the West."[11] Ulbricht told the Soviets in 1970 that the GDR was borrowing heavily in the West to finance imports of machinery and technology. This shift in economic strategy had its roots in economic reforms initiated in the early 1960s. The core idea of the New Economic System launched in 1963 was to simulate market mechanisms without challenging the primacy of central planning. The technological level of East German industry and the efficiency of production units were to be stimulated by so-called economic levers, especially the profits of the publicly owned factories or, later, combines on the basis of a revised pricing system. These reforms were to be introduced incrementally after "economic experiments" in individual enterprises had been carried out. In practice, they soon came under criticism from SED functionaries, and implementation was impeded by the inconsistencies of the planning system and the continuing interest on the part of production units to hide information and propose "soft plans." A new phase of reforms, the Economic System of Socialism announced in 1967, only complicated the situation: a discretionary investment policy resulted in disproportions between the various industrial branches, a lack of consumer goods, and a growing balance-of-payments deficit in hard currencies. The period of economic reform was terminated in 1970–1, when the conservative majority in the Politburo replaced Ulbricht with Honecker as SED party leader and the traditional planning system was more or less restored.[12]

During the various phases of reform policy, foreign trade was increasingly regarded as an important stimulus to economic growth. Before the mid-1960s, the international division of labor had been viewed mainly as a means to close gaps in supply or to realize economies of scale. In official rhetoric, the integration of production, and also of research and development activities, within COMECON always played a key role in the new strategy. But soon it became obvious that the structural weaknesses of COMECON integration would be hard to overcome. Moreover, the partner countries were often unreliable suppliers. After the erection of the Berlin Wall, even

---

[11] Jonathan R. Zatlin, *The Currency of Socialism: Money and Political Culture in East Germany* (Cambridge, 2007), 61.
[12] On the reforms, see André Steiner, *Die DDR-Wirtschaftsreform der sechziger Jahre: Konflikt zwischen Effizienz- und Machtkalkül* (Berlin, 1999).

the Soviet leadership was less willing to make up for short-term shortages of raw materials and other goods.

Under these circumstances, it is not surprising that plans to raise the quality and technological level of East German export products focused in large part on the "capitalist world market." To be sure, the SED still viewed industrial specialization and cooperation within COMECON as a serious task, and the policy of bloc integration was seen as a path toward achieving greater independence from capitalist trading partners in the long run. But after 1964, when the first draft plan for reforming East Germany's foreign trade system was approved, the above-average increase of trade with Western industrialized countries became a more or less official political objective that was intended to compensate for problems of supply and technology in trade with the other COMECON countries. This was a temporary policy focusing on GDR exports necessary to pay for imports that could not be bought from the preferred Eastern bloc trading partners. Nevertheless, the orientation toward export products that met international standards at least implicitly always took the technological level of capitalist economies as a benchmark.

In the last years of Ulbricht's leadership, the East German government adopted a conscious strategy of import-led growth by buying investment goods from the West. This shift in policy was framed in cautious terms, and trade and industrial cooperation with the other COMECON states, especially the Soviet Union, remained an ideological priority. Nevertheless, trade figures pointed to escalating imports of investment goods and raw materials from Western Europe, particularly after 1968. Imports from capitalist countries billed in convertible currencies would, however, have to be financed sooner or later by exports in the opposite direction. The idea of import-led modernization ran up against its limits on this point; the GDR's various attempts at reform had not overcome the structural weaknesses of the centrally planned economy. Incentives intended to redirect East German manufacturing enterprises toward an announced "confrontation" with international markets – above all, the provision allowing them to integrate their hard currency earnings in their operating results and the possibility of closer collaboration with export firms that held branch monopolies in foreign trade – had been introduced half-heartedly. By the end of the 1960s, the international competitiveness of East German industry in traditionally important export branches with relatively high value added had deteriorated. The machine tool, chemical, and electrical industries failed to meet their export targets; that failure, in turn, limited the hard currency available for importing indispensable raw materials and investment goods. The alternative to earning convertible currency from exports was to borrow it. Already in June 1970, the GDR's growing hard currency debts prompted calls for stricter regulation of foreign trade, and it was one of the reasons for the abandonment of reform and the removal of Ulbricht from power.[13]

THE 1970S: A CHANGE IN STRATEGY?

Although Ulbricht's replacement by Honecker definitely marked a break in policy on investment, consumption, planning, and social welfare,[14] its impact on trade and debt should not be overestimated. To be sure, officials at the planning commission and various ministries attempted to limit borrowing from the West by increasing trade with the East in the early years of Honecker's tenure. That effort was also in line with Honecker's move toward closer ideological alignment with the Soviet Union and reversal of Ulbricht's attempt to pursue a more independent policy at least in economic matters. In the spring of 1971, Gerhard Schürer, the head of the planning commission, provided the Politburo with a draft of a new five-year plan that simply cut imports from nonsocialist countries by 0.2 percent each year and envisioned an increase in exports of more than 10 percent. This would have reduced the hard currency debt substantially within a few years. But even on paper, the various industrial ministries could not find a way to work out realistic current plans without incurring negative trade balances.[15]

East German officials soon recognized that imports from COMECON countries could not fill the technology and quality gaps, to say nothing of the more or less permanent bottlenecks affecting all branches of industry. The COMECON member states' adoption of a "complex program" designed to encourage "socialist economic integration" in 1971 did not significantly resolve these problems. The division of labor among the Eastern bloc countries tended to conserve technological levels and methods of production. Moreover, East German manufacturers lost market shares in even the less developed East European countries that were following a strategy of industrialization by imitation. Consequently, the East German share in exports of machines and equipment within COMECON decreased from

[13] For details, see Ahrens, *Gegenseitige Wirtschaftshilfe*, 133–248, 266; Ralf Ahrens, "Normsetzungsanspruch und Weltmarktdynamik: Reformversuche in der Außenwirtschaftssteuerung der DDR in den sechziger Jahren," in *Sozialistische Wirtschaftsreformen: Tschechoslowakei und DDR im Vergleich*, ed. Christoph Boyer (Frankfurt, 2006), 357–93; Steiner, *DDR-Wirtschaftsreform*, passim; André Steiner, "Exogene Impulse für den Strukturwandel in der DDR," in Baar and Petzina, *Deutsch-Deutsche Wirtschaft*, 46–72.
[14] André Steiner, *Von Plan zu Plan: Eine Wirtschaftsgeschichte der DDR* (Munich, 2004), 165–91.
[15] Ahrens, *Gegenseitige Wirtschaftshilfe*, 259.

34.2 percent in 1960 to 23.8 percent in 1973. According to trade statistics, though, industrial specialization seemed to be a success. In 1980, more than half of the East German machinery and electrical industries' exports to the Soviet Union were classified as "specialized" manufactures, as a result of negotiations on bolstering economies of scale by concentrating production lines in individual countries. But these ostensible successes of socialist economic integration were largely limited to older, more traditional industrial products. Moreover, specialization created new dependencies that became obvious when, for example, Soviet suppliers did not deliver machinery necessary for the manufacture of East German products intended for export to nonsocialist countries. Ironically, Eastern bloc economic integration tended to aggravate the problem of indebtedness to the capitalist countries, the very problem it was supposed to help alleviate.[16]

Trade problems with the planned economies of the Eastern bloc thus continued to force attention to trade with the West, but the issue of hard currency debt remained unresolved. The planning experts' response to that issue can hardly be called a strategy and reflected the absence of alternatives. They assiduously drafted plans that mandated an increase of exports to the West by as much as one-third in 1974 and 1975 while imports were to be reduced substantially. Economic reality was not willing to adjust to the plan; the import-export ratio ended up being the opposite of what had been envisioned.[17] One reason for that outcome was a sharp rise in the prices of raw materials on the world market. Moreover, Honecker had begun to try to win popular support for the SED regime by increasing social welfare benefits and supplying citizens with more consumer goods. But it was not only the transfer of national income from investment to consumption that drove the GDR into an irresolvable debt dilemma. Although price increases for imports contributed to increased indebtedness, the structural importance of those increases should not be overstated. Adjusted for inflation, the share of investment goods in total imports from the member states of the Organisation for Economic Co-operation and Development (excluding the FRG) actually increased in the years 1971–5 despite decreasing in nominal terms. In the next five years, it dipped further – from 31.4 to 29.7 percent – on account of a rise in the share of food imports, but that trend was offset by increased imports of investment goods from the FRG.[18]

---

[16] Ralf Ahrens, "Spezialisierungsinteresse und Integrationsaversion im Rat für Gegenseitige Wirtschaftshilfe: Der DDR-Werkzeugmaschinenbau in den 1970er-Jahren," *Jahrbuch für Wirtschaftsgeschichte* 2008, pt. 2, 86–90.

[17] Ahrens, *Gegenseitige Wirtschaftshilfe*, 261–2.

[18] Deutsches Institut für Wirtschaftsforschung, *Handbuch DDR-Wirtschaft*, 3rd ed. (Reinbek, Germany, 1977), 357; Deutsches Institut für Wirtschaftsforschung, *Handbuch DDR-Wirtschaft*, 4th ed. (Reinbek, Germany, 1984), 401, 409.

An increasing though not quantifiable portion of imported machinery was undoubtedly used for the production of consumer goods; thus, the machinery did not enlarge the export-relevant capital stock. In any event, the investment goods import figures reflected the fact that since about 1973, Ulbricht's strategy of import-led modernization and rationalization gained in importance again although it obviously led into a vicious circle: neither traditional nor new exports of important branches like machine building and optical products could meet Western standards of technology, quality, terms of delivery, after-sales service, and availability of spare parts. At the same time, East German industry needed steadily more supplies from the West to turn out export products and to bridge the widening East-West technology gap.[19]

The GDR was not alone in stepping off the path of independent socialist economic development in the 1970s. Other COMECON member states also pursued industrial modernization by importing Western investment goods and technology, and they, too, were unable to finance those purchases with export revenues.[20] The basic problem of trade deficits with Western countries was inherent to an economic system short of incentives for efficiency and innovation. Economic planners could try to mitigate the situation by shifting resources, including hard currency holdings, from consumption to investment. In the second half of the 1970s, Schürer warned with increasing urgency that, within a few years, the GDR would not be able to pay back credits in convertible currency. The result would be growing dependence on Western banks and fewer alternatives for funding desperately needed investment. From time to time, Schürer tried to moderate the policy of consumption by proposing reductions in imports of consumer goods. Günter Mittag, the SED Secretary for Economics, and Margarete Wittkowski, the state bank president, joined him occasionally, but they too failed to persuade Honecker to change direction. Instead, the import of investment goods had to be cut, which intensified the problems of modernizing industry and infrastructure.[21]

[19] See, e.g., Arbeitsgruppe für Organisation und Inspektion beim Vorsitzenden des Ministerrates, Information über Auswirkungen von Reklamationen, 2.5.1973, BAB, DC 20/4416. The shortcomings of the GDR's exports to the West were observed in West German literature in more or less the same manner; see Deutsches Institut für Wirtschaftsforschung, *Handbuch DDR-Wirtschaft*, 296.

[20] Kazimierz Poznanski, *Technology, Competition, and the Soviet Bloc in the World Market* (Berkeley, CA, 1987); Derek H. Aldcroft and Steven Morewood, *Economic Change in Eastern Europe since 1918* (Aldershot, UK, 1995), 162–5.

[21] Hans-Hermann Hertle, "Die Diskussion der ökonomischen Krisen in der Führungsspitze der SED," in *Der Plan als Befehl und Fiktion: Wirtschaftsführung in der DDR: Gespräche und Analysen*, ed. Theo Pirker, M. Rainer Lepsius, Rainer Weinert, and Hans-Hermann Hertle (Opladen, 1995), 309–45; interview with Gerhard Schürer and Siegfried Wenzel, in ibid., 67–120; Zatlin, *Currency*, 92; Steiner, *DDR-Wirtschaftsreform*, 544; Armin Volze, "Zur Devisenverschuldung der DDR – Entstehung,

Eschewing the necessary reorientation of trade and investment policy, GDR officials responded to the country's mounting indebtedness by establishing special crisis management bodies. A Politburo economic commission created in 1976 and a working group on the balance of payments – both under Mittag's leadership – were mainly occupied with concrete problems of exports and currency deficits, as was the "small circle" of Honecker's advisors.[22] The mere existence of these bodies was a sign that the problems of foreign trade and currency deficits were given top priority. But task forces making ad hoc decisions were far from a systematic approach to structural problems. The GDR's inflexible political system not only ignored long-term economic rationality but also limited the response to structural economic problems to piecemeal measures.

THE 1980s: DRIVEN BY DEBT

As long as the fundamental problems continued, task forces could hardly stop the increase of debt, nor could the half-hearted institutional reforms of the foreign trade apparatus implemented in the early 1980s. The same applies to the extension of political control and ideological appeals to managers and workers that fill the files from that decade. Short-term economic stimulus measures also failed to live up to expectations. The government tried to make banks adopt strict control of cash receipts. It also urged enterprises to regard the earning of hard currency as the main target for their exports, but they still gave priority to meeting planning targets for gross sales volume.[23] Only under massive pressure from outside could positive trade balances with the West be achieved temporarily: Western banks stopped credits to Eastern bloc countries after Poland and Romania suffered liquidity crises, and the USSR scaled back its petroleum sales at below-market prices to the GDR.[24]

In response to the massive international increases in the price of oil in the early 1970s, the Soviet Union had imposed a revision of the COMECON price formula in 1974. As a result, the Soviets adjusted the price of oil and

---

Bewältigung und Folgen," in *Die Endzeit der DDR-Wirtschaft: Analysen zur Wirtschafts-, Sozial- und Umweltpolitik*, ed. Eberhard Kuhrt (Opladen, 1999), 157.

[22] See Hertle, "Die Diskussion," 311; Dietrich Lemke, *Handel & Wandel: Lebenserinnerungen eines DDR-Außenhändlers 1952–1995*, 2nd ed. (Zeuthen, Germany, 2004), 839–54.

[23] Gerhard Beil, "Bericht über die Wirksamkeit der Vorgaben für die Valutaeinnahmen aus Exporten an die Kombinate," 13.5.1982, Stiftung Archiv der Parteien und Massenorganisationen der DDR im Bundesarchiv, Berlin (hereafter referred to as SAPMO-BA), DY 30/2661, 259–68. On the institutional arrangements, see Maria Haendcke-Hoppe, "Schwerpunkte der Außenwirtschaftsreformen in der DDR," in *Außenwirtschaftssysteme und Außenwirtschaftsreformen sozialistischer Länder: Ein intrasystemarer Vergleich*, ed. Maria Haendcke-Hoppe (Berlin, 1988), 91–100.

[24] See Volze, "Zur Devisenverschuldung"; Deutsche Bundesbank, ed., *Die Zahlungsbilanz der ehemaligen DDR 1975 bis 1989* (Frankfurt, 1999).

other raw materials to international price movements more quickly than previously. The GDR thus had to supply larger amounts of export products, especially machinery, to obtain indispensable imports of raw materials from its Soviet partner. Between 1975 and 1985, East German exports to the USSR, adjusting for price increases, almost doubled to pay for imports that increased by only 7 percent in real terms.[25] But East German planners found a way to turn the time lag that still existed between international price movements and Soviet adjustments into their most important source of hard currency. Substituting brown coal for oil as a fuel for domestic and industrial use, they sold oil products for hard currency in the West or for *Verrechnungseinheiten* (accounting units) to the FRG. Fossil fuels accounted for roughly 30 percent of GDR exports to nonsocialist countries in 1983; machinery, which had made up about one-quarter of East German exports to nonsocialist states ten years earlier, accounted for less than 10 percent.[26] Leaving aside the question of its ecological costs, the policy of substituting brown coal for fuel oil consumed huge sums of investment funds and generated only short-term hard currency earnings. At the same time, the East German economy as a whole lost money necessary to modernize other sectors like the machinery industry.[27] And even the earnings from the sale of oil products only slowed the growth of net debt for a few years while the interest burden grew.[28]

In one sense, the oil program was typical of Mittag's general policy of aiming for immediate hard currency revenues rather than relying on austerity as a means to redirect resources to investment or research and development. Consequently, East German industry had to come to terms with even more limited imports of Western capital goods and technology.[29] In the medium term, this could only weaken the GDR's position on international markets. Schürer concluded as early as August 1982 that the Politburo's instructions to increase exports to nonsocialist countries could not be followed on account

---

[25] Ahrens, *Gegenseitige Wirtschaftshilfe*, 332 (price basis of these GDR calculations: 1970). Nevertheless, it is open to question whether this "valuable material" could really have been sold to the West, as Zatlin argues (*Currency*, 108).

[26] Figures from Dieter Lösch and Peter Plötz, "Die Bedeutung des Bereichs Kommerzielle Koordinierung für die Volkswirtschaft der DDR," in *Deutscher Bundestag, 12. Wahlperiode: Beschlußempfehlung und Bericht des 1. Untersuchungsausschusses*, Drucksache 12/7600, Anhang, 132–45.

[27] See Harm G. Schröter, "Ölkrisen und Reaktionen in der chemischen Industrie beider deutscher Staaten," in *Innovationsverhalten und Entscheidungsstrukturen: Vergleichende Studien zur wirtschaftlichen Entwicklung im geteilten Deutschland*, ed. Johannes Bähr and Dietmar Petzina (Berlin, 1996), 115–24; Steiner, *Von Plan zu Plan*, 198–200.

[28] Oskar Schwarzer, *Sozialistische Zentralplanwirtschaft in der SBZ/DDR: Ergebnisse eines ordnungspolitischen Experiments (1945–1989)* (Stuttgart, 1999), 154; cf. Volze, "Zur Devisenverschuldung," 162–4.

[29] Zatlin, *Currency*, 105.

of the long-known constellation of problems with quality, technology, marketing, and service. The situation seemed all the more dramatic because the GDR was then facing the threat of an absolute credit boycott by Western lenders. It was above all the electrical and machine tool industries – branches that should have had high levels of value added – that were having trouble earning hard currency.[30] Inadequate export earnings meant less financial scope for investment. The East German industry thus found itself caught in a vicious circle: growing wear and tear on equipment led to higher costs and lower product quality, which in turn increased the difficulty of earning the export revenues needed for capital investment. Additionally, the costs of selling export products to the West – sales commissions, marketing, and transportation – rose sharply in the 1980s, as did penalties for late deliveries and defective goods.[31]

The growing reliance on improvisation in response to grave structural problems is also illustrated by the Commercial Coordination department (Bereich Kommerzielle Koordinierung, commonly known as KoKo) headed by Alexander Schalck-Golodkowski. Independent of the regular foreign trade apparatus and under Mittag's direct control, this institution conducted a rapidly growing part of the GDR's trade with capitalist partners. KoKo's more or less legal methods of operation made it a flexible instrument to redress acute shortages of hard currency or particular products, but KoKo could ultimately do nothing to improve the competitiveness of East German industry.[32] That held also for cooperative ventures with West German companies. Buying licenses to produce Western consumer goods in the GDR and exporting part of the production back to the West had by and large not worked as a strategy to improve the GDR's balance of payments in the 1970s. That strategy was used increasingly in the 1980s to satisfy the domestic demand for modern consumer goods. As a result, however, the GDR – the most industrialized economy of the Eastern bloc – served as a cheap subcontractor for West German capitalism instead of buying simple consumer goods from less developed economies.[33]

The decline in the price of oil on international markets in the late 1980s precipitated the GDR's final economic crisis. In the years 1986–8, the

---

[30] Protokoll der Sitzung der Arbeitsgruppe Zahlungsbilanz beim Politbüro des ZK der SED am 16. August 1982, SAPMO-BA, DY 30/266, 289–95.

[31] Zatlin, *Currency*, 166.

[32] See Lösch and Plötz, "Die Bedeutung des Bereichs Kommerzielle Koordinierung"; Matthias Judt, "Schalcks KoKo: Mythos und Realität des Bereichs Kommerzielle Koordinierung," in *Revolution und Vereinigung 1989/90: Als in Deutschland die Realität die Phantasie überholte*, ed. Klaus-Dietmar Henke (Munich, 2009), 307–15.

[33] Zatlin, *Currency*, 99; Jörg Roesler, "Der Einfluss der Außenwirtschaftspolitik auf die Beziehungen DDR-Bundesrepublik: Die achtziger Jahre," *Deutschland Archiv* 26 (1993): 558–72.

GDR earned DM 4 billion less than had been anticipated in the five-year plan passed shortly before.[34] Because of the time lag in COMECON's adjustments to world market prices, the prices of raw materials from the USSR continued to rise. The GDR thus had to increase its machinery exports to obtain the supplies it needed. The Soviet Union in effect still subsidized its East German partner, though, by accepting export goods that probably could not have been sold in the West.[35] Industrial goods that could take the place of oil products in trade with the nonsocialist countries simply did not exist. East German manufacturers of heavy equipment, for example, were unable to increase their exports; indeed, their export sales dropped by approximately 30 percent between 1986 and 1988.[36]

In the last few years of its existence, the GDR obviously exported whatever it could at any price. According to East Berlin's official figures, the GDR's trade balance with Western countries had improved from the 1970s to the 1980s.[37] Leaving aside the question whether those figures are realistic – the currency basis is not specified in the statistical agency's publications – the possible improvement was certainly not sufficient to offset the loss of earning power demonstrated by the disastrous performance of East German industry on the world market. The average real effort to earn one unit of convertible currency had accelerated moderately in the 1970s but then almost doubled between 1982 and 1988.[38]

New products from traditional export branches like the machine building and electrical industries not only failed to achieve the level of profitability anticipated in the government's plans but even fell short of the average earning power of export goods. In addition to the well-known problems in quality, service, and terms of delivery, these supposedly new products were not up to international technological standards.[39] That was not really surprising, given that the performance of East German industry had long been measured by Western standards, which led to widespread copying of Western innovations. Western advances in microelectronics and other research-intensive new technologies, combined with the export restrictions

---

[34] Zatlin, *Currency*, 156.

[35] Christoph Buchheim, "Die Achillesferse der DDR – der Außenhandel," in *Überholen ohne einzuholen: Die DDR-Wirtschaft als Fußnote der deutschen Geschichte?* ed. André Steiner (Berlin, 2006), 99.

[36] Niederschrift zur Beratung der Wirtschaftskommission des Politbüros des ZK der SED am 28. August 1989, BAB, DE 1/58033.

[37] Statistisches Amt der DDR, ed., *Statistisches Jahrbuch der Deutschen Demokratischen Republik 1990* (Berlin, 1990), 276.

[38] Volze, "Die gespaltene Valutamark," 238; Zatlin, *Currency*, 186; Ahrens, *Gegenseitige Wirtschaftshilfe*, 326.

[39] Floßmann to Mittag, 24.10.1986, SAPMO-BA, DY 30/IV 2/2.101/120. On the individual branches, see André Steiner, "Ausgangsbedingungen für die Transformation der DDR-Wirtschaft: Kombinate als künftige Marktunternehmen?" *Zeitschrift für Unternehmensgeschichte* 54 (2009): 155–6.

imposed by the Coordinating Committee for Multilateral Export Controls (COCOM), accelerated the long-running decline of the GDR's industrial competitiveness.

It is thus no wonder that in the summer of 1989 the Economic Commission of the Politburo acknowledged that not even in theory would the metal processing industry be able to achieve "important increases" of exports to the West; an increase in exports of approximately 20 percent from 1989 to 1990, the commission calculated, would be the minimum necessary to keep the GDR solvent.[40] Consequently, Schürer and other experts sought finally in October 1989 to disillusion the Politburo, stating that the prerequisites for achieving the export surpluses necessary to "maintain the balance of payments" simply did not exist.[41] Only a few days later, the new SED General Secretary, Egon Krenz, was informed by his Soviet counterpart, Mikhail Gorbachev, that the Soviet Union was neither able nor willing to step in as lender of last resort. Gorbachev found it hard even to guarantee the supplies of raw materials already agreed upon.[42]

By the time of the opening of the Berlin Wall, the East German economy still was liquid, but its collapse was clearly only a matter of time. The GDR's absolute indebtedness in convertible currencies represented 175 percent of exports to this trade region in 1989,[43] and it was easily foreseeable that the debt burden would grow further. Trade surpluses in inconvertible currencies like the transferable ruble, which was used as an accounting unit for intra-COMECON trade, obviously could not compensate balance-of-payments deficits with capitalist countries. Moreover, the Eastern bloc's protected trade system was rapidly dissolving along with the communist regimes that had created it. A January 1990 COMECON meeting recommended that trade between the member countries in the future be conducted in convertible currency and at current world market prices. Half a year later, the former communist superpower announced its decision to follow these principles as of 1991.[44] "Socialist economic integration" became history shortly after the GDR lost its most important economic ally.

---

[40] Niederschrift zur Beratung der Wirtschaftskommission des Politbüros des ZK der SED am 28. August 1989, BAB, DE 1/58033.

[41] Hans-Hermann Hertle, *Der Fall der Mauer: Die unbeabsichtigte Selbstauflösung des SED-Staates* (Opladen, 1996), 145; Gerhard Schürer, Gerhard Beil, Alexander Schalck, Ernst Höfner, and Arno Donda, "Analyse der ökonomischen Lage der DDR mit Schlußfolgerungen, 30.10.1989," reprinted in Hertle, *Der Fall der Mauer*, 454–5.

[42] Hertle, *Fall*, 149–53.

[43] Steiner, *Von Plan zu Plan*, 225. On the various calculations of the GDR's balance of payments and net debt to Western countries, see Volze, "Zur Devisenverschuldung"; Zatlin, *Currency*, 123; Deutsche Bundesbank, *Zahlungsbilanz*.

[44] Jozef M. van Brabant, "The Demise of the CMEA – The Agony of Inaction," *Osteuropa-Wirtschaft* 36 (1991): 234–54. On the historical background, see Stone, *Satellites*, 204–46; Mark Kramer, "The

CONCLUSION

The permanent dilemma of East German foreign trade policy, which ultimately led to overindebtedness, can only be understood if one considers
the interrelation of its trade with the East and the West. Trade with capitalist countries was always a necessary evil to compensate the shortcomings
of intra-COMECON trade and Eastern bloc economic coordination. It
became a fundamental problem when the GDR began to rely on imports
that could not be amortized by competitive exports. Trade figures and trade
policy show that the East German economy was lagging behind its Western
competitors from an early point in time; the gap widened more rapidly
in the later decades. The balance-of-trade deficits with Western countries
were ultimately the result of the lack of incentives for efficiency and innovation in the East German economy and in the Eastern bloc trading system
as a whole.

Within this framework, the Soviet Union guaranteed the GDR's economic existence by supplying raw materials and accepting East German
export products at relatively beneficial price relations. When those terms
changed in the mid-1980s, the last pillar of a fragile economic structure
began to crumble. The political debates of the 1980s, when Mittag's policy of maximizing short-term hard currency earnings came under criticism
from Schürer and the Stasi,[45] thus focused only on which option would postpone the final decline the longest. All in all, the shortcomings of economic
planning and of socialist economic integration could not be overcome by
shifts in policy. Nevertheless, the move from medium-term economic programs to short-term muddling through is a sign that not only was the
GDR's economic system trapped by the absence of alternatives but also that
its political system was incapable of institutional change beyond attempts
at crisis management that were dependent on the personal authority of
individual officials.

Collapse of East European Communism and the Repercussions within the Soviet Union (Part 3),"
Journal of Cold War Studies 7 (2005): 3–96.
[45] Zatlin, *Currency*, 190–7; Hertle, "Die Diskussion."

10

Ulbricht's and Honecker's Volksstaat?

The Common Economic History of Militarized Regimes

JEFFREY KOPSTEIN

You can do anything with bayonets except sit on them.

Is there a common economic history of Germany's two twentieth-century dictatorships, East Germany and Nazi Germany? Although I answer in the affirmative, this is a question full of potential minefields, not only because of the obvious differences between the two cases – Nazi Germany started a global war and committed genocide and East Germany did not – but also because of the significant asymmetries in the historiographies of the two cases. It is certainly not my intention to play these differences down. And yet, there is something about the economic history of these two cases that does merit comparison, even beyond the similarities of scope and scale of political authority. Both were militarized societies whose leaderships were constrained in their economic policy choices by popular opinion as mediated through everyday resistance. In both cases, a virtual flood of secret police and political reports about popular opinion made their way through the political hierarchy. In the Nazi dictatorship, political rule was stabilized and everyday resistance was negated, or at least muted, through racism, war, and plunder. Nazism could therefore only fall from "without." The East German regime did not have the "luxury" of war, extreme nationalism, or conquest to act as internal stabilizing factors and was thus paralyzed by everyday resistance, ultimately becoming susceptible to revolution from "within." The commonality, to the extent that it exists, lies in the dynamics of mobilization, constraint, plunder, and war (or absence of war) that the elites of two militarized economies confronted. The East

For Professor Andrew Janos.

German case illustrates with special poignancy the quotation cited at the beginning of the essay (variously attributed either to Napoleon or Thomas Hardy).

This essay is therefore a study in historical political economy rather than economic history per se. In such a short contribution, the arguments I offer can only be adumbrated in outline form. I tender them not to test them in a rigorous fashion but rather for the purpose of exploring and advancing the militarist paradigm as an alternative to developmentalism. The comparison is also useful for highlighting the similarities and differences of the economic histories of the two German dictatorships; it is through analogical thinking that social reality is put into perspective. Even here, however, any complete catalog of the similarities and of the two twentieth-century dictatorships must remain beyond the scope of this essay. I restrict my focus to the impact of everyday resistance on militarized economies. The evidence I offer comes almost completely from the research of others and my own work in East German economic history.

DEVELOPMENTALISM OR MILITARISM?

What was the East German economy? Students of communist countries have generally assimilated the experience of these economies to that of the West for purposes of comparison. The state elites of backward economies, so the argument runs, have little choice but to adapt through "development" and "catching up" to those more advanced economies of the global order. Communism is simply a more extreme and (in the short run) efficient means of the state-led developmentalist model familiar from other economies on the global periphery. Alexander Gerschenkron was one of the early giants of this way of thinking about the Soviet economic experience.[1] In his view, the Soviet Union, in using the strong arm of the state to accumulate capital for industrialization, performed essentially the same function as the Russian state it had succeeded. The entire field of comparative economics, as it unfolded during the Cold War era, essentially accepted the view of the communist world as a variant of developmentalism. It is true that the big divide in comparative economics was between "market" and "planned" economies – with the right championing the former and the left the latter – but the purpose of analyzing this divide was to assess their strengths and weakness as models of development.

---

[1] Alexander Gerschenkron, "Economic Backwardness in Historical Perspective," in *Economic Backwardness in Historical Perspective: A Book of Essays* (Cambridge, MA, 1962), 5–30.

In his corpus of work, the political economist Andrew Janos has proposed an alternative.[2] Acknowledging the contribution of the developmentalist approach to communist political economy, he returns to the question of the fundamental purpose of the economy under communism. In particular, he questions the basic assumptions of the developmentalist model. Whereas the elites of backward economies may choose the path of development and play the game of moving up the international hierarchy of nations through capital accumulation and increasing the domestic consumption of their population, it may be equally or more rational for them to choose to play a completely different game – that of military conquest.

According to Janos, "the most significant alternative to development is the militarization of society with the purpose of external appropriation, or still more generally put, for reconstructing the external environment of a political elite."[3] It is unimportant that such a society is run by the military, but what matters more is that the "cultural norms, social organization, and political institutions alike are adjusted to the 'external orientation' of the state, which the state will use to justify its very existence."[4] Janos's inspiration for this way of thinking draws on the nineteenth-century social theorist Herbert Spencer. Some form of industry is required to field an army for conquest,

but this industry is fundamentally different from the one we find in the history of England. For in a militarized society, "the industrial part continues to be a permanent commissariat, existing solely to supply the needs of governmental-military structures and having left for itself enough merely for maintenance. Hence the political regulation of its activities." If the idiom of modernization is applicable at all, it will apply to the means of destruction and military power rather than the means of producing economic wealth and international economic competitiveness.[5]

Janos attempts to "disentangle" the study of Germany and Russia from what he sees as the deficiencies of the developmentalist model. After dealing with the rise and demise of the German militarism from 1890 to 1945, he turns to the Soviet experience. In thinking about world revolution, Janos maintains, one strand of communist thought tended to global insurrectionism and created the communist international to bring about the new order. Fairly quickly, however, the Soviet elite saw the flaws in this design and

---

[2] Andrew Janos, "What Was Communism? A Retrospective in Comparative Analysis," *Communist and Post Communist Studies* 29 (1996): 1–24; "Modernization or Militarization: Germany and Russia as Great Powers," *German Politics and Society* 14 (1996): 31–65; *East-Central Europe in the Modern World: The Politics of the Borderlands from Pre-to Post-Communism* (Stanford, CA, 2001).

[3] Janos, "Modernization or Militarization," 33.

[4] Ibid.

[5] Ibid.

turned to an etatist approach to the revolution, one that turned away decisively from the incrementalism and private property favored by Bukharin and his allies, to a forced draft industrialization drive. This is what convinced economists and historians that what Stalin was doing was the development of a backward economy. Unlike the English model, Janos writes, "this project was not only driven *by* the state, it was also undertaken *for* the state. . . . The historian of World War I may also describe it as the Rathenau-Ludendorf-Falkenhayn mobilization plan of 1916 writ large."[6] Stalinism, for Janos, was ultimately about extending Soviet power geopolitically for the purposes of empire building and, when the opportunity presented itself, acquiring new resources in the European heartland either through revolution or, preferably, through occupation and conquest. These were elites who viewed their own populations in instrumental terms, and economic development in the Western sense of creating broader public wealth domestically always took second place to the more fundamental "external" mission of "building socialism" first in the Soviet Union, then Eastern Europe, and on to the rest of the world.

The modal economic history of a militarized regime therefore involves a cycle of mobilization of society; accumulation of capital; rapid armament; a thrust into the heartland of the enemy in order to plunder and replenish supplies; and then a period of rest, recovery, and consolidation until the cycle begins again. These stages constitute the basic outline of the approach.

How does the East German experience fit into this schema? Although Janos does not discuss the East German case in any detail, it is relatively easy to assimilate it to the general model. In the first stage, until the early 1950s, Soviet occupation forces plundered East Germany's industrial stock and then incorporated the country's economy into the Soviet orbit as a contributor to the communist security sphere. The work of Rainer Karlsch is crucial in this regard.[7] East Germany's economy was initially hobbled by the Soviets both in terms of industrial stock seized and reparation from ongoing production. In subsequent stages, the German Democratic Republic (GDR) devoted considerable resources to creating a military and supporting the Soviet military presence within Germany (by Karlsch's account averaging approximately 11 percent of national income per year through the early 1980s). Although its weapons production always remained small, the GDR contributed in important ways to the Soviet munitions programs, especially in such fields as optics, chemicals, and machine building. The GDR made

---

[6] Ibid., 50; emphasis in the original.
[7] Rainer Karlsch, *Allein bezahlt? Die Reparationsleistungen in der SBZ/DDR 1945–1953* (Berlin, 1993); "Wirtschaftliche Belastungen durch bewaffnete Organe," unpublished paper (1997).

considerable contributions in personnel and military and intelligence expertise to Soviet adventures throughout the Third World and provided it with crucial raw materials for constructing atomic weapons from its uranium mines in Wismut.

Perhaps just as important, however, was the militarization of East German society and culture through the masculinization of public discourse and the creation of the paramilitary Kampfgruppen der Arbeiterklasse (Combat Groups of the Working Class), the Gesellschaft für Sport und Technik (Society for Sport and Technology), and a string of Olympic gold medals that owed as much to the state pharmaceuticals *Kombinat* as to athletic prowess. Although lip service continued to be paid to the "insurrectionist" tradition of Luxemburg and Liebknecht (with hundreds of "Rosa Luxembourg streets" and "Wilhelm Liebknecht primary schools"), the statist model was never seriously questioned. It is not only the amount of resources devoted to the military per se that categorizes an economy as either developmentalist or militarized but rather the economy's fundamental purpose. As Aaron Friedberg has shown, the United States has spent huge amounts on the military at various points in its history, but the orientations of its elites and masses and the structure of its institutions precluded its transformation into a "garrison state."[8]

There were, then, similarities in the basic economic orientations of Nazi Germany and East Germany. Seen this way, the sense of social solidarity experienced by sympathetic intellectuals and even by ordinary East Germans – a solidarity that is the source of considerable nostalgia today – was not unlike that experienced by Germans during the 1930s and 1940s. It was the solidarity not so much of socialism but of a *Kampfgemeinschaft* (community in arms), in which the health, welfare, and literacy of society were harnessed to a broader geopolitical mission. The military mobilizational model of economy was never discarded and was inscribed into the very DNA of Soviet-style economic structures that were never really abandoned.

But East Germany only joined the Soviet-led communist world in 1945, in a second round of Soviet conquests (after an earlier failed attempt in Poland in 1920, successful expeditions in the Caucasus and Ukraine, and annexations of parts of Poland, Romania, and the Baltic states in 1940), and it was Moscow, not Berlin, that was the center of global conquest. The East German elite attempted to bask in the *Machtprestige* (power prestige)

---

[8] Aaron Friedberg, *In the Shadow of the Garrison State: America's Anti-Statism and Its Cold War Strategy* (Princeton, NJ, 2000).

of the Soviet empire but gained little in the way of booty from communist conquests, which were primarily restricted to the Third World.

If the economic orientations of German Nazi and Communist elites are comparable, this is a far cry from saying that the regimes shared a common economic history. It is to that question that I turn next. I focus the discussion around the question of the relationship between the regime, economy, and society.

ECONOMY AND EVERYDAY RESISTANCE THE TWO
GERMAN DICTATORSHIPS

A pattern of theorization on the Nazi and communist dictatorships has emerged highlighting everyday resistance and collective action (or potential collective action). For some years the study of *Resistenz* in historiography of Nazi Germany constituted a subindustry of sorts. Few historians or social scientists, however, seek to identify the ways in which this resistance influenced economic policy. The reason for most resistance studies is more to show which groups of Germans acted ethically under the most extreme circumstances than to show how resistance affected policy. As interesting as this literature is, from the standpoint of causal explanation it misses the opportunity to say just how resistance actually mattered.

There are exceptions. The most consistent and bold statements on the role of everyday resistance among the working class in the Nazi period were penned by Tim Mason.[9] Mason's arguments are intricate and often subtle. For the purposes of this essay, however, they can be boiled down to a few simple propositions. First, the ideology of Nazi social solidarity, conceived at the broadest level as a *Volksgemeinschaft* (a racial, national community) in which notions of class would no longer inform either workers' consciousness or state policy, were received highly skeptically by most of the population. Second, during the 1930s, policies designed to speed up work, weaken working-class institutions of representation, and increase national rates of accumulation and investment at the expense of wages, met with resistance in the form of shirking, high rates of absenteeism, the occasional and isolated strike, and consistent grumbling – all of which was assiduously reported and sent upward by the political police. Third, Mason argued that this resistance reached a crescendo in 1938–9 as the Nazi leaders were pumping unprecedented sums of money into armaments. Such high rates

[9] Timothy Mason, *Sozialpolitik im Dritten Reich: Arbeiterklasse und Volksgemenschaft* (Opladen, 1977) and *Arbeiterklasse und Volksgemeinschaft* (Opladen, 1975).

of investment created labor shortages, pushed up wages, and yielded to workers a form of power – to withhold their services on an individual and atomized basis – that threatened the rearmament program. The Nazi leadership, according to Mason, feared turning the terms of exchange against the working class more strongly than it already had because workers had demonstrated in 1918 their capacity to bring down an authoritarian government. The leadership was therefore cornered. Fourth, and this is his most controversial point, Mason maintains that the constraints imposed on the leadership by workers' resistance forced Hitler to go to war earlier, three or four years earlier, than he would have preferred because he believed that Germany could not increase its military output further without risking industrial unrest and in that case could not wait any longer. Doing so would mean allowing Germany's opponents the time to increase their military output. These social constraints ultimately determined not only the timing of the war but also shaped the kind of war that Hitler fought. Blitzkrieg was not merely a type of tactic but also a strategy that corresponded to the Nazis' precarious domestic situation. The Nazis needed a war, but they did not want a long one and especially not one that would demand sacrifice from the population.

In a nutshell, this summarizes Mason's oeuvre. It is an original, unified, and in many ways, powerful argument. It is also an argument historians have attacked in almost every conceivable way.[10] First, the new emphasis on race and biological thinking among scholars of Nazi Germany, and especially their work documenting the significant public support for the various aspects of the *Volksgemeinschaft* ideology, has called Mason's Marxist picture of working-class resistance into question. Even if it can be categorized as resistance, however, such resistance may simply have functioned as an outlet for frustrations and in many ways may have stabilized the system by precluding more organized forms of action. The Nazis never had to endure a revolt similar to the one of June 17, 1953, in the GDR. Second, to the extent that workers remained immune to Nazi ideology and developed their own sense of identity and personal space outside of the *Volksgemeinschaft*, it remains far from clear that such attitudes and behavior can be understood in any meaningful sense as "resistance." It can just as easily be thought of as "acquiescence" if not support. Third, Mason's argument that the system faced an economic crisis from overinvestment in the military in the late 1930s has confronted mixed support at best. Some have criticized this characterization as objectively wrong. Others, however, have supported the

---

[10] See, esp., Richard Overy, "Domestic Crisis and War in 1939," *Past and Present* 122 (1989): 138–68.

assertion.[11] Fourth, the notion that the crisis led to war and specifically Blitzkrieg is a conclusion that even people who otherwise buy much of what Mason has to say almost unanimously dismiss as not grounded in facts (other factors, especially foreign policy appear to explain the exact timing of the war much more persuasively) and at best speculative.

It is important to note that Mason's interpretation changed in subtle ways over time. Whereas his early work was a straightforward structuralist explanation for the origins of the war – workers constrained leaders and forced their hand – his later work contained an important cognitive component that did not deny the power of the Nazis to crush working-class resistance.[12] His work did, however, continue to maintain that working-class attitudes, as they filtered their way up to the leadership, influenced just how far Hitler and his cronies were willing to go in forcing savings and suppressing consumption.

PARALLELS

Despite the crucial differences between Nazi Germany and communist East Germany, I have been continually impressed by how the regime's internal interpretations of the attitudes of ordinary people, everyday resistance, and a general fear of unrest to be found at every level in the archives – from the factory reports to the monthly reports of the *Bezirksleitungen* (district leadership), to Central Committee Department reports, to the Stasi at just about every level, all the way up to the Politburo – reflect important continuities in the two German dictatorships. Like the Nazi leadership in Mason's story, the East German leadership from very early on found itself hemmed in by shop-floor resistance of the most elementary sort and, especially after June 1953, feared a mass uprising. It was always prepared to make concessions and always avoided confrontation with workers, especially groups of workers.

It is important to note here that Mason's Marxism and his putative romanticism regarding the role of the working class need not be adopted in order to accept much of his structuralism – a structuralism that may provide clues to a common economic history of the two regimes. It is true that implicit in much of Mason's work is the hope that the working class could become the true driving force of history; he had very high hopes for workers, especially German workers. Ultimately, these hopes were dashed not only in Germany but also in the rest of the world. Yet the essentially

---

[11] Adam Tooze, *The Wages of Destruction: The Making and Breaking of the Nazi Economy* (London, 2006).

[12] See Mason's response to Richard Overy in "Debate: Germany, 'Domestic Crisis' and the War in 1939," in *The Origins of the Second World War*, ed. Patrick Finney (London, 1997).

nonnormative component of his essays may remain intact and the East German case may help us salvage (if only in modified form) the kinds of things that Mason was getting at.

In my own research on East Germany, I have been deeply influenced by both the historians who have documented the regime's early relationship with the working class[13] and those who have explained the constraints the leadership faced in crafting effective institutions within the confines of what I'm referring to here as a militarized economy.[14] These two strains of historiography allow us to draw important parallels with the Nazi experience (even if, to be fair, it was the intention of none of these historians to do so). Resistance to the reintroduction of piece work, labor competitions, and the activist movement during the late 1940s prevented the Socialist Unity Party (Sozialistische Einheitspartei Deutschlands, or SED) from gaining complete control of the shop floor. The archival evidence on this point is quite overwhelming. A cat-and-mouse game between the workers' state and the working class ensued that was never resolved successfully in one direction or another. In the one instance in which the state did seriously attempt to suppress wages through norm and price increases, in mid-1953, ordinary people rebelled en masse (as Port and Pritchard show, 1953 was really a culmination of smaller strikes[15]) and the regime quickly retreated after the protests were put down with Soviet assistance. Never again did the regime try to "tame" (Mason's term) the working class through central policies with any seriousness. The few attempts to increase output or lower the overall wage bill through central policies were always subverted at the enterprise level with the tacit acquiescence of the leadership. The one genuine venture into reforming the militarized state to make it compatible with rising consumer demand, the New Economic System, of the 1960s, was in no small measure prevented from full implementation (whatever that might have been) because of Walter Ulbricht's fears that price increases and "socialist" unemployment might lead to a repeat of June 1953. Such constraints ultimately left Erich Honecker with little alternative when he came to power but to pursue a sort of consumer populism that led to underinvestment, rapidly rising foreign debt, huge state subsidies, infrastructural decay, and, ultimately, political revolution.

---

[13] See in particular Peter Hübner, *Konsens, Konflikt, und Kompromiss: Soziale Arbeiterinteresse und Sozialpolitik in der SBZ/DDR 1945–1970* (Berlin, 1995) and Andrew L. Port, *Conflict and Stability in the German Democratic Republic* (New York, 2007).

[14] Especially Jörg Roesler, *Zwischen Plan und Markt: die Wirtschaftsreform in der DDR zwischen 1963 und 1970* (Berlin, 1990) and Andre Steiner, *Die DDR-Wirtschaftsreform der sechsiger Jahre* (Berlin, 1999).

[15] See Port, *Conflict and Stability*, and Gareth Pritchard, *The Making of the GDR, 1945–1953: From Antifascism to Stalinism* (New York, 2000).

One could argue, however, that such a structural – even *ouveriste* – approach is flawed in the East German case, too. Again, the potential criticisms are reminiscent of the critiques of Mason's work launched by economic and labor historians of Nazi Germany: Nazi workers were encouraged, often successfully, to take pride in their work for the regime. The same, it appears, was true in East Germany, at least in some measure. Rebellious impulses could easily be deflected by segmenting the labor force into groups of more and less loyal, enthusiastic, and productive workers. Between 1953 and 1989, not one instance of collective protest occurred of a magnitude large enough to threaten the regime. Without too much difficulty, one could find groups of ordinary East Germans who benefitted from the regime's policies and who most likely supported it for material as well as ideal reasons. Furthermore, the ubiquity of concern with mass public support emanating from the lower levels, as both scholars of Nazi German and East Germany have found in the archives of two different eras, could simply reflect bureaucratic strategies for increasing resource allocation from the center. "Give us more or we run the risk of unrest" might have been the logic presented by factor directors and *Bezirk* party secretaries to their superiors in Berlin. In a similar vein, it is worth recalling that some of Mason's critics argued that his evidence was drawn disproportionately from Nazi sources, especially political police sources, which, for obvious reasons, had the tendency to cast all attitudes and behaviors in a political light (either pro- or antiregime) even when they did not reflect tendencies that could have been translated into collective action. In short, so the argument might run, objectively the Nazis and the communists need not have worried very much about the working class or ordinary people and therefore neither should we.

But any analysis of the ebb and flow of wage policy, piece rate policy, price policy, housing policy, and consumer goods policy from very early on in both regimes suggests very strongly that both the Nazis and the communists did worry. And it is the discrepancy between the objective political capacities of the state and the society, and the perceived potential for conflict in the militarized economy that is most interesting. It is true that the "hidden transcripts" of everyday resistance may not amount to very much when elites are not aware of them, when they remain hidden.[16] But one thing we know about both of these states (and especially East Germany) is that very little did remain hidden. The leadership of these societies had unprecedented access to the hidden transcript of subaltern groups, including

---

[16] James C. Scott, *Domination and the Arts of Resistance: The Hidden Transcript* (New Haven, CT, 1990).

workers. Perhaps the most we can say for everyday resistance in both German dictatorships is that it fostered a culture of disrespect for authority in the workplace and in society at large. But while such a culture of disrespect may never, on its own, have overthrown the regime, it did lay the groundwork for a potential overthrow, and the leadership of both societies were acutely aware of this. This, I think, is what Mason is really getting at, and I see no reason to discard his approach.

Everyday resistance matters in a totalizing dictatorship and a militarized economy in a way that it does not in a democracy, a capitalist economy, or even in a traditional society. In a democracy, everyday resistance is marginal because the culture that it nurtures can be expressed quite openly in participatory behavior. In a traditional dictatorship, where rulers are satisfied simply to demobilize the population and foster political passivity, everyday resistance is expected and even accepted. Modern dictators who wish to construct a militarized economy designed for conquest, however, because they wish to mobilize the population, to politicize them for instrumental purposes, constantly keep an ear to the ground for signs that their projects might be rejected en masse.

It may be exaggerating to argue that once the June 1953 strikes occurred, the rest of the GDR's history is essentially one of a coercive state over a cowed society. But it is true that the events of the years running up to and culminating in mass unrest in June 1953, and the skirmishes of the class war in the workplace that occur continuously after that, nourished the sentiment in the leadership that the whole operation was far more precarious than it probably was. Like Hitler, Ulbricht and Honecker lived with a "myth of the general strike" that threatened to bring the whole enterprise crashing down. In the communist case, because a general strike really did occur, the fear of unrest was probably more well founded, though it is difficult to say whether this fear shaped East German policies more decisively than it did in the Third Reich.

MILITARIZED ECONOMIES WITH AND WITHOUT WAR

The common economic history of militarized economies suggested by students of the phenomenon, (and here in obvious deference not only to Janos but to Goetz Aly's 2005 work on the relationship between conquest, plunder, and legitimacy[17]) involves a cycle of mobilization, accumulation, armament, a thrust into the heartland of the enemy in order to plunder and

[17] Götz Aly, *Hitler's Beneficiaries* (New York, 2005).

replenish supplies, and then a period of rest and recovery until the cycle starts again. The leaders of these societies are not devoid of rationality but they confront social pressures that are unique to this type of economy and society. The pressures I have described are characteristic of militarism, as opposed to the different kinds of conflict under industrialism.

I believe that this description fits the Nazi experience and the communist world as a whole. The Nazi case is hardly controversial. Analyzing the Soviet case in these terms, however, still runs up against disputes between the right and the left of the Cold War era. What about East Germany? By virtue of having joined the communist militarized division of labor late in the day, only after the age of communist conquest in Europe had passed, East Germans lived through only the accumulation stage (after being plundered itself), missing out on the benefits of acquisition, and proceeding directly therefore to decline. What were left were scraps, meager takings in Cuba, Benin, Angola, Mozambique, Nicaragua, and other destinations in the impoverished Global South.

Although documenting the myriad ways in which East Germany's economy and society were militarized remains beyond the scope of this essay, German scholars since 1989 have provided a number of important studies substantiating this claim. Clemens Heitmann's analysis of civil defense in the GDR, for example, shows just how connected both the economy and other parts of East Germany's society, in both important and trivial ways, remained to the Soviet doctrine of "destroying the enemy on his own territory" and integrated into the broader Soviet project of subordinating the economy and society to military needs. Throughout the 1980s, East German political, economic, and military leaders retained current and detailed plans for surviving a nuclear war and even occupying West Berlin.[18] From sports, to scouting, to the medical profession, the military pervaded almost every nook and cranny of East German life.[19]

Ultimately, however, East Germany's was a militarized economy and society without a war to fight – that was its central contradiction. Who, after all, needed a second, peaceful Germany? After some flirtation with Khrushchevian utopianism in the 1960s, the SED leadership settled into

---

[18] Clemens Heitmann, *Schützen und Helfen? Luftschutz und Zivilverteidigung in der DDR 1955 bis 1989/90* (Berlin, 2005), 83–9; Helmut Göpel, "Die Berlin-Operation," in *NVA: Anspruch und Wirklichkeit nach ausgewählten Dokumenten*, ed. Klaus Naumann (Berlin, 1993), 286–300.

[19] Uta A. Balbier, "Kampf um Gold: Spitzensportförderung in der Nationalen Volksarmee und in der Bundeswehr," *Militärgeschichte: Zeitschrift für historische Bildung* 4 (2003): 16–21; Christian Sachs, "'Disziplin muss geübt warden!' Zur Geschichte und pädagogischen Praxis der Wehrerziehung in der DDR," in *Unter dem Deckel der Diktatur. Soziale und Kulturelle Aspekte des DDR-Alltags*, ed. Lothar Mertens (Berlin, 2003), 137–64.

a conservative, if rather drab, consumer socialism in the 1970s and 1980s. It is difficult to conceive of something similar happening in the Nazi case. War and planning for war was the glue of the Third Reich. Consider, for example, the counterfactual put forth by Robert Harris in his novel (and later to be TV movie) *Fatherland*. The year is 1964. Germany has won World War II. Churchill and his "warmongers" have long ago fled to Canada. Europe is now under Nazi control and all that remains of the fighting is a few guerilla skirmishes in the hinterland of Siberia. The scene in the novel is set for the U.S. President *Joseph* Kennedy to visit Germany and make détente with Hitler. Germany has become stable, a bit shabby, and very conservative. Its officials have become cynical and more than slightly corrupt. Its youth long for jazz, travel, and an end to militarization.

The reason that Harris's Brezhnevite/Honecker-like postwar Nazi Germany does not ring true is that it is terribly difficult to imagine a peaceful Nazi Germany, a country satiated and contented to end the "struggle." It is this constant need for struggle, for outward expansion – for war – that historians have placed at the center of their analyses.

Mason's most bold claim, that Hitler started the war in 1939 because he needed to, may be moving beyond what his evidence might warrant. But even if the causal logic is flawed, the functional logic is compelling. War helped the Nazis. It increased national integration, gained new adherents for the party among the working class, provided new sources of wealth in the form of plunder (the essence of the militarized economy's raison d'etre), and brought "inferior" foreigners to Germany as workers who could perform functions that Germans would have had to and allowed ordinary Germans to occupy a place on the social ladder higher than where they had previously been. To some extent, racism and anti-Semitism were equally integrative.

The depressing part of the comparative story is that Mason is only partially right and on crucial issues he missed something terribly important about the dynamics of a militarized economy. For although Hitler may have "needed" the war, once he started it there was no reason why war would not increase his popularity (until the bombing started at home). One need only read the *Sopade Berichte* for a taste of the pessimism that pervaded Social Democratic thinking on the willingness of Germans to resist Nazi war plans. Once the war had started, the German working class appears to have supported the Nazi state no less strongly than other segments of the society – a *Burgfrieden* of sorts, minus the Social Democrats. The everyday resistance of ordinary Germans was diminished or at least muted by the glories of war and the decadent pleasures of conquest and negative empathies of racism.

That war has an integrative capacity should surprise neither the historian nor the social scientist. We have known this at least since Thucydides.

In East Germany, by contrast, everyday resistance among workers intensified once it was clear that the SED, a nominally working-class party, had taken over. Involved in a cat-and-mouse game from 1947 to 1953 and thereafter paralyzed by the specter of rebellion, a fear reinforced in the millions of pages that flowed upward on the disrespect showed by ordinary people for "socialism," "peace," and the SED, the East German leadership ultimately had very little power to shape its own economic environment. Unwilling or unable to engage in real combat or war, the party (and not only the East German communists but all communists) had to settle for an endless series of phony, ritualized "combat tasks" or what I have called elsewhere the "campaign economy"[20] with such unconvincing, even laughable, militarized slogans as *"mein Arbeitsplatz ist mein Kampfplatz für den Frieden"* (My workplace is my battlefield for peace) in which the disciplining virtues of real war were substituted with the metaphorical language of organizational struggle for something as abstract and boring as socialism. The people quickly sensed the difference.

And yet, even these ridiculous militarized slogans revealed something of the truth. If peace required a socialist East German state and the existence of such a state required prosperity (what else could this slogan possibly have meant?), then that identified the challenge about as clearly as possible. I, as a worker, had to work hard to make socialism work in Germany so there would be no war. Clear enough. But this was not an economy set up to compete with the developmental model of the West along any other lines *but* war. Once the war became a phony war, a war of economies competing over productivity and living standards rather than over territory, this was something that East Germany was destined to lose. Ulbricht did not understand this but his opponents did. His opponents made an equally large category error in believing that peace without prosperity could bring stability.

The history of the two German dictatorships yields some tantalizing clues about everyday resistance: precisely where we might expect it to matter the least, it may matter the most. The greater the *Machtanspruch* and mobilizational demands; the stronger the capacity to infiltrate and monitor the hidden transcript of the oppressed; and the more ambitious and transformative the plans of the leadership – the more leaders may actually care

---

[20] Jeffrey Kopstein, *The Politics of Economic Decline in East Germany, 1945–1989* (Chapel Hill, NC, 1997).

about and react to what ordinary people are thinking as expressed in their everyday acts. Hard as they may try (and the Stasi certainly tried) tyrants can never really know what people are thinking, how far they can be pushed, and what might lead to rebellion. In the language of rational choice theory, dictators always suffer from the problem of preference falsification. For this reason, everyday resistance may matter most in a totalitarian dictatorship.

It is important to note that everyday resistance probably does not matter in the way the more optimistic students of resistance hoped that it might. The lessons of the Nazi period are sobering ones. Whereas people cannot be easily mobilized to build abstractions such as socialism, they can be seduced or bought off by the possibilities for plunder or glory inherent in war. Seen in this way, the nuclear deterrent of the Cold War years begins to loom much larger in an analysis of East German economic history; unable to translate its militarized structures and the impulses that both underlay and derived from them into a real war, the communist world had to substitute an ersatz productivist war that it was destined to lose. Everyday resistance may have played no small part in this defeat.

PART IV

Transformation, Subvention, and Renewal,
1989–2010

11

The East German Economy in the Twenty-First Century

MICHAEL C. BURDA

Twenty years after reunification, the Eastern German economy remains the proverbial glass of water – half-full and half-empty at the same time. As a modern episode of economic growth and convergence it is hard to beat. It is even more difficult to imagine a more daunting challenge than that faced by German policy makers in early 1990: how to raise standards of living fast enough in the East to keep its inhabitants from leaving in droves and thereby validating their own pessimistic expectations, and simultaneously to attract new investment from the wealthier parts of the world. It was precisely the young, the educated, and the productive elites who were first in line to leave, and their departure threatened to make East Germany less attractive for West German and international investors as well as for those left behind. Although it could be viewed as an explicit policy choice made under political constraints, reunification had no viable economic alternative.

For economists, German unification posed questions of central professional interest. Harvard's Robert Barro boldly predicted that it would take thirty-five years for the East to close half of the 70 percent productivity gap with the West.[1] This prediction, based on remarkably robust econometric evidence from the United States, West European regions, and Japanese prefectures, turned out to be less than accurate, unless one is ready simply to ignore sharp increases in productivity in the years 1991–4. The expectation that East Germany would someday merely be a simple replication of the West meant, paradoxically, that initial conditions and the path of adjustment would end up determining the resting point of the system – meaning that it was not unique and was path dependent. In the early 1990s, I argued

---

[1] Rober Barro, "Eastern Germany's Long Haul," *The Wall Street Journal*, May 3, 1991.

This paper was written for a conference of the German Historical Institute, Washington, DC, September 2009. I thank Susanne Schöneberg, Felix Strobel, and Femke Schmarbeck for helpful research assistance.

that one could just as easily imagine an East German economy in 2020 that looked like the highly industrialized Dresden-Leipzig-Halle region in the late nineteenth century, or instead a scenario in which the new states were nothing but a giant national park dedicated to biodiversity of flora and fauna, including that of the legendary Ossi.[2] This multiplicity of potential outcomes must have prompted the government of Chancellor Helmut Kohl to act as it did, arguably with more decisiveness than the economists who advised it.[3]

Considering the initial conditions of the German Democratic Republic (GDR) and the standard of living in other comparable communist states at the outset (e.g., the Czech Republic and Slovakia), the reunification episode has been nothing short of a minor miracle. Real incomes per capita – allowing for regional price differences for goods and services such as lodging, public transportation, and nontraded goods – have virtually converged.[4] Yet the proverbial glass of water remains half-empty in many central respects. Convergence in income per capita does not equate with convergence in productivity per capita or per hour. Eastern productivity remains about three-quarters of Western levels. The overall unemployment rate in the East is now slightly less than double of that in the West.

The Germans insisted on unification their way and paid a heavy price for it. Overall gross domestic product growth has slowed since the mid-1990s, partly due to the new tax burdens induced by reunification, partly for reasons having to do with structural shifts in production patterns. Much of the Eastern German economy was destroyed in 1990 by monetary union, at a stroke of the pen; yet having its own currency would have bought five but certainly not twenty years of prosperity. The extent of structural

---

[2] See Michael Burda and Charles Wyplosz, "Labor Mobility and German Integration: Some Vignettes," in *The Transformation of Socialist Economies*, ed. H. Siebert (Tübingen, 1992).

[3] Karl-Heinz Paqué, *Die Bilanz: Eine wirtschaftliche Analyse der Deutschen Einheit* (Munich, 2009) cites white papers by the Council of Economic Advisors (Sachverständigenrat) as well as the Bundesbank militating against economic and monetary union. For early economic analyses of the German reunification episode, see George Akerlof, Janet Yellen, Andrew Rose, and Helen Hessenius, "East Germany in from the Cold: The Economic Aftermath of Currency Union," *Brookings Papers on Economic Activity*, 1991:1; Michael Burda, "Les Conséquences de l'Union Economique et Monétaire de l'Allemagne," *Revue de l'OFCE* (1990); Michael Burda, "Capital Flows and the Reconstruction of Eastern Europe: The Case of the GDR after the Staatsvertrag," in *Capital Flows in the World Economy*, ed. H. Siebert (Tübingen, 1991); Hans-Werner Sinn and Gerlinde Sinn, *Kaltstart: volkswirtschaftliche Aspekte der deutschen Vereinigung* (Munich, 1991); Irwin Collier and Horst Siebert, "The Economic Integration of Post-Wall Germany" *American Economic Review* 81 (1991): 196–201; Michael Burda and Charles Wyplosz, "Labor Mobility and German Integration: Some Vignettes," in *The Transformation of Socialist Economies*, ed. H. Siebert (Tübingen, 1992); Michael Burda, "Labor and Product Markets in Czechoslovakia and the Ex-GDR: A Twin Study," *European Economy*, July 1991.

[4] Tilman Brück and Heiko Peters, "Twenty Years of German Unification: Evidence on Income Convergence and Heterogeneity," DIW Discussion Paper 925, October, 2009.

change necessary for a planned economy to compete internationally was certainly underestimated by most observers at the time. With aggregate output per capita currently hovering at 70 percent and labor productivity at 80 percent of West German levels, further convergence will be slow because it is not only about equipping East Germans with adequate physical and human capital but also about endowing them with the same level of social, institutional, business, and marketing infrastructure, and the right output mix.[5] As a result, the last mile of convergence in productivity per capita and other measures of long-term economic viability will be difficult without further structural change. Yet because of its initial trial by fire, the Eastern German economy looks much more vibrant and robust than the macroeconomic numbers lead one to believe. Karl-Heinz Paqué has recently presented convincing evidence that the overall "investment" was worth it.[6]

This essay is organized along four themes: (1) economic convergence and its measurement; (2) the mobility race between capital and labor that has taken place since 1990; (3) structural change and the implantation of new institutions that are conducive to economic growth; and (4) agglomeration and economic geography and the roles they can be expected to play in the future of the new German states plus Berlin.

CONVERGENCE: A QUESTION OF BENCHMARKS

The political promise made by Chancellor Kohl to Eastern Germans in the run-up to the elections in March 1990 and that certainly determined its outcome was the prospect of *blühende Landschaften* – "blossoming land-scapes" of economic growth and prosperity. How does one evaluate that promise after two decades of integration?

From the point of view of economic welfare, the central indicator for economists is consumption – those goods and services that bring us pleasure or comfort. Estimates vary, but average consumption per capita in the new states is believed to have reached about 85 percent of the average Western level. This gap is not significantly larger between poor northern and rich southern states in the western part of Germany. These differences in consumption are strongly influenced by prices of nontradable goods such

---

[5] This and related snags in the East-West German integration and convergence process were stressed early on by Joachim Ragnitz, "Warum ist die Produktivität ostdeutscher Unternehmen so gering? Erklärungsansätze und Schlussfolgerungen für den Konvergenzprozess," *Konjunkturpolitik* 45, no. 3 (1999): 165–87.

[6] Paqué, *Die Bilanz*.

Table 7. *East-West German Convergence in the Small:
Fractions of Households Owning Key Durable Goods (%)*

| | Year | | |
| | 1993 | 1998 | 2007 |
Durable Good	East/West	East/West	East/West
Automobile	66/74	71/76	72/78
Landline telephone	49/97	94/97	95/96
Cell phone	–	11/11	82/82
Personal computer	16/22	36/43	70/73
Internet access	–	5/9	56/61
Television	96/95	98/95	97/96
Cable access	–	64/51	61/48
Satellite dish	–	30/29	33/41
Video recorder	36/48	61/63	71/69
Refrigerator	95/95	99/99	99/99
Microwave oven	15/41	41/53	68/69
Dishwasher	3/38	26/49	54/64
Washing machine	91/88	94/91	99/95[a]
Dryer	2/24	14/33	22/44

[a] Year: 2006.
Source: IW Kôln (2009). All households.

as housing, food, and personal services, which are in turn dependent on local levels of wealth and productivity in traded goods. More revealing are consumption levels of individual goods. Consider Table 7, which shows a striking convergence in consumption patterns of Eastern and Western households, with the former sometimes even overtaking the latter. This evidence is largely confirmed by East Germans' assessments of their own individual well-being – abstracting from perceptions of political paternalism or even subjugation by the West.[7] From the perspective of consumption or income, Eastern Germany has done well. Most East Germans enjoyed a relatively high standard of living compared with the rest of the communist bloc before the fall of the Wall, and this relative status has certainly been maintained in the aftermath.

In the light of this evidence it is difficult to deny the impression of "ein Volk." Consumption patterns of Table 7 are mirrored in patterns of labor

[7] In a public opinion poll by the *Tagesspiegel* newspaper and ZDF television in November 2009, 86% of Germans surveyed (85% in West, 91% in the East) described reunification in retrospect as "the right thing to do" (http://www.tagesspiegel.de/politik/deutschland/Deutsche-Einheit; art122,2942683 [accessed April 24, 2013]). In the same survey, however, 60% of West Germans believe that East Germans profited most from reunification, while the largest share of East Germans surveyed (34%) thought that West Germans were the main beneficiaries.

market participation. It is also noteworthy that life expectancy – perhaps one of the most easily agreed-upon indicators of well-being – has converged for East and West German women and nearly so for men, with West German males still expecting only a single year more of life than East German men.[8]

Although consumption is certainly not a sufficient indicator of happiness and well-being, the two are highly correlated. At the same time, self-esteem and self-sufficiency are aspects that also cannot be ignored. Unemployment rates are still roughly double those in the West, even if they have come down considerably in the past five years. Consumption paid for by transfers from a more productive West hardly represents a sustainable situation in the long term. Thus a more careful look at macroeconomic "supply side" indicator of productivity per capita – a measure that captures both productivity per employed labor as well as the employment rate – is an essential component of any comprehensive assessment of unification two decades later.

The macroeconomic picture for the region of Eastern Germany – originally with a population of roughly seventeen million in the late 1980s – has been rather mixed. Table 8 displays the most commonly used macroeconomic measures of convergence. After the introduction of the D-Mark at the exchange rate 1:1 for current transactions, the decimation of East German manufacturing in the early 1990s was unavoidable – Akerlof, Rose, Yellen, and Hessenius cleverly employed the once top-secret *Richtkoeffizienten* of the GDR's planning ministries to infer that less than one-fifth of industry was competitive at a 1:1 Eastern mark-D-Mark conversion rate, and were subsequently proved more than right.[9] After a collapse of Eastern industrial production to about one-third of its 1989 value,[10] it has risen relative to the West steadily ever since – through the recession of 2001–2 and even in the current downturn. In the past fifteen years, more than half of the per-capita gross domestic product gap between the East and West has been closed in less than half the time predicted by Robert Barro.[11] In August 2009, an Eastern German state (Thuringia: 11.1 percent) could boast a lower unemployment rate than a Western one (Bremen: 12.2 percent). If

---

[8] Institut für Wirtschaftsforschung, Halle (hereafter referred to as IWH), "Ostdeutschland Transformation seit 1990 im Spiegel wirtschaftlicher und sozialer Indikatoren," Sonderheft 1/2009.

[9] Akerlof et al., "East Germany in from the Cold." The *Richtkoeffizienten* represented the planning ministries' own assessment of their ability to raise foreign exchange through international trade. By obtaining these numbers at detailed levels of sectoral disaggregation, Akerlof and his colleagues were able to assess competitiveness of individual industries at the time with remarkable accuracy.

[10] Rudiger Dornbusch and Holger Wolf, "Eastern German Economic Reconstruction," in *The Transition in Eastern Europe*, vol. 1, ed. Oliver Jean Blanchard, Kenneth A. Froot, and Jeffrey D. Sachs (Chicago, 1994).

[11] Barro, "Eastern Germany's Long Haul"; and Barro, Robert, and Xavier Sala-i-Martin, *Economic Growth* (New York, 1995).

Table 8. *East-West German Convergence in the Large: Macroeconomic Indicators*
(as % of Western German value)

Year	Consumption	Nominal Wages Per Hour	Nominal Wages Per Worker	Labor Productivity (per hour)	Labor Productivity (per worker)	Gross Domestic Product Per Capita	Unemployment Rate	Participation Rate
1991	62	n.a.	57	n.a.	45	43	165	137
1992	67	n.a.	68	n.a.	57	50	225	121
1993	73	n.a	75	n.a.	67	59	193	111
1994	75	n.a.	77	n.a.	71	64	174	108
1995	78	n.a.	80	n.a	72	67	163	108
1996	79	n.a.	80	n.a	74	68	168	106
1997	79	n.a.	80	n.a	74	68	177	107
1998	80	73	81	68	74	67	186	107
1999	81	74	81	69	75	68	195	106
2000	81	74	81	70	76	67	221	104
2001	80	75	81	72	77	67	235	102
2002	81	75	81	74	79	69	226	102
2003	81	75	81	74	79	69	216	101
2004	80	76	81	74	79	70	214	100
2005	80	77	82	74	79	69	187	103
2006	80	77	82	74	79	70	188	103
2007	80	78	82	75	78	70	200	104
2008	n.a.	79	82	76	79	71	204	104
2009	n.a.	80	83	n.a.	n.a.	n.a.	186	n.a.

Source: Statistisches Bundesamt (Volkwsirtschaftliche Gesamtrechnung der Länder), Bundesagentur für Arbeit.

the persistence of macroeconomic developments is any guide, some Eastern states such as Thuringia and Saxony are well poised to overtake weaker Western states such as Lower Saxony or Schleswig-Holstein.

With hindsight, it is remarkable if not amusing to examine the economic naïveté in political discussion during the early 1990s, which literally expected a phoenix to emerge from the ashes in a matter of a few short years.[12] What could they possibly have been thinking? Estimates of the Central Intelligence Agency in the late 1980s were certainly inflated for reasons related to defense and national security policy. Moreover, it is hard to imagine a market for most Eastern output, even at an exchange rate corresponding to the average *Richtkoeffizient* of 4.4 Eastern marks per D-Mark. The best evidence of this was the collapse of the delivery time for a Trabant or a Wartburg from 4 to 5 years to zero in the months following November 1989.

---

[12] Naturally, it was politically expedient to dismiss the naysayers of the time, such as Oskar Lafontaine, who correctly anticipated the enormous fiscal burden that unification would impose on the West German taxpayer. The rush to reunification can be seen as an effort to override any rational discussion of the economic prospects of East Germany, which may have impeded or even hindered the process.

For this reason, comparisons of East Germany's experience with other ex-communist countries can be highly misleading. Comparisons of output over time and space are never trivial and should not be taken lightly. Can we really consider the quality of consumption for a family driving a Trabant and washing their clothes in a Foron WM66 to a one owning an Opel and a Miele? East German consumers voted with their feet in 1990 and 1991 and sealed the fate of most of existing industry at the time. After two decades, however, manufacturing, in particular of consumer and intermediate goods, has been modernized by billions of euros of new investment and is experiencing an impressive renaissance. Understanding this structural change is essential to constructing scenarios for the Eastern German economy for the decades to come.

To motivate and organize the discussion, it useful to formalize thinking about growth and productivity as follows. Let $\Delta Y/Y$ stand for the rate of growth of real gross domestic product (Y) over a time interval, and similarly let $\Delta K/K$ and $\Delta L/L$ denote the rates of growth of capital (K) and employed labor (L), respectively (the symbol Δ denotes change over a year). The equation at the center of attention is the following representation of the "Solow decomposition,"[13] which tautologically *defines* the so-called Solow residual $\Delta A/A$ through the following relationship:

$$
\underset{\substack{\text{Output} \\ \text{growth}}}{\frac{\Delta Y}{Y}} = \underset{\substack{\text{total factor} \\ \text{productivity}}}{\frac{\Delta A}{A}} + \underset{\substack{\text{output growth} \\ \text{due to capital}}}{s_K \frac{\Delta K}{K}} + \underset{\substack{\text{output growth} \\ \text{due to employment}}}{(1 - s_K) \frac{\Delta L}{L}},
\tag{1}
$$

where s_K is the before-tax share of capital in national income, a number roughly equal to about one-third in developed economies. The Solow residual captures those determinants of economic growth that are not attributable to growth in capital and employed labor. In a quantitative discussion of the East German economy it is useful to augment and rewrite the Solow decomposition as:

$$
\underset{\substack{\text{Output} \\ \text{growth per} \\ \text{capita}}}{\left(\frac{\Delta Y}{Y} - \frac{\Delta N}{N} \right)} = \underset{\substack{\text{growth of} \\ \text{total factor} \\ \text{productivity}}}{\frac{\Delta A}{A}} + \underset{\substack{\text{contribution of} \\ \text{changing endowment} \\ \text{of capital per capita}}}{s_K \left(\frac{\Delta K}{K} - \frac{\Delta N}{N} \right)} + \underset{\substack{\text{contribution of changing} \\ \text{employment rate}}}{(1 - s_K) \left(\frac{\Delta L}{L} - \frac{\Delta N}{N} \right)},
$$

$$
\tag{2}
$$

with $\Delta N/N$ standing for the growth rate of the population. Because ($\Delta L/L - \Delta N/N$) is approximately equal to the change in the employment rate, this equation attributes changes in per capita gross domestic product (per capita

[13] Robert Solow, "Technical Change and the Aggregate Production Function," *Review of Economics and Statistics* 39 (1957): 312–20.

Michael C. Burda

Table 9. *Accounting for Per Capita Gross Domestic Product East-West Gap*

Per Capita Gross Domestic Product East-West Gap (in %)		Attributable to Gap (in %) in . . .		
		Total Factor Productivity	Capital Endowment	Employment Rate
1995	32.2	9.0	17.4	5.9
2000	31.2	10.5	12.1	8.6
2006	26.7	8.9	9.5	8.3

Note: The state of Berlin is excluded from this analysis.

productivity) not only to growth in total factor productivity ($\Delta A/A$) and growth in physical capital stock per capita ($\Delta K/K - \Delta N/N$), but also to improvement in the state of the labor market expressed as the change in the employment rate, the utilization of available working-age individuals.[14] An increase in the employment rate in the East, *ceteris paribus*, is associated with increasing gross domestic product per capita. This explains why the doggedly high unemployment rate observed in Eastern Germany is a brake on regional per capita output. In the next section, we turn our attention to the flow of capital ($\Delta K/K$) into and the flow of people ($\Delta N/N$) out of the new states, for a given employment rate.

Using equation (2) it is possible to account for the per capita productivity gap of the five eastern German states (Mecklenburg-Lower Pomerania, Brandenburg, Saxony-Anhalt, Saxony, and Thuringia), from the average of Western states (again, excluding Berlin) as the sum of parts due to differences in total factor productivity ($A^W - A^E)/A^W$, capital equipment/structures per capita ($(K/N)^W - (K/N)^E)/(K/N)^W$, and employment rates ($(L/N)^W - (L/N)^E)/(L/N)^W$. Table 9 presents estimates of this "lateral output gap decomposition" using data from 1995, 2000, and 2006.

CENTRAL MECHANISMS OF GERMAN INTEGRATION: MOBILITY AND
STRUCTURAL CHANGE

Mobility of Capital versus Labor

Early on, Horst Siebert presciently described the transformation of the ex-communist economies as an "integration shock,"[15] and there is little doubt

---

[14] If the employment rate is denoted by L/N, its percentage change is approximately equal to $\Delta L/L - \Delta N/N$ or $\Delta lnL - \Delta lnN$. It should be noted that, as it is typically defined, the employment rate does *not* equal 1 minus unemployment rate (the ratio of unemployed to the *labor force*, which excludes people of working age who are not actively looking for work).

[15] Horst Siebert, *Das Wagnis der Einheit: Eine wirtschaftspolitische Therapie* (Stuttgart, 1992).

that unification was a surprise to economic agents in both the East and West. To focus discussion, I employ Eichengreen's intuitive definition of economic integration: the achievement of efficient production by two or more geographic regions formed by their union.[16] An integration shock involves several mechanisms. First, internal accumulation of capital in the poor region raises output per capita. This is the mechanism stressed by Barro and Sala-i-Martin and the motivation for Barro's pessimistic prediction.[17] Second, labor moves from the capital-poor to capital-rich region. Third, capital mobility in the form of foreign direct investment (FDI) will benefit the capital-poor region, financed either by international capital markets or at the expense of the capital-rich one (here: West Germany). Fourth, trade between incompletely specialized regions equalizes wages and rates of returns, as capital-rich regions tend to export capital-intensive goods and labor-rich goods tend to export goods that use labor more intensively. Finally, the backward region can adopt technologies, techniques, and "soft infrastructure" from the leading region, heading to convergence of total factor productivity. In this section, I focus on the movement of capital and labor as drivers of East-West German integration.[18] In terms of equation (2), an increase in capital investment in the East ($\Delta K / K > 0$) will increase gross domestic product per capita, as will outmigration ($\Delta N / N < 0$), *ceteris paribus*. Holding unemployment constant, an exodus of population will have an equivalent effect on the capital-labor ratio and thus on output per capita.

The reallocation of capital and labor between the East and West was intense but variable over the past two decades. In the first five years after the Wall fell, more than a million people left the East. Through the early 1990s, this rate declined to a trickle, then rose again after 1995, when growth in the region declined and unemployment rates rose. Similarly, there was a burst of capital investment in the early 1990s, reaching a peak in mid-decade, then declining since then. An unusually large fraction (two-thirds) of the cumulated investment flow in Eastern Germany was dedicated to residential and business structures, compared with about one-third in business fixed equipment. The large run-up in investment spending on structures is frequently seen not only as the outcome of distorted investment incentives, but also as having longer run consequences for the structure

---

[16] Barry Eichengreen, "One Money for Europe: Lessons from the U.S. Currency Union," *Economic Policy* 10 (1990): 117–87.

[17] Robert Barro and Sala-i-Martin Xavier, "Convergence Across States and Regions," *Brookings Papers on Economic Activity* 1 (1991): 107–82; Barro, "Eastern Germany's Long Haul."

[18] This is based on arguments I have made elsewhere more formally: Michael Burda, "Factor Reallocation in Eastern Germany after Reunification," *American Economic Review* 96 (2006): 368–74 and Michael Burda, "What Kind of Shock Was It? Regional Integration and Structural Change in Germany after Unification," *Journal of Comparative Economics* 36 (December 2008): 557–67.

Table 10. *Capital Formation in Eastern and Western Germany (1991–2007)*

Region	Average Investment Rate (% of GDP)		Investment Per Capita (EUR. 2000 Prices)		Average Annual Investment Per Worker Employed (EUR. 2000 Prices)	
	Equipment	Structures	Equipment	Structures	Equipment	Structures
East (excl. Berlin)	11.6	21.7	1836.6	3440.4	4338.3	8126.9
West	9.0	10.2	2372.9	2694.7	4946.3	5616.9
Berlin	8.5	11.3	1928.7	2544.4	4162.6	5491.6

Source: Statistisches Bundesamt, Volkswirtschaftliche Gesamtrechnung der Länder.

of output and factor demands.[19] After a very strong start in the 1990s, investment rates in the East have declined significantly and now are hardly different from those in the West (see Table 10).

Rising capital endowment in the Eastern German economy was thus a prime determinant of the rapid rise in productivity per employee documented in Table 11. It was driven not only by the growth of investment spending but also by labor shedding, especially in the first years following reunification. In some sectors, capital intensity has even overshot Western levels. For example, the official estimate of eastern aggregate capital-labor ratio in manufacturing was virtually at par with the West as early as 2002 at 99 percent; this average concealed variation ranging from 66 percent in textiles/clothing and 81 percent in metallurgy to 125 percent in chemicals and 122 percent in the automobile sector. Even higher ratios could be found in intermediate materials (average 123 percent of the West), basic chemicals (143 percent), and mining and quarrying (184 percent). Overall, however, the capital-labor ratio in Eastern Germany remains, according to the Federal Statistical Office, at 84 percent of the West German level.[20]

Structural Change

Eastern Germany experienced a phase of intensive factor mobility in both directions. Such massive movements of factors of capital and labor are likely to be accompanied by significant structural change. This is a natural process of adaptation of a region long cut off from economic forces of

---

[19] Hans-Werner Sinn, "EU Enlargement and Lessons from German Unification," *German Economic Review* 3 (2000): 299–314.

[20] Bundesministerium für Verkehr, Bau und Stadtentwicklung, *Jahresbericht der Bundesregierung zum Stand der Deutschen Einheit* (2009).

Table 11. *Membership in Employers' Associations, Union*
Coverage and Pay in Eastern Germany, 1993–2003

	1993	1998	2003
Share of all firms which are	36	21	10
	76	45	29
Share of all firms paying less	35	41	47
Share of all			

Source: DIW. This survey has been discontinued and comparable, more recent data on unionization are unavailable.

international specialization and trade. The recovery of economic activity since the early 1990s in the new states has by no means been uniform. As already mentioned, Akerlof and his colleagues showed, using internal statistics maintained by the central planners of the GDR, that only about 20 percent of industry was internationally competitive at a 1:1 Ostmark-D-Mark exchange rate immediately following unification.[21] The extent of this structural change can be seen in Figure 6, which documents the relative overall evolution of gross sales in industrial sectors in the period 1995–2008. Noteworthy is not only the strikingly uneven recovery of East German industry but also the relative reallocation of production from the West toward the East in the vast majority of sectors. It is also noteworthy that this shift is consistent with at least a partial restoration of the preeminent position held by Central Germany's industrial economy until World War II.

The strikingly heterogeneous behavior of eastern German industry suggests that aggregate indicators conceal enormous structural shifts under the surface of the East German economy. Just as Friedrich Hayek would have described it, many sectors continue to discover their role in the world economy, with exports from the East maintaining a secular growth path relative to Western states. But other aspects are also at work, mostly reflecting the scars of four decades of socialist planning as well as misguided West German policies post-Wall. The boom in construction during the 1990s when generous tax breaks were offered to investment in residential buildings led to an artificially oversized building sector.[22] Reunification did not imply an immediate scale-back of the level of East German government to West German standards but required a steady effort that faced great political obstacles.[23] In terms of real gross domestic product, Eastern Germany

---

[21] Akerlof et al., "East Germany in from the Cold.
[22] Sinn and Sinn, *Kaltstart*; Sinn, "EU Enlargement."
[23] Paqué, *Die Bilanz*.

Relative Evolution of Industry Turnover, 1995–2008 (1995=100)

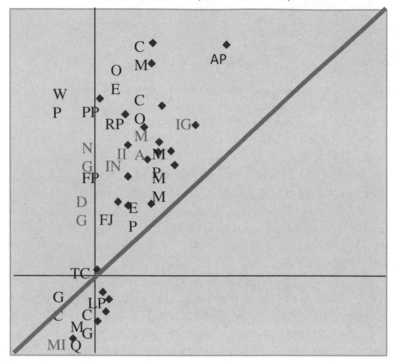

Eastern states

Western states

Figure 6. Structural Change in Germany, 1995–2008. *Note:* Each point corresponds to one of the following industrial sectors: mining and quarrying (MQ); coal mining, peat, oil, and gas production (CG); food processing and tobacco (FP); textiles and clothing (TC); leather production and processing (LP); wood products excluding furniture (WP); paper and printing (PP); coke and oil refining (CO); chemical manufactures (CM); rubber and plastic products (RP); glass, ceramics, and stone processing (GC); metal production and processing (MP); machinery and machine tools (MM); office equipment, data processing, and electronics (OE); automotive and automobile production (AP); furniture, jewelry, and musical instruments (FJ). In addition, the following aggregated sectors are marked red: mining, quarrying, coal, oil, peat, and gas production (MI); durable manufactures (DG); nondurable manufactures (NG); intermediate goods (II); all manufacturing (M); investment goods (IG); and total industry (IN). *Source:* Statistisches Bundesamt, author's calculations.

including Berlin has grown since 1992 by roughly 2.7 percent annually, and by 3.7 percent if Berlin is excluded – compared with 1.5 percent per annum real growth in the West. If only the manufacturing industry is considered, real growth amounted to 5.5 percent in the East (including Berlin) and a whopping 8.1 percent without the (remarkably nonindustrial) capital city. It is safe to say that the deindustrialization of the East has been stopped and reversed to a surprising extent.

Although Eastern Germany continues to account for a smaller fraction of total output than its population share, and although growth rates reflect its low initial condition in the early 1990s, this does not hold uniformly across sectors of activity. Shifts of the output mix across sectors with different growth outcomes will influence overall macroeconomic performance and will do so more positively in the future as slumping sectors disappear and strong ones grow. In manufacturing, the Eastern German states excluding Berlin now account for 9 percent of total German value-added in that sector, up from 7.6 percent in 2000 and 5.6 percent in 1995. In striking contrast, the East German value-added share in broadly defined services has hardly risen since 1995 from 11.2 percent to 11.7 percent. This reflects a shrinking government and growing private services. The share of construction fell from 27.8 percent in 1995 to 16.9 percent in 2005, and remains oversized compared to its West German counterpart.

Given the extent of the transformation of the Eastern German economy, it is inevitable that this structural change would spill over to the West. Concomitant with the expansion of manufacturing in the new states is a visible change in economic structures in the old Western states. The two panels of Figure 7 provide evidence for this claim.[24] The first shows how the employment shares in the West began changing significantly after 1990, the year of German unification. Since 1990, the West German economy has lost roughly one-fifth of its socially insured employment in industry while significantly increasing the number of jobs in services, especially business-related services.[25]

The second panel displays the evolution of indexes of disparity in sectoral employment growth as proposed by Lillien.[26] These numbers, which are similar in behavior to weighted standard deviations of employment growth rates, show a marked increase in entropy of sectoral employment. This

---

[24] Reproduced from Robert Bachmann and Michael C. Burda, "Sectoral Transformation, Turbulence, and Labor Market Dynamics in Germany," *German Economic Review* 11 (2010): 37–59.
[25] Ibid.
[26] David Lillien, "Sectoral Shifts and Sectoral Unemployment," *Journal of Political Economy* 90 (1982): 777–93.

a) Sectoral fraction of socially insured employment

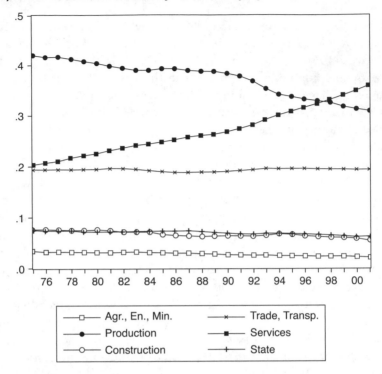

	Agr., En., Min.		Trade, Transp.
	Production		Services
	Construction		State

b) Lillien index of employment growth turbulence at different lags

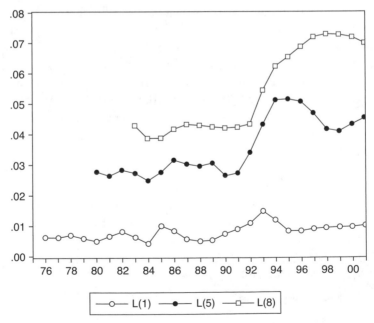

L(1)   L(5)   L(8)

Figure 7. Indicators of Structural Change in Western Germany: (a) Sectoral fraction of socially insured employment; (b) Lillien index of employment growth turbulence at different lags. *Source:* Bachmann and Burda (2010).

conjecture appears even more valid when the changes are measured over longer periods, that is, when short-term fluctuations are filtered out by measuring employment growth over longer intervals. Note that the increase in the indexes begins around 1990, the year of German unification.

One of the most important focal points of structure change is the labor market. Eastern Germany has experienced wrenching structural change – the loss of more than half of all industrial jobs by some estimates – and this outcome has starkly limited the strategy space of players in collective bargaining. Table 11 depicts the dramatic loss of influence of the vaunted (West) German collective bargaining model in the East. Following an initially successful campaign for legitimacy in wage bargaining in the first years following unification, membership fell from well more than 50 percent to now less than 20 percent. At the same time, growing frustration with a collective bargaining system has driven eastern German companies to abandon employers' associations (*Arbeitgeberverbände*), weakening legitimacy of collective bargaining at the industrial-regional level, which is typically strong in Germany.[27] The result has been a steady reduction of unit labor costs in the new states, once decried by Gerlinde and Hans-Werner Sinn as having the highest in the world,[28] are now lower than in Western Germany and represent a source of competitive advantage for new FDI (Figure 8). Overall, Eastern Germany looks to emerge as a foil for labor market rigidities frequently stressed in the discussion of West German labor markets.[29]

Wild Cards: Agglomeration and Location

It is certainly possible to paint a gloom and doom picture of East Germany – the region continues to lose population each year absolutely, with outmigration at about forty to fifty thousand per year. Investment has stabilized at levels that, while significant, do not match record levels in the mid-1990s.[30] Even the neoclassical model with constant returns to scale would link this to a permanent reduction in the steady state of the economy and, under certain technical conditions, to "hysteresis" – when long-run

[27] Boeri, Tito, Alison Booth, and Lars Calmfors, *Unions in the Twenty-First Century* (Oxford, 2007).
[28] Sinn and Sinn, *Kaltstart*.
[29] Christian Merkl and Dennis Snower, "The Caring Hand that Cripples: The East German Labor Market after Reunification," *American Economic Review* 96, no. 2 (2006): 275–382.
[30] This potential scenario, driven by increasing returns and the loss of critical mass in labor market networks, was highlighted in the writings of Marshall and has been applied to the East German case by Harald Uhlig, "Sectoral Transformation, Turbulence, and Labor Market Dynamics in Germany," *German Economic Review* 11 (2006): 37–59.

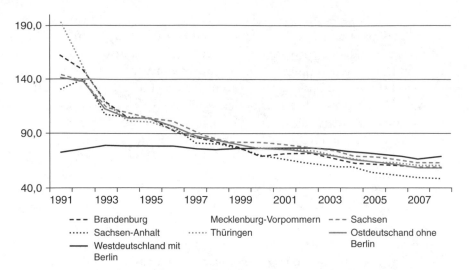

Figure 8. Unit Labor Costs (total wage compensation in manufacturing per employed worker in current prices relative to union coverage and pay) Western Germany and Eastern German States, 1991–2007. *Note:* Unit labor costs in manufacturing measured as index of gross pay per worker divided by index of nominal value of output added per worker × 100. Berlin is counted as part of western Germany. *Source:* IWH (2009). Reproduced with permission.

outcomes are path dependent and history matters.[31] This would rather speak for the national park outcome for Eastern Germany rather than *blühende Landschaften*. As long as people of working age continue to leave Eastern Germany, the long-run physical and human capital resources needed for sustainable development will also diminish commensurately.

The implications of this analysis for economic policy are strikingly anti–*laissez-faire*. A significant positive policy move that led to increased investment in the East would alter the expectations of workers and firms, which would in turn militate against a migration decision; the retention of workers increases the productivity of investment in the region and increases the rate of return, attracting more investment, and so forth. The creation of a virtuous cycle was certainly behind the policies of the Kohl government – pouring hundreds of billions of euros over the first decade of the unification episode. As the preceding analysis suggests, too much investment occurred in residential construction at the expense of productive workplaces for Eastern Germans.

[31] See, e.g., Burda, "Factor Reallocation"; Sebastian Böhm, "Stabilität und Eindeutigkeit von Gleichgewichten in Modellen der räumlichen Faktormobilität in diskreter Zeit" (diploma thesis, Humboldt-Universität zu Berlin, 2009).

Yet there is more reason to question the Panglossian critique of economic intervention for Eastern Germany. Agglomeration is defined by economists as the violation of the neoclassical assumption in the spatial dimension, in particular, that a doubling of the scale of economic activity *in the same economic space* will lead to a more than doubling of its output. The reasons for agglomeration are manifold, but a convincing case for them has been around at least since Alfred Marshall in the late nineteenth century. Marshall argued that large markets can support more product diversity and more efficiency in connecting input producers and users of intermediate inputs, where "support" means the payment of fixed costs. Areas in economic decline face the opposite effect, with smaller communities in Eastern Germany facing ever-rising average costs of infrastructure put into place in the go-go years of the past decade. Cuts in services and institution of usage fees have in turn led to more out-migration, aggravating the process. This logic can be extended to many phenomena in the private domain, including labor market "thickness," which can lead to a vicious cycle of slow but inexorable regional decline.

After almost two decades, the force of agglomeration has begun to show up in an increasingly latticelike development of Eastern Germany. Figure 9 displays net population changes in 2007 at the level of *Landkreis* (comparable to counties) that appeared in a recent review of the East German economy.[32] Although the mechanism of endogenous decline clearly appears to be operative, there are many recognizable points of light in the figure – at least ten light-colored nodes of population growth in this year, besides Berlin. Evidently, those who have stressed the depopulation of Eastern Germany have underplayed internal migration, not just to Berlin but also to larger cities such as Dresden, Leipzig, Jena, and a number of cities associated with the hinterlands (the so-called *Speckgurtel*) of Berlin. As pointed out by Jennifer Hunt and Michael Burda,[33] East Germans have proved to be less mobile than econometric evidence predicts, judging solely from wage gains available through migration. In retrospect, a selective policy of regional development focused on these areas (and perhaps extended to smaller cities such as Chemnitz, Cottbus, Gera, Magdeburg, Rostock, and Schwerin) might have a better alternative to a carte-blanche subsidy approach that ended up in poorly chosen infrastructure projects. Arguably, a

---

[32] IWH, "Ostdeutschland Transformation."

[33] Jennifer Hunt, "Staunching Emigration from East Germany: Age and the Determinants of Migration," *Journal of the European Economic Association* 4 (2006): 1014–37; Michael C. Burda and Jennifer Hunt, "From Reunification to Economic Integration: Productivity and the Labor Market in East Germany," *Brookings Papers on Economic Activity* 2 (2001): 1–71.

Michael C. Burda

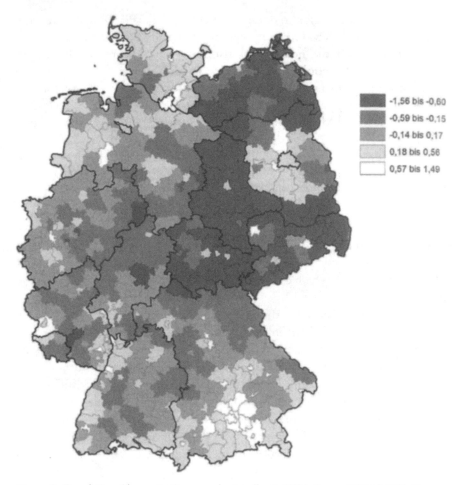

Figure 9. Population Change in Germany by Landkreis, 2007. *Source:* IWH (2009). Reproduced with permission.

tough triage policy might have saved more of East Germany from economic decline.

A little-considered advantage of Eastern Germany that will interact with the effects just described is related to the region's proximity to growth markets of the next two to three decades. Poland, Czech Republic, Slovakia, Hungary, and other markets of Central and Eastern Europe have grown rapidly in the past decade and their demand for consumer and investment goods has spilled over to Germany, and given the importance of location in trade and foreign investment, it is no surprise that East Germany has benefited from this demand. At the same time, FDI activity from Germany in these countries (especially Poland) has been nothing short of phenomenal. The deepening integration of Eastern Germany with Poland and other growing economies, combined with the accumulation of wealth there, is likely to lead to a renaissance of border communities and a stabilization of real estate values. This may be the ultimate triumph of economics over nationalism when East Germany begins to benefit from inward foreign investment by Polish and Czech firms and real estate acquisition by wealthy Polish and Czech families.

CONCLUSION

Eastern Germany, with approximately the land mass of Tennessee yet with a population density nearly three times as great, offers economists with a fascinating case study in economic integration two decades after the fact. The region can expect a highly heterogeneous economic future – not only in the qualitative sense but also in both a sectoral and spatial sense. Its experience contains lessons for the future of Central and Eastern Europe. In this integration process, production factors move in opposite directions, even as output is rising. This mobility race, combined with deep structural change, has severely constrained the options available to policy makers. For example, the adoption of a second currency would have yielded little gain in the absence of money illusion and, in the light of high labor mobility, real wages denoted in an Eastern German currency would have risen as much as they did under monetary union. Factor mobility has been the hallmark of the German integration episode distinguishing it from similar episodes in economic history. Barriers related to language, institutions, and culture in unified Germany are negligible; convergence of behavior in the past fifteen years has been so significant that one can really speak of a common representative household.[34] It is testimony to this that German economic policy achieved a high level of consumption for its citizens early on, tackling the harder problem of sustainability in a second, more prolonged phase.

At the outset of the postunification period, Eastern Germany was isolated from world trade and was burdened with an outdated capital stock and uncompetitive structure of output.[35] The lack of brands, corporate

---

[34] Recent research suggests a convergence in the behaviour of Eastern and Western Germans over time. See Burda and Hunt, "From Reunification to Economic Integration"; Nicola Fuchs-Schuendeln, "Adjustment to a Large Shock – Do Households Smooth Low Frequency Consumption?" mimeo, Harvard University, 2005; and Thomas Dohmen, Armin Falk, David Huffman, Jürgen Schupp, Uwe Sunde, and Gert Wagner, "Individual Risk Attitudes: New Evidence from a Large, Representative, Experimentally-Validated Survey" DIW Discussion Paper 511, September 2005.

[35] Akerlof et al., "East Germany in from the Cold."

headquarters, and R&D centers also hampers the achievement of West German levels of total factor productivity. Yet in the absence of market distortions, the neoclassical economic paradigm sets a high bar for justifying policy interventions. Naturally there are significant deviations of the German economy from this benchmark in product, labor, and financial markets. One could have justified and did justify any number of interventions, all of which were rejected in the pressure-cooker atmosphere of reunification as impractical (such as *Bleibeprämien*, "premiums for staying") or subject to massive problems of political economic capture ex-post (e.g., wage subsidies and Eastern exemptions from value-added tax). In the current German fiscal environment such policies are even less likely to be pursued.

Looking forward, I venture to assert that the glass is more half-full than half-empty. The decades to come will see relatively strong growth in Eastern Germany, which by virtue of its location will be closer to the growth markets of the future in Central and Eastern Europe. By virtue of the reunification episode, Eastern German labor markets are more flexible than their western counterparts; the brunt of the recent collapse in demand for high-end investment and durable goods is likely to induce further patterns of structural change in the West, which the East has already experienced. Although structural change and adaptation will save a core of highly efficient industry in the new states, the steady drain of population to the West guarantees that the East of the twenty-first century will be a lattice of growth poles alternating with areas of chronic outmigration, transfer dependency, and local economic decline. Given that East Germany comprises the land mass of the equivalent of the state of Tennessee (108,333 km^2 or 41,828 sq mi), this may not seem like a problem, but it is important to keep in mind that the population density of the former GDR (including all of Berlin) remains roughly 150 persons/km^2 compared with 265 and 58 in Western Germany and Tennessee, respectively.

For these reasons, I conclude a much more nuanced and optimistic view of the Eastern German states than my colleagues Sinn or Harald Uhlig.[36] A slow bleeding of population is inevitable, but will ultimately be dominated by a North-South divide in which old locational advantages and traditional agglomeration patterns in the southern Eastern states are reasserted and reinforced. Radical structural change in product and labor markets in the past two decades has steeled East Germany for the challenges of globalization and made it particularly poised to profit from the continuing

---

[36] Sinn, "EU Enlargement"; Harald Uhlig, "Regional Labor Markets, Network Externalities and Migration: The Case of German Reunification," *American Economic Review* 96 (2006): 383–5.

growth and prosperity of the new market economies of Central and Eastern Europe. It would not surprise me if the population trend is reversed in the next decade, as East Germany reassumes its role — after more than a half-century of dormancy — as a new growth pole for the European economic area.

12

The Social Policy of Unification and Its Consequences for the Transformation of the Economy in the New Eastern States

GERHARD A. RITTER

As a historian with a special interest in the comparative history and the present problems of the welfare state, I have spent some time investigating the social policy of German unification and its economic effects. I wrote a monograph on this subject from which this essay is derived.[1] In preparing the book-length study, I had access to a wide range of unpublished sources both from the German Democratic Republic (GDR) and the Federal Republic of Germany (FRG). These included the records of the GDR team that negotiated both the treaty on monetary, economic, and social union with the Federal Republic[2] and the treaty of unification[3]; the records of the Federal Chancery and Federal Ministry of Finance; the records of the ministries in both countries that dealt with social policy; and the minutes of the meetings of the major parliamentary parties in the GDR and the Federal Republic. An examination of these materials makes it clear that the new Eastern federal states had little choice but to take over the political, economic, and social order of West Germany. Nonetheless, there were mistakes in the handling of the process in specific fields.

EASTERN GERMANY'S TRANSFORMATION FROM A PLANNED TO A MARKET ECONOMY COMPARED TO OTHER EASTERN EUROPEAN STATES

One of the consequences of reunification in Eastern Germany was the loss of about 3.5 million jobs. Agriculture and manufacturing were particularly

---

[1] Gerhard A. Ritter, *Der Preis der deutschen Einheit. Die Wiedervereinigung und die Krise des Sozialstaats*, 2nd ed. (Munich, 2007); *The Price of German Unity: Reunification and the Crisis of the Welfare State* (Oxford, 2011).

[2] Presse- und Informationsamt der Bundesregierung, ed., *Der Vertrag über die Schaffung einer Währungs-, Wirtschafts- und Sozialunion zwischen der Bundesrepublik Deutschland und der Deutschen Demokratischen Republik. Erklärungen und Dokumente* (Bonn, 1990).

[3] "Vertrag zwischen der Bundesrepublik Deutschland und der Deutschen Demokratischen Republik über die Herstellung der Einheit Deutschlands – Einigungsvertrag," *Bundesgesetzblatt II* (September 28, 1990): 889–1245.

hard hit. Over a four-year period, the agricultural sector, which had been overstaffed, dropped about three-quarters of its workforce, while the manufacturing sector lost about half of its jobs. The former GDR was largely deindustrialized; the new states would later struggle to set up manufacturing firms that could compete on the international market.

This development set Eastern Germany apart from other East Central European states such as Poland and Czechoslovakia, which were initially more successful in preserving jobs.[4] In contrast to those states, however, the GDR had the advantage of taking over the time-tested legal, economic, and social system of the Federal Republic. The GDR thus did not have to develop a new system in the midst of a lengthy – and inevitably controversial – political process. But this advantage also came with the disadvantage of keeping the GDR from being able to adjust the new order to suit its particular needs.

Monetary union came as a sort of shock therapy. Large numbers of skilled laborers and those best suited to make a new start economically left the territory. In my opinion, however, no political or economic alternative would have stopped this drain of talent. Different exchange rates for wages, salaries, and pensions would not have been feasible. Wages in East German currency had, on average, reached only one-third of nominal West German wages by the end of 1989, and, moreover, the East German mark was trading at an exchange rate of between five and ten to one against the D-Mark on the black market. The West German Federal Ministries of Finance and the Economy and the Bundesbank suggested that East German wages and salaries be exchanged at a rate of two to one.[5] Yet even with the considerable increases in Eastern German wages in the first half of 1990, compensation at that level would still have remained too low to significantly inhibit the massive migration to Western Germany. Young and skilled persons in particular were departing in droves, which threatened to precipitate the collapse of Eastern Germany's economy. One issue that ought to have been handled differently was the debt of GDR firms incurred before 1990. It was decided that firms should pay these debts off at a rate of two to one. The Treuhand Agency – the body that oversaw the privatization of Eastern German enterprises – ultimately had to write off this debt in all but a few instances in order to attract investors. The policy thus served merely to complicate the transition to a market economy.

---

[4] On this comparison, see Ritter, *Price*, 76–8.
[5] Ibid., 152. The ministries also suggested that there should be some form of compensation for the loss of subventions that the GDR had provided to subsidize the cost of housing, transportation, energy, and many goods as well as for the sharp increase in social welfare contributions.

In short, Eastern Germany was forced to make a "cold start" (*Kaltstart*).[6] Thrown into the fray of international competition, it was not able to use low exchange rates and wages to improve its competitiveness. Its transition to the international economy, which included acute competition with Western Germany and other international exporters, was much more abrupt than in these other ex-communist states, which were able to use trade policies to lengthen the period of adjustment. Whereas the East Central European states could use national economic policies to insulate their domestic markets to some degree, the disappearance of the internal German border created in unified Germany a single market in which the sharp differences in wages, salaries, and social benefits that had existed before between West and East Germany became nearly impossible to maintain.

A more advantageous contrast between the new Bundesländer and the other ex-communist states of East Central Europe was that the former received considerable financial and administrative help from the Federal Republic. This aid helped bring the infrastructure there up to the same standard as in Western Germany in a remarkably short time. However, private investment in the economy was far too low for the development of competitive new enterprises. Too much public investment went into consumption; the construction of residential and commercial buildings (which now often stand vacant); and, in particular, the creation of a secondary labor market and the provision of comparatively generous social benefits.

Many factors combined to produce a tremendous recession in the East after unification: overstaffing in most branches of the economy, years of inadequate investment, low productivity, long neglect of infrastructure (especially in telecommunications), severe damage to the environment, and the failure to keep up with new technological developments. One may also ask whether serious mistakes were made in the process of unification. Was it right, for instance, to adhere to the principle of restoring socialized property to its owners rather than providing them with financial compensation? Though largely revised by later laws, this practice was an obstacle to private investment in the years immediately following unification. Should currency union have been postponed? The early adoption of the D–Mark in Eastern German probably made it more difficult to prevent the collapse of the GDR's extensive trade with the Soviet Union and other member states of the Council for Mutual Economic Assistance.

---

[6] Economists Gerlinde and Hans-Werner Sinn used this expression in their bestseller *Kaltstart. Volkswirtschaftliche Aspekte der deutschen Vereinigung*, 3rd ed. (Munich, 1993).

THE TREUHAND AGENCY

One oft-debated topic is whether there were alternatives to the Treuhand Agency's policy. Established by the government headed by Hans Modrow of the Socialist Unity Party (Sozialistische Einheitspartei Deutschlands, or SED), the Treuhand Agency was completely reorganized after the first free elections to the GDR's parliament, the Volkskammer, on March 18, 1990, by the newly formed coalition government under Lothar de Maizière.[7] The agency was charged with privatizing, reorganizing, or closing down roughly eight thousand state-owned companies that together employed four million people. Initial estimates projected a profit of as much as DM 600 billion from the sale of companies to private-sector owners.[8] The treaties between the GDR and the Federal Republic – one on monetary union (May 18, 1990) and one on unification (August 31, 1990) – stipulated how the eventual profits from the sales were to be used: first, to help finance the structural transformation of the Eastern German economy; second, to pay off public debt; and finally, to compensate GDR citizens who had lost monetary assets as a result of the monetary union.[9] In the end, though, the Treuhand Agency failed to make a profit and instead ran a deficit of DM 230 billion,[10] which it incurred mainly by investing in companies to make them attractive to buyers willing to preserve at least a small portion of existing jobs.

The Treuhand Agency initially prioritized rapid privatization, believing that the best way to revitalize firms. Later, it shifted its priorities and focused on reviving firms itself, assuming their financial burdens and attempting to repair the environmental damage that many of them had wrought. Increasingly, these tasks were seen as prerequisites to prolonging the existence of the companies. In negotiations with potential purchasers, the Treuhand Agency often offered substantial financial support in exchange for private investment and pledges to retain at least a portion of the workforce. The agency's expenses increased markedly after the government decided in early 1993 to preserve and revamp existing industrial centers in Eastern Germany

---

[7] On the establishment and organization of the Treuhand Agency, see Dieter Grosser, *Das Wagnis der Währungs-, Wirtschafts- und Sozialunion. Politische Zwänge im Konflikt mit ökonomischen Regeln* (Stuttgart, 1998), 121–4, 348–59.

[8] Rudi Schmidt, "Restrukturierung und Modernisierung der industriellen Produktion," in *Arbeit, Arbeitsmarkt und Betriebe*, ed. Burkard Lutz, Hildegard F. Nickel, Rudi Schmidt et al. (Opladen, 1996), 227–56; here, p. 240. In a statement before the Volkskammer on February 20, 1990, Modrow said that the national assets of the GDR were worth 1,400 billion East German marks. *Protokolle der Volkskammer der Deutschen Demokratischen Republik 1989/90*, 9th election period, 17th meeting, 473.

[9] Article 10, Clause 6 of the Treaty of May 18, 1990, and Article 25, Clause 6 of the Treaty of August 31, 1990.

[10] "Treuhandanstalt costete 230 Milliarden DM," *Süddeutsche Zeitung*, July 21, 2000.

and to ensure that promising new ventures received adequate financing. As a result, the Treuhand Agency functioned as a holding company of sorts for several years before its dissolution.[11]

It comes as no surprise that the Treuhand Agency made many mistakes in its decisions on the privatization and reorganization of thousands of businesses. In addition to cases of corruption, fraudulent candidates were sometimes favored to take over a company. The agency had, however, been charged with a nearly impossible task. Criticism of its actions came from two opposing camps: from those who wanted more government control over the process of privatizing state-owned businesses and those who wanted less. Some in the former group argued that, in "selling off" East Germany, the agency had placed too much trust in the market and in self-regulation. They believed that public ownership and a mixture of public and private ownership should have been given more of a chance. They also argued that there was too much time pressure to sell and that the state should have guided this process and extended the time frame. The other group of critics, including most economists, believed that the state's attempts to reconstruct the economy from above and its policy of subsidizing existing companies resulted in firms becoming perpetually dependent on taxpayer support. This group felt that the change of priorities from privatization to reorganization and, in particular, the policy of maintaining industrial centers ran counter to basic market principles and increased the cost of German unity. Although valuable historical work has been done on the Treuhand, a detailed history based on the tremendous body of sources available remains to be written.[12] Such a history would need to address the very different situations in the various industrial sectors and regions and the specific conditions of individual companies, a task that would require a large research team.

The basic problem Eastern German companies faced was the challenge of developing products in a very short time that could compete on the open global market. It could not be solved by generous financial help alone. Rather, a skilled workforce, employers with initiative willing to take risks, and knowledge of the market were also needed. Some Eastern German companies – in the brewing industry, for example – had products with

---

[11] Gerhard A. Ritter, *Wir sind das Volk! Wir sind ein Volk! Geschichte der deutschen Einigung* (Munich, 2009), 135.

[12] See Birgit Breuel, ed., *Treuhand intern. Tagebuch* (Frankfurt, 1993); Birgit Breuel and Michael C. Burda, *Ohne historisches Vorbild. Die Treuhandanstalt 1990–1994* (Berlin, 2005); Wolfgang Seibel with the cooperation of Hartmut von Maaßen, Jörg Raab, and Arndt Oschmann, *Verwaltete Illusionen. Die Privatisierung der DDR-Wirtschaft durch die Treuhandanstalt und ihre Nachfolger* (Frankfurt, 2005); Mark Cassel, *How Governments Privatize: The Politics of Divestment in the United States and Germany* (Washington, DC, 2002); an important source is Treuhandanstalt, ed., *Dokumentation 1990–1994*, 15 vols. (Berlin, 1994).

well-established reputations dating back to before the GDR and were able to adjust successfully to the new conditions. They modernized production, adapted their products to meet current market demand, launched professional advertising campaigns, and, in some cases, won significant market share in Western Germany.[13]

THE TRANSFER OF THE WEST GERMAN SOCIAL SYSTEM
TO EASTERN GERMANY

The Offer of Monetary Union

The Federal Republic's surprising offer of monetary union on February 7, 1990, was the most important and most difficult decision the Bonn government made in the process of unification. Most West German economists were opposed to monetary union, and both the German Council of Economic Experts (Sachverständigenrat zur Begutachtung der gesamtwirtschaftlichen Entwicklung)[14] and the Bundesbank, which had not even been informed of the decision beforehand, had warned Bonn against such a move. According to the most prevalent economic theory, monetary union between two states with such massive differences in economic systems and performance could only be achieved by means of a long, drawn-out process of adaptation. Known as the *Krönungstheorie* (crowning theory), this view held that the GDR economy would have to assimilate to the Federal Republic's in a number of stages. Although the Federal Republic would provide some support, East Germany would progress mainly on its own resources until monetary union became possible as the crowning achievement of the process. This theory failed, however, to take the pull of the West German labor market into account and underestimated the length of time – potentially decades – adaptation would require. It was open to question whether that process would succeed, given the breakdown of the Eastern German economy, nor was it likely that Easterners would be willing to wait that long.

West Germany's offer of monetary union was primarily intended to send a signal to East Germans that they should remain in the East. Together with the Volkskammer elections on March 18, 1990, which gave the parties in favor of rapid unification an overwhelming mandate, the offer of monetary

---

[13] For examples of such success stories, see Karl-Heinz Paqué, *Die Bilanz. Eine wirtschaftliche Analyse der Deutschen Einheit* (Munich, 2009), 56–60.

[14] See the letter of February 9, 1990, from the expert commission to Kohl, in "Sachverständigenrat zur Begutachtung der gesamtwirtschaftlichen Entwicklung," *Jahresgutachten 1990/91*: 306.

union reduced but did not completely stop the westward migration of Easterners. The offer of monetary union was also a device to open the path to German unification without the stages of a "treaty community" (*Vertragsgemeinschaft*) and a confederation as originally planned. However, it also reflected West Germany's conviction that the GDR would not be able to transform itself from a planned economy to a market economy on its own.

The offer of monetary union was conditional upon the enactment of comprehensive economic reforms, but it did not carry the concomitant promise to transfer the West German social system to the East. Hans Tietmeyer, the head of the West German delegation negotiating the Treaty on Monetary, Economic and Social Union, later made it quite clear that he had consciously left social union off the agenda. He thought that the Federal Republic's very complicated system of social and labor law, with its detailed regulation and generous benefits, should not apply in the East until after a period of transition. This would ease the East's transformation from a planned economy to a market economy and stimulate private investment from Western Germany.[15] The Federal Ministries of Economy and Finance, which also wanted to reduce the financial burdens of unification, shared this view. But this perspective did not prevail at the political level.

THE EASTERN AND WESTERN DEBATES ON SOCIAL POLICY

In the GDR, all political forces were in favor of a complete transfer of the West German social system. On top of that, they wanted to maintain some of the GDR's so-called social achievements (*soziale Errungenschaften*), including, for example, family policies, work security policies, and the system of minimum pensions. In particular, they wished to extend the GDR's constitutionally guaranteed right to work to the new common state.

It was the Central Round Table in the GDR that first worked out a social policy program. Established on December 7, 1989, this institution, modeled closely on a Polish precursor, consisted of an equal number of representatives of opposition groups and of the parties in the governing coalition headed by the SED. The Central Round Table set a date for free elections and controlled the government and the Volkskammer. It considered itself a temporary organization whose task was to set things up for the new freely

[15] Hans Tietmeyer, "Erinnerungen an die Vertragsverhandlungen," in *Tage, die Deutschland und die Welt veränderten. Vom Mauerfall zum Kaukasus. Die deutsche Währungsunion*, ed. Theo Waigel and Manfred Schell (Munich, 1994), 57–117; here, p. 66.

elected Volkskammer. It thus paved the GDR's path from a dictatorship to a parliamentary democracy.

After long deliberations, the Central Round Table, which had many parallel organizations on the local level, decided on a social charter (*Sozialcharta*) with a comprehensive program of social rights, including the right to work, the right to housing, and the right to free education from elementary school through university. It also called for company lockouts to be prohibited, and for firms to be required to maintain – and expand – the GDR's system of employer-provided social benefits. Moreover, the charter mandated that a comprehensive unitary system of social insurance largely financed by the state with minimum pensions should be guaranteed.

The Modrow government endorsed this program, as did the old Volkskammer in its last session on March 7, 1990.[16] In practice then, the program was addressed not to the Modrow government but to the new government that would be formed after the elections on March 18. The idea was that the new government would take the program into the negotiations with Bonn, which would ultimately have to pay for it. The program, its supporters argued, would create a social market economy that was truly social. Had it been pushed through, this comprehensive social system would have increased the cost of unification tremendously and would have made Eastern Germany's transformation into a market economy nearly impossible. Observers in the Federal Republic criticized it above all for its lack of realism. Horst Seehofer, then parliamentary secretary in the Federal Ministry of Labor, stated in an article entitled "Das faule Ei vom Runden Tisch" (The Rotten Egg of the Round Table) that the program amounted to "socialist castles in the sky" (*sozialistische Luftschlösser*). It gave the state far too great a role in the economy, Seehofer argued, and failed to recognize the role of responsible employers. Moreover, it betrayed a lack of understanding of the concept of social partnership and of the role of performance (*Leistung*) in the social welfare system.[17]

The coalition government established on April 12, 1990, and headed by Lothar de Maizière, the leader of the Christian Democratic Union/East, also adopted a social policy program in its coalition agreement. It demanded not only the transfer of the generous West German system of social benefits but also the maintenance of many of the GDR's "social achievements."[18]

---

[16] *Protokolle der Volkskammer der Deutschen Demokratischen Republik 1989/90*, 9th election period, 18th meeting, 548, and printed paper of the Volkskammer 83.

[17] Horst Seehofer, "Das faule Ei vom Runden Tisch," *Bayernkurier*, March 17, 1990.

[18] Federal Ministry of Inner German Relations, ed., "Grundsätze der Koalitionsvereinbarungen zwischen den Fraktionen der CDU, der DSU, der DA, der Liberalen (DFD, BFD, FDP) und der SPD," *Informationen* 8 (April 24, 1990).

This program largely reflected the attitudes of the Eastern Social Democrats, who belonged to the coalition.

It was impossible to persuade the government of Chancellor Helmut Kohl to accept this program in the negotiations on monetary union even though the trade unions and opposition Social Democrats in West Germany favored many of its elements.

Given the unrealistically high expectations of the East German negotiators, the complete transfer of the West German social system was the least that they would accept and the most that the West Germans were willing to offer, with some minor, mostly temporary adaptations to accommodate the special situation in the East, as the basis for the monetary, economic, and social union. West German Federal Minister of Labor and Social Order Norbert Blüm had strongly advocated that the monetary and economic union offered by the West be supplemented with a social union.[19] That view was backed by all of the federal ministries that deal with aspects of social policy, a large majority of the Christian Democratic Union/Christian Social Union Bundestag caucus, and Kohl, who had the upcoming Volkskammer and Bundestag elections in view.

THE PENSION SYSTEM

In aligning the social policies of East and West, an arrangement had to be made concerning the GDR's statutory pension system. Despite the resistance of the West German Federal Ministry of Finance, it was agreed that East German pensioners with forty-five years of insurance would receive a pension equivalent to 70 percent of their preretirement net income and that pensions in the statutory pension system would be guaranteed to be at least equal to the amount they would have been in the GDR. The agreement was especially generous to widows who were not entitled to pensions from a period of paid employment; like war victims, they had been very harshly treated as unproductive persons in the GDR pension system. The Eastern system of minimum pensions – which was not part of the West German system – was maintained in the new Bundesländer until December 31, 1996, as an alternative to the West German system of social assistance. The average pension was increased from 475 marks in June 1990 to DM 1,214 over the course of four years.[20]

Although the great majority of pensioners profited greatly from this transformation of old-age insurance, those who had been beneficiaries of

---

[19] Ritter, *Price*, 145–6, 148.
[20] Bundesministerium für Arbeit und Sozialordnung, *Sozialbericht 1997* (Bonn, 1998), 311.

"special pension systems" (*Sonderversorgungssysteme*) and many of those privileged with participation in one of the GDR's sixty-one "supplementary
pension plans" (*Zusatzversicherungssysteme*) did not. The pensions paid in the
special pension systems for members of the People's Army (Volksarmee),
the People's Police (Volkspolizei), the Customs Service, and, in particular, the hated State Security Service (Staatssicherheitsdienst) could be reduced. The same applied to the members of the complicated system of
supplementary pensions. Pensions were paid under these schemes to a wide
variety of groups with close connections to the GDR systems, including
employees of parties, trade unions, and other organizations; employees of
the state and of the most important state-owned combines; and professional
elites such as professors, teachers, and the scientific and technical intelligentsia. However, many of those negatively affected by the curtailment and
incorporation of their pensions into the general statutory pension insurance,
which some of them called a pension criminal law (*Rentenstrafrecht*), sued
the federal government, occupying its courts and legislation until after the
turn of the century, and the courts often decided on corrections in their
favor.

It should be noted that the extension of the West German pension
system to include Eastern Germans was possible only because it is a "pay-
as-you-go" system funded by the contributions of current employees and
employers. If pensions were paid from earnings from capital – as, for example, life insurance benefits are – the state would have had to bear the costs
of East German pensions until sufficient capital had been accumulated.

One significant feature of the social union was a large increase in early
retirement. The trend had begun under regulations enacted under the
Modrow government and was accelerated by the provisions of the Unification Treaty and later laws. By 1993, approximately 850,000 Easterners
over the age of fifty-five had opted to take advantage of this program.[21]

LABOR MARKET POLICY

Another social issue that needed to be addressed was the reduction of unemployment through labor market policy. Although the GDR had not had an
unemployment insurance system since 1977, establishing one in Eastern
Germany was not controversial. What was controversial in the West was
transferring active West German labor market policy to the East. Objecting
strongly, the Federal Ministries of Finance and Economics feared that if West

---

[21] Ritter, *Price*, 237.

German–style short-term allowances or wage support payments (*Kurzar-beitergeld*: money given to make up for wage and salary reductions result-ing from cuts in working hours) were made in the East, "the adaptation of particular branches of the economy would be delayed and the existing unsatisfactory structure would be conserved."[22] They could not, however, prevent the stipulation in Article 19 of the Treaty on Monetary, Economic, and Social Union that the GDR would, in close collaboration with the Fed-eral Republic, develop an unemployment insurance system that would also provide for employment promotion (*Arbeitsförderung*) measures. Active labor market policy was greatly expanded and supplemented with new instru-ments when extended to the new Eastern states. Wage support payments acquired a wholly new meaning in the East: recipients might have been formally employed but not actually working. In the first year after mone-tary union, up to two million persons in the East – more than double the number of those officially unemployed – received wage support payments. At the time, these payments were the most important tool for ameliorating the negative social consequences of the economic upheaval. In the severe financial and economic crisis that emerged in September 2008, the support of short-term labor proved to be the most important and successful means to prevent unemployment from rising dramatically in Germany.

From the end of 1991 on, *Arbeitsbeschaffung*, or measures to provide work, and measures to support training and retraining courses (*Umschulung*) with the financial support of the Federal Labor Office (Bundesanstalt für Arbeit) largely replaced wage support payments. These new measures were all very expensive. In 1993, active labor market policy in the East accounted for DM 43 billion of the Federal Employment Agency's DM 50.5 billion in total expenditures in the East – that is, 18 percent of East Germany's gross national product.[23] Although the very generous expansion of West German labor market policy smoothed the process of economic transformation and drastically reduced unemployment, it also delayed necessary changes in the economic structure of Eastern Germany. It failed to build a bridge to the normal labor market as many had hoped, and it proved to be no remedy for low productivity, the Achilles's heel of the East German economy.

---

[22] Working paper "Arbeitslosenversicherung" of February 24, 1990, of the Federal Ministry of Finance, II c 1, Bundesarchiv, Zwischenarchiv Dahlwitz-Hoppegarten, Bundesministerium für Finanzen B 126/114047.

[23] Friedrich Buttler and Knut Emmerich, "Kosten und Nutzen aktiver Arbeitsmarktpolitik im ostdeutschen Transformationsprozess," in *Die Wettbewerbsfähigkeit der ostdeutschen Wirtschaft. Aus-gangslage, Handlungserfordernisse, Perspektiven,* ed. Gernot Guttmann (Berlin, 1995), 61–4; here, p. 62.

In my view, using the solidarity structures of old-age insurance and unemployment benefits to finance a considerable part of the cost of unification was a major mistake. DM 140 billion – or nearly one-quarter of the DM 615 billion in net transfers from the West during the period from 1991 to 1995[24] – was paid by the employer and employee contributors to those insurance programs. This disproportionally burdened middle and lower income groups and drove up nonwage labor costs (*Lohnnebenkosten*). Together with the drastic expansion of early retirement, this set a vicious circle in motion: increased employer/employee social welfare contributions drove up labor costs and led to an increase in unemployment, which in turn placed additional burdens on the social welfare system. That burden affected not only the Eastern German economy but the economy of Germany as a whole, impeding growth through the 1990s and into the new century. In a September 2005 interview, Bundesbank president Axel Weber said that unification was two-thirds responsible for the German economy's "underperformance."[25]

LABOR RELATIONS

Finally, the West German system of labor relations also had to be transferred to the East. In the first phase after the fall of the Wall, the Deutsche Gewerkschaftsbund (Confederation of German Trade Unions) and individual German trade unions attempted to cooperate with unions in the East that had been under the close control of the ruling SED. They soon abandoned hope, however, that those unions would undertake comprehensive democratic reforms. Consequently, the West German trade unions extended their organizations to the East, recruiting the members of East German unions collectively and individually. As there were significant differences between the unions, some of them allowed lower and mid-level functionaries to continue their work in the East. Employers' organizations, which had no counterpart in the East, had to be built from the ground up under the influence of the West German organizations.

Two different courses were followed in collective wage agreements within the various sectors of the economy. Agreements were made either for a very short period or for a multiyear period with stepwise increases in wages and salaries. The most important agreement, concluded in March 1991, was for 1.2 million employees in the metal-working and electrical industries. It provided for a series of three wage increases that would bring Eastern

---

[24] Ritter, *Price*, 91–2.
[25] *The Guardian*, September 10, 2005.

standard wages to Western levels by April 1, 1994.[26] Amid a recession affecting Germany as a whole and as productivity growth in the East failed by far to meet expectations, employers gave notice that they intended to terminate this agreement in February 1993. This triggered a widespread strike in the Saxon metal industry that finally ended in a compromise: the period of assimilation was extended to the middle of 1996, and individual firms would be allowed, under certain conditions, to pay workers less than the agreed-upon industry standard.[27] This process became rather typical, in Eastern Germany at first and later, to a more limited extent, in the rest of the country. The rigid system of *Flächentarifverträge* – industrywide collective wage agreements for an entire region – became more flexible and more often allowed special arrangements for individual firms. With increasing frequency, employers also sought to solve their problems by ignoring the wage agreements or leaving employers' organizations altogether.

It is nonetheless significant that in the first years after unification, employers' organizations and trade unions, which were both dominated by functionaries from the West, were jointly responsible for allowing agreements that provided for rapid increases in Eastern wages without taking the continued Eastern lag in productivity into account. Both labor and management did not want to see Eastern Germany become a permanent low-wage region. The unions regarded such an arrangement as a threat to high wages in the West, and employers were concerned that it would foster competitors in the East. Both sides obviously saw the East mainly as a market for West German products and not as a place of production.

The economists Gerlinde and Hans-Werner Sinn have suggested that this misguided wage policy, grounded in the understandable expectation that workers in both parts of Germany would soon be earning similar wages, could have been prevented by offering employees shares in their firms.[28] This suggestion has sparked a controversy among economists. Giving employees shares was not politically feasible politically and would have been complicated, as there were no reliable figures on the value of individual firms. Also, employees with shares would have had to bear the double risk of losing their jobs and their shares. Investors would have feared the influence of trade unions, which might have tried to interfere in the companies' operations if, as the unions demanded, central funds were built up in this way.

---

[26] Lothar Clasen, "Tarifverträge 1991. Schrittweise Angleichung," *Bundesarbeitsblatt* 4 (1992): 5–10.
[27] Bernd Keller, "Arbeitspolitik in den neuen Bundesländern. Eine Zwischenbilanz des Transformationsprozesses," *Sozialer Fortschritt* 45 (1996): 88–102; here, p. 100.
[28] Sinn and Sinn, *Kaltstart*, 251–61.

We can conclude that the transfer of the laws, institutions, and actors of social policy from the West to the East was accomplished very effectively and thus represented a considerable achievement of political forces, public administration, and, in particular, the self-governing organizations of the German welfare state. The transfer of West German social policy smoothed the process of transformation in the East and probably prevented social unrest. However, it also enormously increased both the material and intangible costs of unification, taking up the energy of those involved for three or four years and postponing necessary reforms. Another intangible cost concerned the socialization of people in the East, whose belief that the state was, in the last resort, responsible for the economy and for the well-being of society was only strengthened by it.

THE EASTERN GERMAN ECONOMY TWENTY YEARS AFTER UNIFICATION

Much has changed since the mid-1990s. As Karl-Heinz Paqué persuasively demonstrated in his penetrating economic analysis of German unity, *Bilanz*, it would be very wrong to argue that the reconstruction of Eastern Germany has been a failure and that the former GDR will become a German Mezzogiorno (albeit Mafia-free) if major changes are not enacted.[29] Labor productivity in manufacturing rose from about 30 to 35 percent of Western productivity in 1991 to about 78 percent in 2008. Real wages nonetheless remained significantly lower in the East than in the West. As a result, unit labor costs in manufacturing in Eastern Germany dropped from 200 percent of the Western level (1991) to 86 percent (2008). An East German employee is on average 34 percent cheaper than a West German one. East German firms have thus gained a competitive advantage regarding labor costs.[30] After a nearly complete collapse in the early 1990s, the industrial sector in Eastern Germany rebounded and was growing more rapidly than its Western counterpart by the twentieth anniversary of unification.[31] While net monetary transfers from the West to the East from 1991 to 2006 amounted to €1200 billion,[32] they are now much lower; a second solidarity agreement reached in 2004, which replaced the solidarity agreement of 1993, provides for these monetary transfers to expire in 2019.

By 2010, the Eastern Germany economy, excluding Berlin, was able to support a workforce of 5.8 million people without financial assistance

---

[29] Former German Chancellor Helmut Schmidt said this in an interview with the weekly *Focus*, May 23, 2005.
[30] Paqué, *Die Bilanz*, 146–51.
[31] Ibid., 142–5.
[32] Ibid., 184.

from the West. Transfers were still necessary, however, to provide benefits to retirees and the unemployed. New industries – particularly in micro-electronics and the renewable energy sector – have been developed that are leading in Europe, though they are threatened by particularly strong competition. Traditional industries have been renewed. In agriculture, Eastern Germany's mainly large cooperative farms had probably become more competitive than the mostly small and medium-sized farms in Western Germany. Tourism emerged as an important source of economic growth in some regions of the East.

The differences between developed and less developed areas have become more and more apparent in the East as well as in the West of Germany. There are boomtowns like Potsdam, Dresden, Leipzig, Chemnitz, Greifswald, and Jena in the East. Eastern Germany's infrastructure is now at least on the same level as in the West. The telecommunications system, which was severely underdeveloped before 1990, is now probably the most modern in the world. Most of the great environmental pollution has been removed. Life expectancy, which was three years below that of the West before unification, is now nearly the same.[33] Most of the old buildings neglected by the East German regime have been modernized. The old town centers and their beautiful cathedrals in the Hanseatic cities of the north, many of which stood in ruins, have been restored.

However, there have been setbacks. Unemployment is still significantly higher there than in the West. Eastern firms are often only *Werkbänke* (workshops) owned by Western German companies. Only 5 percent of the seven hundred biggest German companies have their headquarters in the East, and even these are often dependent subsidiaries of larger Western German companies.[34] Accordingly, research and development, as far as it is not financed by public sources, is much weaker in the East. There is still a stream of skilled labor and young people – especially young women – from East to West.

---

[33] For 1990, see Sachverständigenrat für die Konzertierte Aktion im Gesundheitswesen, "Jahresgutachten 1991," in *Das Gesundheitswesen im vereinten Deutschland* (Baden-Baden, 1991); for 2009, see *Der Tagesspiegel*, November 9, 2009.

[34] Deutsche Bank Research, September 2, 2009, 8.

13

German Economic Unification

A View through the Lens of the Postwar Experience

HOLGER C. WOLF

The postwar economic experience of West Germany began with sustained – and initially unexpected – growth. As the early rebound gave way to organic expansion, living standards rose and millions of newcomers were integrated into the labor force. When the Berlin Wall came down in 1989, the challenge of unification at first evoked a sense of déjà vu. From a dysfunctional monetary system to distorted relative prices and regulated trade, the economy of the German Democratic Republic (GDR) exhibited features reminiscent of the spring of 1948 before the enactment of currency and economic reforms. The overlap of the reform programs of 1948 and 1990 accentuated the seeming parallels between the two eras, raising hopes for a second immediate "economic miracle." It was not to be, though the longer-term performance has been quite impressive.

This essay revisits the comparison between West Germany's postwar experience and East Germany's experience of unification with the benefit of two decades worth of hindsight. It argues that, although the two episodes are more dissimilar than first appearances might suggest, the postwar experience nonetheless provides a useful analytical framework for assessing the postunification reforms. Perceptions notwithstanding, initial conditions – from the state of the capital stock to labor market constraints and international conditions – were substantially more propitious in the postwar period. Psychology differed as well. The postwar experience commenced with dismal expectations that subsequently were dramatically exceeded. Over time, the unexpectedly good performance translated into strong popular support for the economic model behind the reforms. By contrast, the postunification episode commenced with overly optimistic expectations.

I am very grateful to conference participants and in particular to Uta Balbier, Anne-Marie Gulde, and David Lazar for helpful comments.

Although the pronounced difference in initial conditions and the broader environment limits the usefulness of the initial postwar experience as a predictive model for the early postunification period, the comparability of the two episodes increases markedly when the focus is shifted to the phases of sustained growth that followed the periods of initial adjustment. By the mid-1990s, the differences in infrastructure and capital stock between the "old" and "new" states of the Federal Republic of Germany (FRG) had narrowed; the institutional transition was largely completed; and the agency responsible for privatizing GDR state enterprises, the Treuhandanstalt, had completed its work. The subsequent experience – productivity-oriented wage policies supporting sustained growth in export and manufacturing – displays greater similarity with the 1950s, albeit it with some marked exceptions.

THE POSTWAR ECONOMIC EXPERIENCE OF WEST GERMANY

Expectations in the early postwar years were shaped by the visual impact of bombed-out inner cities and the daily experience of shortages. Hopes for economic recovery were modest; predictions envisioned continued rationing and extended waiting times even for basic goods. The future seemed to hold little promise beyond prolonged economic stagnation.

These expectations proved wrong, and spectacularly so. The West German economy not only rebounded from the postwar lows but also continued to enjoy rapid growth for the next two decades. Millions of newcomers were successfully integrated into the labor force during the 1950s, and living standards rose markedly. The stark gap between expectations and outcomes prompted the popular moniker for the period: *das Wirtschaftswunder*, the "economic miracle." A voluminous literature on the causes behind this "miracle" points to the combination of initially underappreciated starting strengths, supportive domestic policy choices, advantageous international developments, and – not least – a dose of good fortune.[1]

---

[1] The literature on West Germany's postwar economic recovery, dating back to Henry Wallich, *Mainsprings of the German Revival* (New Haven, CT, 1955), is too sizable to reference adequately. Recent books exploring the economic, political economy, and intellectual background of the *Wirtschaftswunder* include Alan Kramer, *The West German Economy 1945–1955* (1991); A. J. Nicholls, *Freedom with Responsibility: The Social Market Economy in Germany, 1918–1963* (Oxford, 1994); Alfred C. Mierzejewski, *Ludwig Erhard: A Biography* (Chapel Hill, NC, 2004); and James van Hook, *Rebuilding Germany: The Creation of the Social Market Economy, 1945–1957* (Cambridge, 2004). See also Herbert Giersch, Karl-Heinz Paqué, and Holger Schmieding, *The Fading Miracle: Four Decades of Market Economy in Germany* (Cambridge, 1994) and Werner Abelshauser, *Wirtschaftsgeschichte seit 1945* (Munich, 2004) for two takes on the longer-term postwar economic history.

Initial Conditions

Aerial photographs from 1946 conveyed the impression of a country in ruins. The remains of collapsed houses, painstakingly cleared away by the *Trümmerfrauen* (rubble women), framed popular perceptions. Yet under the ruins, the postwar economy was in a considerably less dire state than was apparent at first sight.[2] The country's spatially dispersed industrial capital stock had suffered only moderate damage outside of urban centers and was of relatively recent vintage; while the labor force was expanded by a continued influx of refugees. Yet output remained depressed. The low implied productivity reflected shortcomings in physical and institutional infrastructure. Transportation networks operated at low capacity, hobbled by damage to critical nodes. International and interzonal trade remained constrained by the low capacity of the transportation network and by policy decisions. Although employment carried the benefit of higher rations, workers had little incentive to increase their productivity as monetary incomes at controlled wages had limited purchasing power in the increasingly important black markets. Similarly, firms facing price controls, prohibitive marginal taxes, and uncertainty about the economic and political future had few incentives to increase output or invest.

These challenges were eventually addressed – at quite moderate cost – prompting a rapid – and, in the popular perception of the time, miraculous – increase in output as productivity recovered. Repairs to the transportation system spurred an initial rebound, and focused the spotlight on factors constraining production from reaching capacity. The reform package of the summer 1948 – combining a tough monetary reform with an (at the time quite controversial) supply side reform comprising price liberalization alongside tax reductions – addressed the most important of these, restoring sound money and incentives.[3]

The reforms had an instant effect. Long absent products suddenly filled shop windows, bolstering popular acceptance of the new currency. As incentives improved, official sector output rebounded. Yet not all was well. Unemployment rose rapidly as firms facing hard budget constraints cut

---

[2] See, e.g., Kramer, *West German Economy*; Wendy Carlin, "West German Growth and Institutions, 1945–1990," in *Economic Growth in Europe since 1945*, ed. Nicholas Crafts and Gianni Toniolo (Cambridge, 1996), 455–97; and Abelshauser, *Wirtschaftsgeschichte*.

[3] The contribution of different factors to the initial growth performance, and specifically the role of the June 1948 reforms, remains the subject of debate. See, e.g., Giersch, Paqué, and Schmieding, *Fading Miracle*; Carlin, "West German Growth"; Abelshauser, *Wirtschaftsgeschichte*; and Barry Eichengreen and Albrecht Ritschl, "Understanding West German Economic Growth in the 1950s," SFB 649 Discussion Paper 2008-068 (Berlin, 2008), available online at http://sfb649.wiwi.hu-berlin.de/papers/pdf/SFB649DP2008-068.pdf (accessed September 19, 2012).

back on employment and as the inflow of refugees continued. As the initial
euphoria after the monetary reform wore off, critical voices became more
prominent. The focus on supply side policies, which stood in sharp contrast to the dominant Keynesian approach at the time, provoked growing
skepticism among both the Western German public and the Allies.[4] Calls
for a more interventionist government role – for measures ranging from a
return to price controls to fiscal demand stimulus – grew louder.

Contrary to the widely held view of the June 1948 reforms as a clear
demarcation point for the start of the postwar recovery, both economic
developments and public perceptions were thus quite volatile. Criticism of
the ordo-liberal model as an ivory-tower conception ill-suited to postwar
realities remained a prominent theme in the early postreform period. The
Christian Democratic Union's narrow victory in the Federal Republic's first
parliamentary election provided a time window for the model to establish its
credentials. Following a final crescendo in early 1951, the criticism abated
in the face of organic capacity and employment growth.

Steady Growth

West Germany's sustained growth during the 1950s was the result of several interdependent factors that, in a positive feedback loop, allowed for
the simultaneous expansion of both real wages and employment. Most
importantly, moderate wage growth, typically below or matching prior
productivity growth, assured stability in unit labor costs.[5] Stable labor costs
in turn stimulated investment, as did a decline in political and macroeconomic uncertainty[6] and fiscal incentives favoring retained earnings. Initially
seen as a serious challenge, the continued inflow of skilled and motivated
refugees became a major advantage in this context. The mobile newcomers
alleviated bottlenecks, eased sectoral and spatial adjustments, and played a
significant role in the establishment of new firms.[7]

---

[4] For in-depth analyses of the domestic policy debate, see Mierzejewski, *Ludwig Erhardt*, and van Hook, *Rebuilding Germany*.

[5] The causes of West Germany's generally stable industrial relations and relative wage constraint are a matter of debate. Complementary explanations include concern for the political stability of the new republic, restrained union bargaining power in the face of high unemployment and continued labor force growth, the importance attached to nonwage objectives (notably codetermination), and uncertainty about the durability of productivity growth. See, e.g., Charles Kindleberger, *Europe's Postwar Growth: The Role of Labor Supply* (Cambridge, MA, 1967); Giersch, Paqué, and Schmieding, *Fading Miracle*; and Carlin, "West German Growth."

[6] See Helge Berger, *Konjunkturpolitik im Wirtschaftswunder: Handlungsspielräume und Verhaltensmuster von Bundesbank und Regierung in den 1950er Jahren* (Tübingen, 1997) for a discussion of macroeconomic policy in this period.

[7] See Kindleberger, *Europe's Postwar Growth*, for an early view emphasizing labor supply as a crucial facilitating factor in sustained postwar growth.

A favorable external environment played a supportive role. Following the initial impetus provided by the European Recovery Program, demand for exports was further stimulated by expansionary policies pursued by West Germany's trading partners, an attractive real exchange-rate valuation (in turn supported by the moderate labor cost trends), declining barriers to intra-European trade, and, not least, Germany's sectoral concentration on capital goods in high demand during a period of rapid global economic expansion.[8]

Assessment

For a comparative assessment of the postwar and postreunification experiences, several points seem particularly noteworthy. First, in contrast to the popular perception of the 1948 reforms as a discrete demarcation point separating different growth processes, the academic literature paints a more complex picture. Some rebound growth occurred before the reforms, while economic volatility extended into the early 1950s, accompanied by a debate on whether the ordo-liberal model could effectively address the needs of postwar West German economy and society.

Second, the evidence suggests that the depressed level of industrial output immediately after the war reflected low productivity rather than a scarcity of capital or a lack of skilled workers. Addressing the causes behind depressed productivity – primarily problems in the physical and institutional infrastructure – allowed for a onetime rebound effect. The resource costs of addressing the challenges were modest. Aside from repairs to infrastructure, the main obstacles to economic recovery were the monetary disequilibrium – resolved by the June 1948 reforms implemented by the Allies – and disincentives – reduced by the supply side reforms accompanying the currency reform and, later, by external trade liberalization.

Third, labor market developments were largely conducive to continued economic expansion and contributed to reinforcing feedback effects. In particular, the alignment of wage increases with productivity growth allowed for a joint increase in real wages and employment, driven by sustained investment also buttressed by stable macroeconomic policies and fiscal incentives. Fourth, the international economic setting – expansionary policy by trading partners, coordinated liberalization, and an attractively valued real exchange rate – was propitious.

---

[8] See, e.g., Christoph Buchheim, *Die Wiedereingliederung Westdeutschlands in die Weltwirtschaft* (Munich, 1990); Kramer, *West German Economy*; Giersch, Paqué, and Schmieding, *Fading Miracle*; van Hook, *Rebuilding Germany*; and Barry Eichengreen, "Institutions and Economic Growth: Europe after World War II," in Crafts, Nicholas and Gianni Toniolo, eds., *Economic Growth*, 38–72.

THE POSTUNIFICATION EXPERIENCE

From monetary disequilibrium to distorted relative prices, controlled external trade, and pervasive government influence in the allocation of resources, the list of similarities between Germany's Western states in early 1948 and its Eastern states in early 1990 is striking on first sight. So, too, is the overlap in the reform measures implemented in the summers of 1948 and 1990. The apparent similarity of initial conditions and reforms raised hopes at the time of reunification of a second economic miracle, hopes disappointed as employment fell and production shrank in the two years following the enactment of the reforms.

On closer inspection, the opening phases of the two episodes are less similar than they appear at first sight. Both the initial conditions and broader frameworks in which reforms were enacted differed in several crucial aspects. The postwar and postreunification experiences are, however, markedly more comparable in the period following the initial adjustment.

Initial Conditions

The apparent disconnect between the seemingly similar starting conditions and diverging outcomes can be attributed to quite dissimilar developments in factor supplies (and thus capacity output) and demand as well as to differences in the reform challenges.[9]

Initial growth in the postwar period benefitted from a sharp rise in the productivity of existing resources following repairs to physical infrastructure and reforms of the institutional framework. In the postunification period, a comparable initial rebound was constrained by considerably less favorable dynamics on both the capital and the labor side. A significant part of the capital stock in the new states became obsolete upon unification, unable to meet the technological, environmental, and energy efficiency standards of the Federal Republic.

In labor markets, skilled workers could avail themselves of the option to work in the old states by either commuting or moving. The mobility option,

---

[9] For evaluations of the postunification experience, see George A. Akerlof, Andrew K. Rose, Janet L. Yellen, and Helga Hessenius, "East Germany in from the Cold," *Brookings Papers on Economic Activity* (1991): 1–87; Gerlinde Sinn and Hans-Werner Sinn, *Jumpstart: The Economic Unification of Germany* (Cambridge, MA, 1992); Michael Burda and Jennifer Hunt, "Reunification to Economic Integration: Productivity and the Labor Market in Eastern Germany," *Brookings Papers on Economic Activity* (2001): 1–71; Abelshauser, *Wirtschaftsgeschichte*; and Karl-Heinz Paqué, *Die Bilanz: Eine wirtschaftliche Analyse der Deutschen Einheit* (Munich, 2009). On the economic history of the GDR generally, see André Steiner, *Von Plan zu Plan*; published in English as *The Plans That Failed: An Economic History of the GDR* (New York, 2010).

coupled with optimistic economic expectations, contributed to a sharp rise in wages in the new states in the early postunification years. As relative wages rose ahead of relative productivity, relative unit labor cost increased sharply, with further adverse effects on the economic viability of the capital stock. The supply side effects on capacity output were aggravated by less favorable demand-side developments. Whereas pent-up demand boosted domestic production following the 1948 reforms, consumers in the new states spent a significant share of their hard currency income on goods produced in the old states. At the same time, traditional trading partners in Eastern Europe switched demand to Western goods.

In consequence, the scope for an output recovery driven by higher productivity of existing resources was more limited. The rebound potential was further constrained by the differences in the institutional reform challenge that were not always fully appreciated at the time. In large part, the postwar reforms entailed "stroke of the pen" removals of restrictions imposed on a market economy with private ownership of resources. Lifting those restrictions created incentives to exploit newly available opportunities, and the incentives were eagerly embraced. After reunification, the new states faced a far more complex array of challenges, ranging from the time-consuming task of privatization to the adoption of a new institutional and regulatory system. The more encompassing and complex reform challenge complicated firm-level adjustment in the years immediately following reunification.

Steady Growth

Following the initial recovery, postwar Germany experienced sustained growth in output, exports, employment, and real wages. Some of the features supporting postwar growth were present in the 1990s; others were absent. Although a full discussion exceeds the scope of this essay, the following section takes up three core issues: the role of labor market dynamics, the availability of financial support, and the performance of the manufacturing sector, including exports.

The Labor Market

Postwar economic growth drew important support from a skilled and motivated labor force augmented by the continued inflow of refugees. Productivity-oriented wage settlements stabilized unit labor costs, supporting investment and allowing real wages and employment to grow in tandem.

When the Wall came down, the relative scarcity of skilled workers in the Western states provided some hope that large-scale, employment-generating investment in the new Eastern states would fuel a similar dual growth of employment and real wages. A very different dynamic, however, developed in the postunification period. The option to move to the old states put tight limits on the sustainable real income divergence between the Eastern and Western states.[10] Wage increases exceeding productivity growth raised unit labor costs above the level in the old states – themselves exhibiting one of the highest levels globally – reducing the scope for labor-intensive production.[11] As firms adjusted to sharply higher labor costs coming atop the demand contraction, real wage growth was followed by a sharp decline in employment, reversing the postwar sequence.

While the mobility constraint – a core difference between the early postwar and the postunification periods – remains in place, labor market dynamics in the new states have changed materially since the mid 1990s. Wage differentiation and firm level flexibility in the new states have increased substantially – including relative to the old states. A sustained period of productivity-based wage growth – strongly resembling the experience of the 1950s – has cumulatively reduced relative unit labor cost in the new states below those in the old states, supporting labor demand.[12] The postwar and postunification periods thus display greater similarity if attention is focused on the phase following initial adjustment.

Financial Support and Social Insurance

The inclusion of postwar Germany in the European Recovery Program sent a crucial political signal and provided targeted financial support for core sectors. In the postunification period, large-scale transfers from the old to the new states – amounting to a very large share of the Eastern states' gross domestic product and reflected in extraordinary national current account deficits – similarly provided crucial support. The funds were partly used to

---

[10] On migration determinants and effects, see Jennifer Hunt, "Staunching Emigration from East Germany: Age and the Determinants of Migration," *Journal of the European Economic Association* 4 (2006): 1014–37, and Paqué, *Bilanz*. Empirically, the initial increase in relative wages was associated with a sharp decline in movement from the new to the old states. Net migration, however, began to rise again starting in the mid-1990s and has recently held steady in the annual range of 50,000.

[11] Paralleling the discussion of the causes of wage restraint in the postwar period, the role of various (complementary) reasons for rapid wage increases in the postunification period has been debated. See, e.g., the works cited in note 8 and Dennis Snower and Christian Merkl, "The Caring Hand That Cripples," IZA Discussion Paper No. 2066 (Bonn, 2006), available online at http://ftp.iza .org/dp2066.pdf (accessed September 19, 2012).

[12] See, e.g., Paqué, *Bilanz*.

close the significant East–West gaps in transportation and communications infrastructure, removing an important obstacle to investment.

In contrast to the postwar period, a significant part of the external funding supported social transfers, primarily through the extension of the social insurance systems as part of the German economic, monetary, and social union.[13] The transfers allowed real consumption gains to be broadly spread[14] and supported demand for the nontraded sector in the new states[15] while also influencing feasible wage paths and thus the nature of the adjustment process.

Manufacturing and Exports

The postwar recovery was supported by strong output and export growth in the manufacturing sector. West German manufacturers had the good fortune of specializing in capital goods during a global investment boom. A competitive real exchange rate supported by stable unit labor costs, the removal of trade barriers, and strong global growth helped sustain the manufacturing boom and allowed firms to reestablish and expand traditional trading relations.

The situation in the postunification period differed markedly. Firms in the new states had to radically alter trade patterns, both spatially – away from the collapsing Council for Mutual Economic Assistance and toward highly competitive markets in the European Union – and in composition, as there was limited demand for many traditional East German products in those new markets. While firms in the postwar period were gradually exposed to increased international demand, firms in the new states not only faced immediate competition on both domestic and international markets but also had to cope with a strong real exchange rate and, in the early years, with sharp increases in relative unit labor costs.

The much less benign starting conditions were reflected in a dramatic initial decline in exports. As in the case of labor markets, the two episodes become more similar once the focus is shifted from the initial period to sustained performance. As labor markets became more flexible, relative unit labor costs declined. The southeast in particular was able to leverage its

---

[13] See Gerhard Ritter, *Der Preis der deutschen Einheit* (Munich, 2007) for a detailed assessment.

[14] The difference was perhaps most pronounced for retirees. Whereas retirees in the postwar period had to wait until the 1957 pension reform to participate in sustained real growth, the extension of the public retirement program implied rapid real income gains for retirees in the new states.

[15] For an analysis of the economic importance of transfers see Harald Lehmann, Udo Ludwig, and Joachim Ragnitz, "Originäre Wirtschaftskraft der neuen Länder noch schwächer als bislang angenommen," *Wirtschaft im Wandel* (2005): 134–45.

rich industrial history to reenter global markets as both old and new firms modernized their product portfolios. Following the initial sharp contraction, manufacturing output and exports have shown impressive and quite persistent growth, displaying marked similarity to the postwar experience.

CONCLUSION

The perceived outlook for Western Germany's economic future was dim in 1946. Prolonged stagnation appeared the most likely scenario. But instead the Federal Republic enjoyed two decades of heady growth. Millions of newcomers were integrated into the workforce while living standards rose sharply. Some forty years later, the former GDR faced its own economic transition. As the new states were plagued by many of the same obstacles confronting postwar Western Germany – a dysfunctional monetary system, distorted prices, misallocated resources, and regulated trade – hopes ran high that a package of reforms similar to those enacted in 1948 would bring about a second economic miracle. Yet just as postwar expectations had proved too pessimistic, predictions of a postunification boom turned out to be too optimistic. Although living standards rose in the East – supported by large-scale transfers – economic activity and employment contracted sharply.

This essay argues that a number of structural differences limit the comparability of the two episodes in their first few years. Appearances notwithstanding, initial conditions in the postwar period were more favorable than perceived at the time. West Germany, at its core a private-property market economy, was operating far below potential as a result of both localized damage to core infrastructure and disincentives. It enjoyed rapid initial growth as relatively low-cost repairs to both the physical and the institutional infrastructure allowed output to rise toward capacity. Although an inefficient initial factor allocation likewise seemed to provide some scope for a postunification rebound, the new states suffered a significant adverse shock to their capital stock, faced an internal migration constraint on wages, and confronted a far more radical and comprehensive institutional reform and privatization challenge. Taken together, these constraints counteracted any efficiency gains reflecting resource reallocation.

Beyond the initial recovery in the Federal Republic, longer-term growth into the 1960s was supported by a range of factors linked by positive feedback loops, some fortuitous, some traceable to initial conditions, and some deliberate policy choices. Externally, the West German economy benefited from the push for European economic integration, strong global demand for capital goods, and a favorable exchange rate. Domestically, investment was supported by fairly tranquil industrial relations, stability-oriented fiscal and monetary policies, fiscal incentives, and moderate labor cost growth. Labor force growth allowed for a smooth adjustment of sectoral and regional imbalances, supported wage moderation, and facilitated sustained expansion.

The economy of the new Eastern states benefited from fewer positive growth factors than the West German economy had in the early 1950s and was buffeted by additional challenges. Although global growth again provided support, established and new firms in the new states faced a harder challenge in trying to establish footholds in international markets in the face of immediate, comprehensive trade liberalization and a highly valued real exchange rate. While the pool of skilled labor again provided support for sustained investment-based recovery over the longer term, the favorable real labor cost dynamics of the postwar period could not be reestablished as concerns about the effects of the large-scale movement of skilled workers to the old states and initial optimism about the economic outlook contributed to large wage increases running ahead of productivity.

Whereas labor cost and exchange-rate trends were less favorable, the postreunification recovery benefitted from other factors. The adoption of the D-Mark and of the established institutional framework of the Federal Republic along with membership in the European Union provided immediate credibility that supported investment – even if they also ruled out fine-tuning institutions and policies to the specific needs of a transition economy. As part of unified Germany, the new states – in contrast to other transition economies – benefited from substantial transfers financing the modernization of Eastern Germany's physical infrastructure and housing stock as well as allowing for a social buffering of the adjustment process and supporting a broadly shared real consumption increase.

What, then, can be said about the relevance of West Germany's postwar experience in assessing the economic dynamics of postunification Eastern Germany? In his early and influential assessment of the multiple influences determining the postwar economic experience, Henry Wallich concluded the fact *"[t]hat all these things came together at the right time and place is the real German miracle."*[16] The new states were not as fortuitous along all dimensions. The postwar period thus remains exceptional, the rare case in which substantial scope for an initial rebound followed by organic growth is supported – and enhanced – by a range of initial conditions, policy choices,

---

[16] Wallich, *Mainsprings*, 2; emphasis added.

external developments, and good fortune. That said, the comparative picture brightens once attention is shifted beyond the initial years of declining employment and output. In particular, manufacturing sector output and exports in the new states have experienced sustained growth since the nadir, building on traditional strengths, and have done so in an environment of enhanced labor market flexibility, declining real unit labor costs, and strong export focus – features reminiscent of the postwar growth experience.

Index